Nikki Fairchild

Genders and Sexualities in the Social Sciences

Series Editors: **Victoria Robinson**, University of Sheffield, UK and **Diane Richardson**, University of Newcastle, UK

Editorial Board: **Raewyn Connell**, University of Sydney, Australia, **Kathy Davis**, Utrecht University, The Netherlands, **Stevi Jackson**, University of York, UK, **Michael Kimmel**, State University of New York, Stony Brook, USA, **Kimiko Kimoto**, Hitotsubashi University, Japan, **Jasbir Puar**, Rutgers University, USA, **Steven Seidman**, State University of New York, Albany, USA, **Carol Smart**, University of Manchester, UK, **Liz Stanley**, University of Edinburgh, UK, **Gill Valentine**, University of Leeds, UK, **Jeffrey Weeks**, South Bank University, UK, **Kath Woodward**, The Open University, UK

Titles include:

Jyothsna Belliappa
GENDER, CLASS AND REFLEXIVE MODERNITY IN INDIA

Edmund Coleman-Fountain
UNDERSTANDING NARRATIVE IDENTITY THROUGH LESBIAN AND
GAY YOUTH

Niall Hanlon
MASCULINITIES, CARE AND EQUALITY
Identity and Nurture in Men's Lives

Brian Heaphy, Carol Smart and Anna Einarsdottir (*editors*)
SAME SEX MARRIAGES
New Generations, New Relationships

Sally Hines and Yvette Taylor (*editors*)
SEXUALITIES
Past Reflections, Future Directions

Meredith Nash
MAKING 'POSTMODERN' MOTHERS
Pregnant Embodiment, Baby Bumps and Body Image

Meredith Nash
REFRAMING REPRODUCTION
Conceiving Gendered Experiences

Lucy Nicholas
QUEER POST-GENDER ETHICS
The Shape of Selves to Come

Barbara Pini and Bob Pease (*editors*)
MEN, MASCULINITIES AND METHODOLOGIES

Victoria Robinson and Jenny Hockey
MASCULINITIES IN TRANSITION

Yvette Taylor and Michelle Addison (*editors*)
QUEER PRESENCES AND ABSENCES

Yvette Taylor, Sally Hines and Mark E. Casey (*editors*)
THEORIZING INTERSECTIONALITY AND SEXUALITY

Kath Woodward
SEX POWER AND THE GAMES

Genders and Sexualities in the Social Sciences
Series Standing Order ISBN 978–0–230–27254–5 hardback
978–0–230–27255–2 paperback
(*outside North America only*)

You can receive future titles in this series as they are published by placing a standing order. Please contact your bookseller or, in case of difficulty, write to us at the address below with your name and address, the title of the series and the ISBN quoted above.

Customer Services Department, Macmillan Distribution Ltd, Houndmills, Basingstoke, Hampshire RG21 6XS, England

Queer Post-Gender Ethics
The Shape of Selves to Come

Lucy Nicholas
Faculty of Health, Arts and Design, Swinburne University, Australia

First published 2014 by
PALGRAVE MACMILLAN

Palgrave Macmillan in the UK is an imprint of Macmillan Publishers Limited, registered in England, company number 785998, of Houndmills, Basingstoke, Hampshire RG21 6XS.

Palgrave Macmillan in the US is a division of St Martin's Press LLC, 175 Fifth Avenue, New York, NY 10010.

Palgrave Macmillan is the global academic imprint of the above companies and has companies and representatives throughout the world.

Palgrave® and Macmillan® are registered trademarks in the United States, the United Kingdom, Europe and other countries.

ISBN 978–1–137–32161–9

This book is printed on paper suitable for recycling and made from fully managed and sustained forest sources. Logging, pulping and manufacturing processes are expected to conform to the environmental regulations of the country of origin.

A catalogue record for this book is available from the British Library.

A catalog record for this book is available from the Library of Congress.

Typeset by MPS Limited, Chennai, India.

To the memory of my father, Brian George Nicholas,
1946–2013

Contents

Acknowledgements

This book owes acknowledgements to a great many inspirational and supportive people. Firstly it owes a legacy to those gender theorists, feminists and queers whose ideas have been such an inspiration. In this way, like any work (as with any person), my ideas have been a collaborative project.

Professor Liz Stanley has been the best academic mentor that I could wish for, whose prolific ideas have been an inspiration. Likewise, Dr Kate Orton-Johnson's support and persistence deserves my thanks. To my illustrious and insightful proof readers, my eternal gratitude: Dr Deb Dempsey, Dr Glenda Ballantyne, Dr Chris Agius and James Slater.

I would like to acknowledge the patience, support and unconditional love of my family: Danny, Bec, Mum and Mike and I thank them for sticking by me in all that we have all been through in the last few years. Kylie Lewis, Carmen Seaby, Lauren Kenny, Roz Ward and EJ Scott remain a consistent inspiration and changed my life and way of thinking about gender, and the rest, for the better.

Previous iterations of some of the ideas in this book have been published in Haworth, Robert (ed.) *Anarchist Pedagogies: Collective Actions, Theories, and Critical Reflections on Education*, PM Press, Oakland and in Nicholas, Lucy 2009, 'A Radical Queer Utopian Future: A Reciprocal Relation beyond Sexual Difference', *Thirdspace: A Journal of Feminist Theory and Culture*, 8(2).

I would also like to acknowledge the support of The International Network for Sexual Ethics and Politics, the University of Edinburgh, sociology at the University of Portsmouth, the Arts and Humanities Research Council, Dr Victoria Robinson, the comments of the anonymous reviewer and the team at Palgrave Macmillan.

Introduction

The existing, oppositional categories of gender and biological sex are being increasingly challenged in social and cultural life. Intersex communities are pushing for greater self-determination and resisting the medical assignment of 'ambiguous' infants to dualistic sex categories (see ISNA 2013; OII 2013). In Australia, Germany, Nepal and elsewhere there are moves towards the expansion of legal sex/gender categories on official documentation, including those which offer a third option (Bibby 2013; Davidson 2014; Knight 2012; Nandi 2013). Facebook has announced the expansion of users' gender options to an alleged 58 options (Goldman 2014). There is growing grass-roots international interest in truly gender-transcendent childrearing or the withholding of infants' sex/gender (Green & Friedman 2013; Leonard 2011; Parafianowicz 2009) as well as encouraging 'gender-free' toys (Ditum 2012; Orenstein 2011). Some preschools are trying to eliminate gendering (Hebblethwaite 2011) and some countries are introducing gender-neutral pronouns (Bahadur 2013). Androgynous 'male' models are modelling 'women's' clothes in fashion magazines and on runways (Morris 2011), and androgynous 'female' models are doing the reverse (Peppers 2013). And there are thriving underground radical queer scenes, which strive for gender-deconstructive practices – for example, it is common to ask a person in this context what pronoun/s they prefer, and not uncommon for this to be non-gendered (either 'they' or an invented set of pronouns such as those used throughout this book[1]) (Vanelslander 2007).

In academia such normative visions have been less frequent. However, in per foreword to the nineteenth-century memoirs of Herculine Barbin, Foucault interpreted (and perhaps idealised) Barbin's intersex existence, imagining that an identity-transcendent mode of existence and sexuality is possible, where:

> Everything took place in a world of feelings – enthusiasm, pleasure, sorrow, warmth, sweetness, bitterness – where the identity of the partners ... had no importance ... the happy limbo of a non-identity. (Foucault 1980: xiii)

In feminist thought, disparate thinkers have long argued that the problems of gender would best be tackled by challenging the categorisations themselves, for example, Delphy's assertion that 'Perhaps we shall only really be able to think about gender on the day when we can imagine nongender' (Delphy 1993: 9). More recently, queer theory has proposed the deconstruction of identity categories, in particular binary categories, and some thinkers are now moving to consider how such a deconstructive impulse of 'non-identity' can also underpin a positive ethics or sociality without undermining its own premises of celebrating limitless differences. Some thinkers are now considering what positive, but still identity-deconstructive, 'queer bonds' may look like:

> Queer bonds reach beyond sexual self-recognition because we need a theory of queer sociality that cuts across identitarian positionings that will remain forever incommensurate, and that articulates a bond spanning differences that may remain irreducible. (Weiner & Young 2011: 227)

This gesturing towards the possibility of an ethically and politically preferable transcendence of gender identity is what motivates this work. That is, while much research has established that gender is not a natural or necessary social formation, has undesirable effects, and possibly that subjective and social life would even be preferable without it, there has been limited academic extension of these claims to the corollary of exploring *how* it might be eradicated and what preferable mode of being could replace it. How might we understand ourselves and the world without gender? The time is ripe to consider that the deconstruction and eradication of sex/gender difference might benefit everyone, and reconstructively think through how it might be challenged, and what a post-gender ethics might consist of.

This work stems partly from my impatience with gender theory that is either 'explanatory-diagnostic' (Benhabib 1985: 405) but not utopian or practicable, or work that is utopian but less strong in the analysis of the realities of gender and how it might be challenged. Indeed, Claes & Reynolds lament that in sexual ethics and sexual politics there is

> a common thematic character in broken dialectics between theory and practice, abstract thinking and embodied doing, building within and subverting orthodox positions and the relationship between ethics and politics. (2014: 9)

Much theory that seeks to explain the social causes of the constitution and operation of gender is invaluable, such as Judith Butler's oeuvre, and the work of ethnomethodologists Kessler & McKenna (1978), West & Zimmerman (1987), and later Fenstermaker & West (2002) who diagnose the constitutive and interactional power of sex/gender. However, I find myself itching to consider the implications of this for social change. I wonder what it means for how we may understand ourselves and others differently, and what the limits for alternatives are, that is, what is truly *given* and how that may shape what is possible. When and where proposals for challenging gender do appear, they tend to stop short of calling for its eradication, implying its necessity, and retaining the spectre of dualism. For example, in much queer and transgender literature, alternative formulations exist only to the extent of suggesting an expansion through a different typology or system or way of seeing gender, not its eradication (Bornstein 1994; Feinberg 1998; Halberstam 1998). A limited number of thinkers have interrogated the ethical question of the desirability of transcending gender altogether (Bem 1995; Gunnarsson 2011; Hird 2004a; Van Lenning 2004), and even fewer have considered the practical questions of whether and how this might be achieved. Judith Lorber remains one of the few academic thinkers to take seriously, if briefly, the practical consideration of fostering 'a world beyond gender' (Risman, Lorber & Sherwood 2012; cf. Lorber 2000, 1986).

Meanwhile, there is a growing intersection of gender theory and biology, concerned with developing more sophisticated ontological accounts of the true nature of 'biological' sexual difference, and considering the social implications of this. Much of this has led to a denaturalising of the material essentialism of the dualistic nature of two biological sex categories (i.e. sexual difference), ideas that have been emanating from feminist biology (e.g. Fausto-Sterling 2012) and accounts sometimes grouped together under the monikers 'new materialism' (Hird 2004b), 'feminist corpomaterialism' (Lykke 2010a) or 'post-constructionism' (Lykke 2010b). These thinkers argue that the biological dimorphism that tends to be taken for granted (the idea that there are two distinct sex categories of humyn bodies) is actually a gendered *social* ideal imposed on to a more variable, less fixed and more 'emergent' nature. This has exciting implications for reconstructive accounts of identity as it allows for the possibility that culture shapes the development of bodies as well as how we interpret them, and thus they might be enabled to develop differently.

While there is exciting work about the nature of sex/gender, normative (normative in the sense of 'ethical justification' (Butler 2007: xxi)) or political calls or visions for an 'end to gender' are rare. Some exceptions include less than contemporaneous feminist sci-fi or speculative fiction (e.g. Anderson & McIntyre 1976; Piercy 2001 [1979]), more contemporary radical queer zines[2] and the radical queer communities from which they come (e.g. skullyadams n.d.; Heckert 2002), or fairly isolated social practices such as the aforementioned recent spate of gender-neutral childrearing in diverse parts of the world. Many of these tend understandably to lack explicit and sophisticated accounts of the nature of being or biology as a foundation for their utopian visions.

In an academic context, however, a robust and practicable account that combines these two impulses, the deconstructive diagnostic and the reconstructive ethical and political, towards a conceptualisation of post-gender existence, is still lacking. This work is an attempt to do just this: to present a robust account of the nature of sexual difference and gender, and to consider the implications and possibilities this presents for post-gender ethics.

Many thinkers concerned with gender justice have identified that 'Feminists need both deconstruction *and* reconstruction, destabilization of meaning *and* projection of utopian hope' (Fraser 1995: 71). Conceding, this book takes the form of what Benhabib would call both 'explanatory-diagnostic' and 'anticipatory-utopian critique' (1985: 405). This ontological, moral and political exposition then underpins the exploration of what *could* and *should* replace gendered modes of perception. That is, the consideration of what ways of being, and being sexual and desiring, are ethically preferable to gendered modes. Like Simone de Beauvoir, my central opening question is why 'the sexual relation [is] experienced as a difference and an opposition ... [and whether this is] necessary?' (Heinamaa 1999: 115). Most innovatively, though, in asking whether sexual difference itself might be transcended, it questions how this may be done, and what positive means of understanding ourselves and others, and what shared norms (what I called 'queer bonds' above) might come after it that will not replicate its problems.

This underpins my original theory of post-gender ethics. The central project of this book is the development of an androgynous, but not homogenous, mode of thought that could inform the ways that we come to understand ourselves and the ways that we understand each other and relate socially. This could effectively replace the role of sex/gender difference, offering a more proliferated and less predetermined alternative. It allows me to think through what a sense of self, relationships and sexual conduct organised around ethics, freedom and pleasure, rather than fixed identities, might 'look like'. Finally, I am concerned with the political and practical problems of how this post-gender ethic might be carried out, and present various practices and sites for intervention that demonstrate this. A particular strength of this contribution to academic conversations about gender is the incorporation of real-world practices that offer credence to the claims that such an androgynous way of perceiving is possible and can have positive implications. It is original therefore as a comprehensive and practice-oriented consideration of a possible and preferable model of identification/recognition to that of sexual difference, in particular for sexuality.

Queer theory

I position this work within the broader project of queer theory, as an attempt to extend its deconstructions of sexuality and gender to reconstructive ethics. The disruptive term 'queer theory' is attributed to Theresa de Lauretis (Marinucci 2010: 33) in 1990, who was drawing on the multiple meanings of 'queer' to articulate the anti-normalising potential of challenging the naturalness and dominance of heterosexuality. Queer theory is generally understood to be a challenge to the limiting and exclusionary impulses, or 'heteronormativity' (Warner 1991), of both compulsory heterosexuality *and* the assimilationist political strategies and the identity categories of gay liberation or identity politics (Butler 1990; de Lauretis 1991; Halperin 1995; Phelan 2004; Sedgwick 1990). As part of this project of challenging normalisation, it presents critique of essentialism (the belief that identity is innate) and of oppositional binaries and hierarchy in understandings of selfhood. This is the notion of identity as 'an effect of identification with and against others' (Jagose 1998: 79). Influenced by poststructuralism, the critique of oppositional binaries, for example, hetero/homo, man/woman, masculine/feminine, is political and ethical, constituting a critique of hierarchy and exclusion. It departs from the argument that the nature of binary thinking is that one half of a binary will dominate as the 'norm', inevitably subordinating the 'other' term, which is always understood in relation to it. Warner coined the influential term 'heteronormativity' in a germinal paper, 'Fear of a Queer Planet', in 1991, to denote just this, the extent to which society implicitly assumes heterosexuality to be stable, essential 'thing', and to be the norm and, more than this, implicitly maintains and promotes it through both formal social institutions and more informal social norms and culture. Queer theory is concerned not just with sexuality, but with sex/gender, as it assumes that neither of these cultural categories makes sense without the other, and both are normatively constructed according to fixed binaries. You cannot claim the permanent and fixed identity of homo/heterosexual if you do not have one fixed gender, such that you can posit your attraction to the purportedly same/opposite gender. Some thinkers have argued that the 'story' of two complementary, oppositional sexes or genders is a 'heterosexual fairytale' (Martin 2006), defined by heteronormativity, such that 'gender hierarchy serve[s] a more or less compulsory heterosexuality' (Butler 2007: xiii).

The notion of heteronomativity shares much with earlier feminist ideas such as those of Beauvoir who critiqued the idea of the oppositional impulses underpinning the othering of women against the universal human man in *The Second Sex* (1997 [1949]), an idea now referred to as alterity. Likewise, Ortner (1972) charted the prevalent cultural mode of thought in 'Western' societies, which categorises everything in hierarchical binaries, with the submissive term always being understood as feminine, in 'Is Female to Male as Nature to Culture?' This idea is also extended in Irigaray's 'The Sex Which Is Not One' (Irigaray 1985), where ze characterises man as subject against its binary and subjugated opposite of woman as object. While these thinkers did not all extend this analysis to the corollary that sexual difference itself ought to be eradicated, this naturalised notion of oppositional difference was problematised, and is perceived in this project as the problem inherent to gender, which makes its eradication the most efficacious solution. In Chapter 1 this will be justified by outlining the extent to which bigenderism continues to dominate our ways of understanding ourselves, even in the face of attempts to challenge it and expand gender, by always appealing back to oppositional difference.

Given this critique of binarism, queer theory has therefore tended to celebrate multiplicity, seeing identity as 'provisional and contingent' (Jagose 1998: 76) and the alternative ideal as 'proliferation' (Butler 2007 [1990]: 46), and to avoid reduction or appeals to fixed essence. Doty, for example, defines queer as 'a flexible space for the expression of all aspects of non- (anti-, contra-) straight cultural production and reception' (in Jagose 1998: 97), wherein all kinds of queerness are the alternatives to straight, rather than a fixed opposite of 'gay'. Queer theory is usually understood as a position or an impulse of critique, then, rather than an identity or a positive theory *of* something. This understanding of queer theory as undoing and critique of gender and sexual identity has led to it being sometimes characterised as a completely negative position (Edelman 2004: 4; Giffney 2004; Halberstam 2011), and developed by some more contemporaneously into 'the so-called antisocial thesis' (Weiner & Young 2011: 224). Such a denormatising project I would deem essential in a world dominated by compulsory oppositional gender and heteronormativity. However, increasingly, queer thinkers are calling for more positive, utopian characterisations of the original queer impulse and considerations of how it may impact on positive social change, such as Muñoz's *Cruising Utopia*, which asks readers to 'approach the queer critique from a renewed and newly animated sense of the social' (2009: 18). But there have also been calls for *more explicit, practicable* accounts of how queer theory may inform reconstructive ideas about politics, social relationships ('sociality') and understandings of the self and others (see Butler 2011c, de Lauretis 2011 and others in a special issue of *GLQ* on 'Queer Bonds'). It is hoped that by building on the insights developed by queer theory in its process of *deconstructing identity* that a *workable* positive mode of thought and sociality might be possible.

This very oppositional nature of queer theory *is* a moral impulse, a positive value: 'the antisocial force of (queer) sex is fundamental to the world-making inventiveness that queer bonds also name' (Weiner & Young 2011: 226). The catalyst for such deconstructions is indeed critique of the exclusions wrought by heteronormativity. Continuing this, I argue that queer thinking offers stimulating ethical, reconstructive potential as a premise for another way of understanding ourselves and others, and a more ethical way of conducting ourselves that does not perpetuate these exclusions, or at least minimises them. This critical basis from which queer theory developed can be seen as a strength that might help any reconstructive ideas to avoid too much prescription, one of the central problems of compulsory gender categories.

I will now briefly address one of the most commonly cited challenges to a proposal such as mine: appeals to an essential, biological sexual difference which, to differing extents, is thought to influence gender. I identify that some approaches to gender studies have tended to perpetuate this by 'bracketing off' and reinforcing biological sex in the pursuit of theorising a purely social gender. However, it is this assumption that serves as an enduring spectre of gender, maintaining oppositional thinking in identity. I suggest instead that seeing 'sexual difference' as a social mode of constructing and producing (that is, *constituting*) the body offers more exciting and enduring reconstructive potential, an approach I will revisit in greater depth in Chapter 2. There I will propose an alternative ontology, or way of understanding the self, that argues that bodies *can* be understood in non-binary ways, and in fact that their 'nature' is one of multiple potentiality that *lends* them to this. This underpins and allows for ethical argument for a truly androgynous, non-binary, post-sex, post-gender ethic.

Sex/gender/sexuality/difference

Recent ways of conceptualising sex and gender offer potentially radical and effective premises on which to base an argument for post-gender queer sociality. The notion of a natural biological sexual opposition is taken for granted in social life, and in much academic work. It has become the orthodoxy in sociological and much gender literature (with some significant exceptions, to be elaborated below) to posit a distinction between biological sex – understood as physical differences between men and women – and a more socially understood gender, which is the way that these differences inform social formations. From this 'sex/gender divide', gender then becomes the proper object of study in many works, and sex left alone with a variously theorised factitious influence on gender. This became an established way to use the concepts in Anglophone contexts after Ann Oakley's *Sex, Gender and Society* in 1972, and has proven fruitful for the ability to interrogate the social aspects of gender away from essentialist understandings about the differences between men and women, as well as a useful teaching tool. Using this, it became possible to justify many claims for greater equality in areas that had previously been underpinned by implicit biological reasoning.

It is important to note, however, that many non-Anglophone languages do not have equivalent discrete terms for sex/gender, making such a strategy less easy (Lykke 2010b: 13; Widerberg 1998) and provoking divergent thinking around the issue. Many other thinkers have never considered this conceptually useful, or as the only way to challenge gender essentialism. In gender studies, West & Zimmerman (1987), for example, emphasised early on that such an opposition is often not organic for those first reflecting on gender studies. They challenged the supposed immutability of the biological and supposed mutability or plasticity of the social, a move that undermines the sex/ gender divide. As such they, and others, have always included what we understand to be biological sex in their *social* analyses of gender. Congruently, Kessler & McKenna maintained in 1978:

> We will use gender, rather than sex, even when referring to those aspects of being a woman (girl) or man (boy) that have traditionally been viewed as biological. This will serve to emphasise our position that the element of social construction is primary in all aspects of being female and male. (1978: 7)

More recently, there has developed a growing body of work explicitly critiquing the sex/gender divide that interrogates 'the intertwining of sociocultural and biological dimensions' (Lykke 2010b: 13). This move seeks not to re-essentialise gender, but to also de-essentialise and complicate biological sex using empirical evidence. As outlined above, these are commonly grouped under the monikers 'new materialism' (Hird 2004b), 'feminist corpomaterialism' (Lykke 2010a) or 'post-constructionism' (Lykke 2010b), or emanate from feminist biology (Fausto-Sterling 2012). These accounts tend to eschew the choice between essentialism (i.e. appealing to innate characteristics as in notions of biological sex) or social constructionism (which can downplay or bracket off biology as with notions of gender), choosing instead to consider the reality of how bodies develop. As a result of situating my work alongside these accounts, I use the 'consciously ambiguous' (Lykke 2010b: 13) term 'sex/gender', following the lead of ethnomethodologists Kessler & McKenna (1978) and West & Zimmerman (1987), Scandinavian gender theorists Lykke (2010b) and Widerberg (1998), and feminist biologists Fausto-Sterling (2012) and Hird (2000, 2004a, 2004b). This situates my work among corporeal thinkers who argue that 'in order to transgress dualist philosophy ... feminist analysis of subjectivity and identity should take corporeality ... as its point of departure' (Lykke 2010b: 111).

This analysis means that the classification of people according to sex/gender can be understood as arbitrary and 'underdetermined' (Marinucci 2010: 34–35). 'Underdetermination' used in this way is the position that there is no empirical reality that dictates the categorisation of people according to two supposed pre-existing categories of 'sex'. This combination of characteristics understood to make up a 'thing' called sex, which consists of two discrete categories, is a humyn construction imposed on to bodies. This is an argument made exhaustively and convincingly by feminist biologists (Hird 2000, 2004a 2004b; Fausto-Sterling 2003, 2012) who challenge the classificatory coherence of all of the conventional means by which sex has been, and is, empirically and definitively posited as a clear category (capacity to reproduce, genitals, reproductive organs, hormones and chromosomes). People with different-coloured eyes could similarly be classified, for example, as discrete and fundamentally different categories of people. Dimorphism is, according to these thinkers, a humyn construct.

A key premise of this book is that people continue to be defined according to oppositional or dualistic understandings of biological sex and of gender whether they choose to or not (i.e. this is socially compulsory), and that it is the compulsory placing in hierarchical, oppositional difference that makes the concepts inherently ethically problematic and negative. I will demonstrate this in Chapter 1 by drawing on evidence that sex/gender does what Bourdieu characterises as a 'symbolic violence' to most people by restricting the 'cognitive instruments' through which they may understand themselves and others, which in turn restricts their potentiality and capacities (Bourdieu 2004: 339).

What sex and gender share is an inseparability from, and origin in, oppositional sexual difference. It is this impulse of fundamental difference that I challenge using the new materialist approaches introduced above, queer theory and other theoretical approaches, and to which I offer an alternative herein. This shift to difference as the root problem that maintains gender's persistence and negative impacts is shared by other gender theorists dedicated to diagnosing the oppressive mechanisms inherent to gender. For example, Fenstermaker, West and Zimmerman's vocabulary shifted from 'doing gender' to 'doing difference' (West & Zimmerman 1987; Fenstermaker & West 2002) when they took into account the ways that all types of difference are 'done' simultaneously to produce different social meanings. They conclude that it is the doing of *difference* that is the underlying 'mechanism ... for producing social inequality' (Fenstermaker & West 2002: 96). Likewise, bringing all of these types of difference into one analysis of the problem of gender, it is Butler's premise that:

> The univocity of sex, the internal coherence of gender, and the binary framework for both sex and gender are ... regulatory fictions that consolidate and naturalize the convergent power regimes of masculine and heterosexist oppression. (Butler 2007 [1990]: 46)

Such reasoning is compatible with queer theory as I explained it above and its diagnosis of the co-constitution of sex/gender/difference. Empirical evidence that gender is inherently exclusionary and hierarchical, alongside the position that sex/gender is not essential or naturally occurring allows me to make the argument that people need not be understood in this way, and go on to make the more moral, ethical, practical argument in the bulk of the book for a post-gender alternative:

> the recognition that the standards established by contemporary western categories of gender, sex and sexuality are socially constructed does not eliminate the impact of these categories. It does, however, serve as an invitation to construct alternative categories. The goal is not to exchange one empirically underdetermined set of categories for another empirically underdetermined set of categories. Instead the goal is the proliferation and multiplication of categories. (Marinucci 2010: 35–36)

Approach

One of the preoccupations in the form and content of this book is attempting to find strategic ways around theoretical and practical problems and debates that have become impasses. In doing so, I methodologically use whatever conceptual approaches can aid this aim. Many of the issues in this book have become mired in dualistic either/or reasoning – such as sex/gender, material/social, self/other, sameness/difference, idealism/realism. My promiscuous methodology is therefore invested in finding positive solutions for thinking beyond these oppositions. I see this as the more reciprocal, more 'androgynous' mode of thought for which I will argue in action.

In offering a detailed justification for, overview of, use of and extension of, work explicitly about getting rid of gender, it is necessary to transcend restrictions to disciplines, and I take a methodologically 'queer' (Browne & Nash 2010), 'scavenger' approach (Dahl 2010: 149; Halberstam 1998: 13). My work is at the intersections of queer and feminist theory, social and cultural theory, sociology, psychology, philosophy and ethics, political theory, biology and social movement theory. This diversity allows me to develop an holistic social diagnostic, utopian, practical account of why and how the reifications of sex and gender might be overcome, and – reconstructively – what they might be replaced with. Such a thorough attempt requires thinking through the issue metaphysically and ontologically, normatively and morally, and politically and pragmatically.

My understanding of the research process transcends another dualism, that of theory/practice, by being premised in the epistemological assumptions shared by Stanley's (2013) notion of 'feminist praxis'. The premises of this are defined by Stanley as 'a shared feminist commitment to a political position in which "knowledge" is not simply defined as "knowledge *what*" but also as "knowledge *for*"' (15). Further, in terms of the implications of this for method, praxis is considered 'a social science endeavour which rejects the "theory/research" divide, seeing these instead as united manual and intellectual activities which are symbolically related (for all theorising requires "research" of some form or another)' (Stanley 2013: 15). This practically oriented position establishes a concern that runs throughout the project, with the normative justifiability, usefulness and practicability of the ideas that I draw on and develop, especially in cross-cultural contexts and non-ideal circumstances.

In particular, fresh approaches and ways of thinking through the 'problems' of sex/gender difference are made possible by my use of non-traditional terrains of theory-making, and I take inspiration from solution-based real-world practices that have occurred in communities and groups of people as means of moving ideals forward. In sociology, along with Sennett (2012: ix), who has 'tired of theorizing as a self-contained pursuit', Stein & Plummer have conversely noted that 'useful as they can be, empirical studies have tended to be unreflective about the nature of sexuality as a social category' (Stein & Plummer 1994: 179). Thus my concurrent use of academic and everyday theorising, woven together in my 'exposition' or 'narration' (Rorty in Barker 2008: 33–34) to answer theoretically explicated practical questions. Some work has considered the practices, everyday theorising and ethical impulses around gender and sexuality from social movements such as contemporary queer movements and communities, and from individuals and groups in society. For example, work around international Queeruption gatherings and other queer social movements has been undertaken in human geography (Brown 2007a, 2007b) and sociology (Driver 2008; Heckert 2010; Hennen 2004; Vanelslander 2007), and in my previous work. There I indicated the fruitful intersections between such practices and ethical ways of thinking about the self, others and social organising (Nicholas 2009, 2012), which have nuanced notions about the nature of being, politics and of ethical conduct. In researching anarchist and queer communities (Nicholas 2009, 2012), I have witnessed praxis that organically developed from practice and reflection. As such, it seemed fitting that such informal theorising should be taken seriously and the actually existing practices that were developed in response to this be considered alongside academic positions. This book attempts to embody praxis by fusing the insights of empirical work and theory, making the insights of empirical work less simply descriptive and more analytical and prefigurative, and considering the practical implications of abstract theory. I have contributed to making theory useful for social change by crafting what I argue is a thorough, 'feasible, practicable and enactable' (Critchley 2011: n.p.) reconstructive ethic of gender deconstruction.

In addition to this dedication to an awareness of and attempt to resolve, transcend or move beyond dualistic impasses in thinking, and in line with praxis, I attempt in this book to prefigure some of these sexual-difference transcendent or androgynous practices that are explicitly argued for. Most notably, the book will be written using gender-neutral pronouns and language, as discussed in the first endnote to this chapter, and I expand on gender-neutral pronouns as part of post-gender practice in Chapter 8. This is a performative attempt to deconstruct preconceptions and foster reflection on the imposition of sexual difference in reading practices while also intending to prefigure and reconstruct a form of reading that is less preconceived and provokes agency in both the reader and 'subject'.

The argument and structure: deconstructing sexual difference, reconstructing ethical selves

The argument is given a non-foundational ontology of *potentiality*, that a preferable way of perceiving the world, that is ethos, to that of sexual difference, can be found in a particular understanding of androgyny. More procedurally, this androgynous ethos could inform a reciprocal code of conduct, that it could be enacted by an ethics of reciprocity. If the 'self' is constituted by pre-existing resources, then these are able to exemplify alternative cultural resources to replace the sexual difference that currently shapes our being in the world. In essence, I will make a thorough, programmatic argument for the eradication or rejection of sexual difference (and thereby sex/gender) as a dominant ethic through which subjectivity, intersubjectivity (relations between people) and social life are understood, and for its replacement with an androgynous, relational ethic of reciprocity. I will do so thoroughly through the argument of this book, sharing the premise that 'it is now time to find ways to undercut the first principle of the gendered social order, the division into "men" and "women"' (Lorber 2000: 83).

Chapter 1 will present the problem: the endurance and omnirelevance of a dedication to binary 'gender' perceived as an essential aspect of selfhood, either as biologically or subjectively determined, in the popular imagination and even in theories that seek to deconstruct gender. Here I will outline the impossibility of the expansion of gender, and its perpetual return to binary opposition or 'bigenderism'.

Chapter 2 is an explanation for the persistence of gender and a foundation for reconstruction. Elaborating on how bigenderism is a result of not challenging biological sexual difference, this chapter draws on contemporary new materialist feminist theory to argue for an understanding of bodies that challenges the naturalness of sexual difference, and offers more 'malleable' characterisation of matter. It also demonstrates how gender is understood as a doing or as performative, and maintained socially. Finally, given its persistence and proposing that sex/gender constitutes a 'symbolic violence' with negative impacts on cisgendered ('normatively' gendered) *and* gender-variant people, it outlines the premise that the best way to challenge the problems of sex/gender is to eradicate it.

Chapter 3 will demonstrate the extent to which dominant, liberal ethico-political paradigms can or cannot challenge the 'symbolic violence' that sexual difference imposes. This chapter will propose that these ethico-political paradigms that have attempted to offer more 'just' alternatives to how the self and others are understood are limited in their efficacy by their reluctance to deconstruct sex/gender and challenge the dominant epistemological foundation of self/other. They cannot therefore conceptualise a truly post-gender ethics and sociality. I will then argue that there are some important insights to be taken from ethics developed in contradistinction to these individualistic, liberal ethical formulations, such as feminine ethics, poststructuralist anarchism and communitarianism.

Chapter 4 offers the key philosophical argument and justification for post-gender ethics. Using Simone de Beauvoir's lesser known existentialist 'ethics of ambiguity', alongside Judith Butler and Michel Foucault's work, as well as ideas from other feminist philosophers, it uses metaphysical and ethical reasoning to argue that getting rid of sex/gender is both possible and desirable. This chapter offers a lucid account of Beauvoir and Butler's notions of self, the kind of freedom or 'agency' that they allow for and the ideals they explicitly and implicitly argue for, to underpin a reconstructive alternative ethics of reciprocity.

Following the ontological and normative arguments that justify an androgynous, post-gender mode of being, I will then attempt to fill out what an ethic premised on such ontological ethical foundations may 'look like', and, given the ontological premises, how it may be achieved and maintained. Chapters 5–8 will apply the theoretical insights developed in the first half of the book to social and political practice and vice versa.

Chapter 5 charts the usefulness of queer theory's original deconstructive impulse, and considers how a reconstructive ethic can avoid congealing in to an imposing identity or norm. This chapter seeks to characterise a 'queer bond' and a sexual ethics of pleasure, rather than identity, that is useful cross-culturally. It develops an ethos or mode of thought with which to perceive others, to underpin a truly androgynous and reciprocal ethics (way of being) and sexuality. It engages in 'the recognition debates' using Beauvoir's ethics to transcend the universal/particular positions usually proposed for recognition, and argues for an ideal ethic of 'universalised particularism' to replace the necessity of sex/gender in social life and in sexuality.

Chapter 6 then considers how attempts to realise such a way of being can avoid sliding into privileging either means or ends. Following the idealistic, utopian sketch of Chapter 5, Chapter 6 will consider how such ideals might be implemented in 'impure' contexts that might create the need for value judgements. This will allow me to strengthen the normative bottom line of a reciprocal ethic that could make it utilisable and applicable, without betraying its own premises. Drawing on existentialist ethical deliberations about 'strategic violence' (Beauvoir 1978, 2004; Fanon 1974; Sartre 1974) and debates in deconstruction about the inescapability of dominant discourses (Critchley 1999; Spivak 1994), I will consider here the need for strategic engagement with practices, or means, at odds with the normative ends of reciprocity, and what strategies can minimise the reification of such strategic action.

Chapters 7 and 8 are accounts of how such a post-gender ethic might be applied or practised on the multiple levels of subjectivity, intersubjectivity and culture that have traditionally perpetuated gender. Chapter 7 is concerned with strategies for how individuals might be as enabled as possible to be self-determined or 'purposive' in their identity, and thus able to resist gendering. To this end, it uses the ideal of Foucault's critical subject to consider the capacities a person would require to make autonomous choices about themselves and others that are not predetermined by sex/gender. Queer pedagogy is identified as a key practice for 'teaching' the capacity for androgyny and reciprocity, and broadly pedagogical practices from queer, anarchist and other communities are presented as practices for transcending gender. Finally, gender-neutral childrearing is considered for its potential and effectiveness in actually fostering post-gender ethics.

Chapter 8 considers how relationships and interaction, as well as social institutions and practices can be more androgynous and less gendered towards the end of post-gender society. It outlines how interaction might be more androgynous and reciprocal, such that people are relationally enabled with greater self-determination than gender allows for. Social sites for post-gender intervention, including gender-neutral language and intersex legal and medical rights, are considered for their transformative effectiveness in creating post-gender social contexts or cultural resources. Finally, reconstructive community responses to sexual assault will allow me to briefly address how ethical 'sexuality' might look without compulsory sexual difference or sex/gender identity, but nonetheless with ethical evaluation, premised on a relational ethic of pleasure and reciprocity.

Like feminist theory, which developed from an explicitly normative, ideological motivation, my interest in this topic has developed from an explicitly 'democratic' and queer impulse. My impetus for this project, then, is to consider in a thorough manner what an impulse of maximum purposiveness might look like in terms of identity, behaviour and relations, and my starting point is that it would need to be without sex/gender identity. The first two chapters present the 'problem', in terms of outlining how persistent oppositional sex/gender difference remains, and how it serves as a 'symbolic violence' for all who are shaped by it. These chapters will underpin the reconstructive component of the project by demonstrating how the deconstruction of sex/gender 'sets in to question the *foundational* restrictions on feminist political theorizing and opens up other configurations, not only of genders and bodies, but of politics itself' (Butler 2007 [1990]: 194).

1
The Resilience of Bigenderism

This chapter will illustrate how resilient and compulsory dualistic gender is and how much it continues to be conceptually tied to and co-constitutive with notions of material sexual difference. I will present empirical examples of the personal and social difficulty of trans and intersex selfhood and how they offer evidence for the notion of bigendersm (Gilbert 2009). The ongoing omnirelevance of bigenderism in the virtual contexts of the internet – where assumptions about sex and gender and their relationship between each other continue to shape our sense of self and the ways that we interact, even though these contexts are 'disembodied' – helps to diagnose the problem of gender. I also demonstrate how ostensible challenges to binary sex/gender are persistently recuperated, for example in gender deconstructive theories and activism. I will go on to argue that these examples are demonstrative of the limits of attempting to challenge the persistence of gender without challenging oppositional modes of thought more widely, especially dualistic understandings of bodies.

The omnirelevance of sex/gender identity

It has been widely asserted in sociology that gender is a compulsory and 'omnirelevant' (Garfinkel 1967; West & Zimmerman 1987) aspect of selfhood and social life, 'a precondition for the production and maintenance of legible humanity' (Butler 2004: 11; see also West & Zimmerman 1987). This compulsorily binary understanding of selfhood, and its persistent relationship to notions of biological materiality, is made particularly apparent in the treatment of intersexuality in many countries. Despite proposed statistics that around 1.7% of births demonstrate some level of genital 'anomaly' (Fausto-Sterling 2000; Hird

2004a: 123), it is still the case that 'The birth of a baby with ambiguous genitals constitutes a "social emergency" in the delivery room' (Turner 1999: 467), to the extent that an attribution of singular sex, and thus gender, and physical reconstruction is still routinely undertaken as soon as possible (Hird 2004a). This compulsory and non-consensual gendering of the biology of intersexed infants has led to an 'intersex rights' social movement that advocates for the freedom of people to choose their own physical attributes and social identifications (Chase 1998), for example Organisation Intersex International (Bock 2013) and the Intersex Society of North America (ISNA), which advocated for intersex rights between 1993 and 2008 (Chase 1993).

ISNA founder Cheryl Chase suggests that intersex is inherently disruptive of the sex/gender order: 'I am forced to wonder whether our culture's concept of sexual normalcy, which defines the sex organs of as many as 4 per cent of newborn infants as "defective," is not itself defective' (Chase 1993: 3). The prevalent medical practice of gender assignment for intersex infants, usually judged according to the ability to engage in penetrative sex (Chase 1993: 3; Feinberg 1998: 8), illustrates not only the social imperative to label babies as either boys or girls and the discourse of complementarity between these oppositions (Hird 2004a: 17), but also the inextricability of gender, sex and sexual orientation. It indicates that these notions make sense, and are definable, only in terms of the others. This 'gender assignment' is actually a matter of physically assigning biological sex, from which gender is supposed to follow, categories which themselves allow for stable sexuality categories (hetero/homo require fixed gender), but which are also defined by heteronormativity, as demonstrated by the justifications for choices made regarding the sex category to assign. Intersexuality and gender assignment has gained public attention in recent years (Bock 2013; Fausto-Sterling 2012; Nandi 2013), but the extent to which there is slippage in medical and popular accounts between biological sex and gender identity demonstrates the limits of feminist attempts to separate sex and gender, which I will discuss in greater depth in the next chapter. This slippage has been illustrated in public discourse around 'intersex' athletes (Fausto-Sterling 2012: 1–2; Kenney & Akita 2013), wherein sporting government bodies have been discussing 'gender tests' that pertain to biological signifiers of 'sex'.

Transgender is understood in different ways. Kessler & McKenna (2000) taxonomise these as first an incongruence *between* physical 'sex' and gender, which leads to permanent physical transition into the opposite 'gender', which retains adherence to binary understandings of sex and gender. Second is a less final or permanent crossing wherein bodily sex is incongruent with gender identity, which again adheres to the binaries. And finally, gender ambiguity or variance that transcends the binaries, such that no clear gender attribution can be made. However, the social or interactional difficulty of *all* of these different trans identities also demonstrates this 'omnirelevance' of polarised gendered modes of perception in understandings of the self and others that rely on correlation between sex, gender and sexuality. The interactional problems that this presents further illustrate the negative impacts of sex/gender.

Feinberg argues that violence against transgender people – which ze defines as people who present a gender display at odds with their biological sex, or whose sex or gender are not clear – is prevalent enough to conclude that 'Trans people are still literally social outlaws' (Feinberg 1998: 10). Indeed, research by Lombardi, Wilchins, Priesing & Malouf (2001) found that at some time 59.9% of the transgender respondents from the USA who participated in the research had 'experienced either violence or harassment' (Lombardi et al. 2001: 95) on account of being transgendered. An overview of US research into violence against transgender people found that '43–60% of participants report past experiences of physical violence … and 43–46% report they had been victims of sexual assault' (Testa et al. 2012: 453). These statistics only take into account certain types of violence – the Lombardi research only counted 'assault with a weapon, assault without a weapon, rape, sexual assault, or attempted assault' (Lombardi et al. 2001: 92) – and there are many qualitative accounts of the extent to which gender-ambiguous or gender-variant people more generally find themselves informally policed and under scrutiny, what Bourdieu (2004) would characterise as more 'symbolic violence'. For example, Wyss's empirical research in US high schools supports the prevalent position in previous research that 'trans and genderqueer youth who refuse to conform to the gender pressures that they face are likely to experience isolation and are at very high risk for assault' (2004: 715). As well as being social outlaws, trans and intersex folk often experience difficult relations with state and legal institutions, for example the case of Norrie, whose registration with the registry of births, deaths and marriages in New South Wales, Australia was changed to 'sex not specified' but then reversed in a high-profile case (Bibby 2013).

Also paradigmatic of the institutional and social maintenance of sex/gender is the well-documented 'toilet problem' (Browne 2004; Feinberg 1993; Halberstam 1998; McLaughlin 2005; *Truckface* zine).

The sex-segregated public toilet is a site of heightened sex and gender awareness and regulation: 'In a 2002 survey conducted by the San Francisco Human Rights Commission, nearly half of all transgender respondents reported having been harassed or assaulted in public restrooms' (McLaughlin 2005: n.p.). The prevalence of this violence demonstrates that 'the bathroom problem is much more than a glitch in the machinery of gender segregation and is better described in terms of the violent enforcement of our current gender system' (Halberstam 1998: 25) or a form of discrimination that Browne calls 'genderism' (2004). The impacts of this problem are more than the immediate physical threat. The difficultly that this co-constitution of the spatial and social presents to trans and intersex folk in everyday life reflects and contributes to an increased subjective sense of exclusion. Vade goes as far as to say 'Segregated public bathrooms threaten people's safety, job security and access to education. They also tell us every day, several times a day, that the only viable gender options are female and male' (Vade n.d.: n.p.). The violent enforcement of normative gender 'can be highly detrimental to one's bodily, emotional and mental health' (Wyss 2004: 718) and be internalised, with most of the participants in Wyss's study exhibiting responses consistent with 'a belief that one's oppression is justified' (Wyss 2004: 718).

Additionally, trans people who are gender-variant or ambiguous, that is, who do not 'pass' as either a man or woman, face pressures not only from wider society, but also from within trans communities. Gagne & Tewkesbury's research concluded that for most people in their study, pressure from within the transgender community meant that 'the need to avoid social erasure compelled a complete (even if temporary) transformation' (Gagne & Tewkesbury 1998: 86). This demonstrates that, even in communities where sex and gender and the relationship between the two are somewhat complicated, there remains a binary, difference-based understanding of self and others, derived from oppositional and complementary categories of male/female and masculine/feminine. Indeed, it has been emphasised how much presentations of ambiguity can be recuperated by those seeing it into familiar binary-based understandings: 'Ambiguous gender, when and where it does appear, is inevitably transformed into deviance, thirdness, or a blurred vision of either male or female' (Halberstam 1998: 20). Goffman (1956) and Garfinkel (1967) have effectively demonstrated this point by emphasising the extent to which social participants are willing, or in fact bound, to read the behaviour of others according to conventional categories and will 'recuperate' transgressions. Gilbert (2009), referring to Garfinkel and, later, Kate Bornstein's development of a set of 'generally accepted gender rules,' states that

> According to the rules there is no such thing as someone whose sex or gender diverges from their birth-designated sex, which means that trans folk cannot exist. However, a corollary says that if anyone does change sex it must be from one of the two sexes to the other. The one thing that is absolutely not allowed is a gender that does not fall neatly into one of the two categories. (Gilbert 2009: 95)

Ze characterises this simply as 'bigenderism'. However, to further illustrate what this social formation of gender along these lines means for social life, the case of a self-identified gender-transcendent student senator Toby Hill-Meyer asked that, in an article about per, the University of Oregon newspaper use gender-neutral pronouns,[1] later explaining that ze uses these pronouns as ze perceives per gender to be neither male nor female (Abraham 2004: n.p.). The way that this act was received demonstrates that not only is gender ambiguity socially sanctioned, it is usually not even *possible* as it is understood by others on the basis of being a transgression of something else, such as sexuality norms. The way that ze was read by others demonstrates the reference back to (binary) sex as congruous with (binary) gender and the collapse of both of these with (binary) sexuality: 'Unless we're missing something dramatic here, he's (oops) a gay man. Which is fine. More power to Toby Hill-Meyer' (Olly 2004). This drives home the two related points that will be developed below: that sex, gender and sexuality are inextricably linked in the popular imagination, and thus the mechanism that underlies them and maintains their resilience – sexual difference – is the real problem; and that sex and gender are social problems, intersubjectively (i.e. in relations between people) or *attributionally* maintained or perpetuated.

The 'disembodied' nature of sex/gender

Following from this example of the recuperation of an attempt to expand gender, the conservative ways that gender plays out in the virtual space of the internet allows me to begin considering what the real 'nature' of gender is, and to diagnose why individual attempts to challenge it are destined to recuperation. It illustrates how much gender is a social category that is compulsorily attributed regardless of subjective identity, and how much these attributions are made with fairly flimsy, social cues, rather than biological ones, what Kessler and McKenna call 'cultural genitals' (Kessler & McKenna 1978: 154). This precedes my challenge to the usefulness of the sex/gender divide, when commonsense perpetually appeals back to presumptions about biological sexual difference and its relationship to gender in 'placing' people in interaction.

These attributions of Hill-Meyer were made online, by social partici-pants who made diagnoses of Hill-Meyer's 'true self' from visual clues using the generally accepted rules of sex/gender, which they assume to be essential, fundamental, binary and universal. This same subjective and intersubjective attribution of dualistic and biologically essential sex/gender identity accounts for the subversive failure of the virtual, where 'the rules' are still held by social participants and attributions according to them irresistible.

The 2007 book *Alter Ego: Avatars and their Creators* (Cooper 2007) is paradigmatic of what Braidotti calls 'the imaginative poverty of virtual reality' (Braidotti 1996: n.p.) in relation to gender, and this example clearly illustrates how little gender attribution has to do with biol-ogy. As I have outlined before (Nicholas 2009), it presents a data set of 66 avatars ('computer generated visual representations of people or bots' (Nowak & Rauh 2005: n.p.)) alongside portraits and stories about their creators. Of this international collection of participants in virtual worlds, an overwhelming 56 of the 66 avatars, are directly gender-referential, in that the declared gender of the avatar is continuous with the sex category presented or declared by the creator. Additionally while six avatars are entirely non-human, five of these are anthropo-morphised and therefore gendered. Only one avatar is non-human *and* non-gendered (the 'Flying Spaghetti Monster'). This demonstrates not only the *compulsarity* of gender as a marker of legible identity, but also the *bigenderism* that limits the proliferation of gender categories so that, at best, there can be an incongruence between the choice of which binary sex and which binary gender a social participant holds. Indeed, avatar research by Nowak & Rauh (2005) further demonstrates the inter-subjective imperative of gender online. These researchers sought to test the importance of the stable establishment of gender for interaction in online interaction where no bodily cues are available. In asking research participants to evaluate a series of pictures of avatars, they discovered that the more androgynous and less humyn the avatars, the more difficult people find it to communicate with them:

The responses to the images were consistent with what would be predicted by uncertainty reduction theory. The results show that the masculinity or femininity (lack of androgyny) of an avatar, as well as anthropomorphism, significantly influence perceptions of avatars. (Nowak & Rauh 2005: n.p.)

Uncertainty reduction theory suggests that the more familiar and understandable the other person is in an interaction, the more likely we are to trust and like them. It also states that, in order to reduce uncertainty about a stranger, in the 'initial entry stage of interpersonal interaction' we attempt to place them according to pre-existing behavioural norms and categories (Berger & Calabrese 1975: 99). This avatar research demonstrates that this 'placing' holds true for online interaction where there are no bodily cues, and that placing gender is an integral part of placing someone in familiar terms in social interaction. This research challenges early futurological predictions of the internet as a space in which traditional identity would be challenged by demonstrating that the same rules of social interaction apply in virtual contexts as in real life. Rather than demonstrating greater freedom in the virtual, this demonstrates the gendered limits to the qualitative possibilities of self-presentation and of intersubjective understanding, and the persistence of gendered selfhood and interaction in virtual interactions (O'Brien 1999; Warhol 2002). Importantly, this revelation illustrates that gendered assumptions *precede* biological sex, rather than following from them, just as they do in the 'sexing' of newborn infants.

Supporting these findings, in an early consideration of the possibilities for gender in virtual worlds, while asserting that theoretically 'users are able to create a virtual self, outside the normally assumed boundaries of gender, race, class, and age' (Reid 1995: 181), Reid also acknowledged that 'many obviously feel very uncomfortable and at a disadvantage in interacting with others whose gender is unclear and feel even more discomforted on discovering that they have been interacting under false assumptions' (Reid 1995: 180). As well as highlighting the imperative of stable gender certainty, the notion of 'false assumptions' underscores the way that the virtual is rooted in humanistic concepts of self-hood and of gender as a reflection of a true aspect of the material self. On this theme, Rak's (2005) research into blogging demonstrates people's ongoing attachment to humanistic ideas of subjectivity even in the virtual, to the extent that actual uses of virtual reality are predicated on a liberal notion of unified subjectivity, on 'the assumption that experience congeals around a subject, and makes a subject who can be written and read' (Rak 2005: 166) according to existing frames.

More sophisticated research about online social dynamics (see e.g. Hine 2003; Wajcman 2004) has moved from viewing the virtual as a *place* with certain inherent characteristics, to understanding it rather as a sphere of interaction and considering the co-constitution of technology and the social. In emphasising this resilience of gender as a central defining characteristic even in the virtual, Wajcman, for example, has theorised the internet as a 'new technology with the same old narratives' (Wajcman 2004: 70). Exemplary of these analyses is sociotechnical studies, which would support this by theorising the causal relationship between technology and the social beyond even an interactive view to a more radical 'seamless web view' (Bijker & Law 1992: 201). This marks a break from early futurological and optimistic accounts of the internet as a space that would allow for free play of identity. It also accounts better for the resilience of gendered interaction, emphasising instead 'the continuation of pre-established relations' (Webster 2006: 5). Extending the notion of 'performativity' – which views being as an ongoing practice or repetition that gives the illusion of stability – to this relationship in an approach comparable with performative geographies, proponents of this sociotechnical account assert that the distinction between 'machines and those who operate them ... [is] an accomplishment' (Bijker & Law 1992: 201). Importantly here, this is all demonstrative of the relatively small part that pre-existing biology plays in this construction of gender, so that sex can perhaps be understood to be a result of gendered interpretation, rather than a pre-existing entity.

The imaginative limit of social interaction in the virtual, then, is presentation of a binary gender that is not continuous with the binary sex a social participant is assumed to hold. This is the extent of the challenge to the gender rules given the pervasiveness of stable social attributions of sex/gender and ultimately to greater or lesser degrees, social interaction online ensures that bigenderism itself is upheld. As the notion of 'false assumptions' discussed demonstrates, even this transgression can sometimes be too challenging to commonsense understandings of sex/gender. This same limit is, I argue, apparent in some queer theory, trans identity politics and queer or trans activism that call for or envision alternative gender models. Ultimately they tend to leave biological sexual difference and binary understandings of sex and gender undisturbed. Like sex/gender in the virtual, attempts to challenge the binary aspects are recuperated in to conventional understandings, once again illustrating that the truly limiting mode of thought here is compulsory oppositional dualism.

The binary limits of trans identity politics

Some alternative models for gender have been proposed by queer and trans theorists and activists to offer more freedom for gender non-conformists (Bornstein 1994; Ettling 2005; Feinberg 1998; Halberstam 1998; Vade n.d.), but ultimately these tend not to challenge the omnirelevance of gender of some sort for understandings of one's self and others in social life. Additionally, the limits of these models tend to be the separation of gender from biological sex, resulting in a fixed category of masculine/feminine gender not continuous with male/ female sex, or the idea of an expansion of gender displays such that this is more variable, but still with a fixed, binary bodily sex. Many of these alternative formulations for understanding gender are important for expanding identity choices significantly and thus making life more liveable for those who do identify with them. However, in relying on the sex/gender divide these identity options are illustrative of the very limits that I have outlined above: they variously fall back into a bina-rism so that usually 'if anyone does change sex it must be from one of the two sexes to the other' (Gilbert 2009: 95). They also assume that a separation of sex and gender is socially viable, that is, that people can 'read' a discontinuity between sex and gender, that the two can be understood as separate by the majority of people in interaction. Finally, these accounts tend to assume that these models could be implemented on an individual level, downplaying the weight of social and cultural attribution in sex/gender identity, and overemphasising how volun-taristic this process could be. Understanding why these approaches, which *do* nonetheless constitute some new socialities, collapse back into bigenderism (just as with attempts at ambiguity on the internet), and why they do not present a post-gender sociality, will help me to better diagnose the causes of bigenderism and understand what is needed for an approach that can truly obviate gender.

In formulating alternative gender visions, many thinkers argue for better representation of their own accounts of what *they* perceive as gender's 'true nature'. Many of these positions share the tendency cited above of going only as far as separating and rearranging the *combinations between* 'sex' and 'gender', rather than multiplying within the categories of sex and gender. This is apparent in Halberstam's *Female Masculinities*, wherein masculine gender is separated from male sex in the pursuit of liberation for masculine women: 'masculinity must not and cannot and should not reduce down to the male body and its effects' (Halberstam 1998: 1). Likewise, Feinberg explicitly articulates the way that ze understands this discontinuity between sex and gender to be inherently subversive and progressive for more freedom of gender expression:

> So why do I sometimes describe myself as a masculine female? Isn't each of those concepts very limiting? Yes. But placing the two words together is incendiary, exploding the belief that gender expression is linked to birth sex like horse and carriage. (Feinberg 1998: 9)

What is called for ultimately by such accounts is a separation of gender from the perceived biological of sex, and a multiplying of this social gender – what Feinberg calls 'gender variance' (Feinberg 1998: 10) – not the eradication of gender. The first of these aims – the option to identify with a gender identity that is discontinuous from your biological sex category – is of course a progressive aim considering that much common-sense assumption is that your behaviour is determined by your biology, but its possibility for extension to challenge the oppositions themselves is questionable. Kessler & McKenna describe this particular use of 'trans', which allows for identification with the gender opposite to your sex, as 'a previously unthinkable combination of male and female' (Kessler & McKenna 2000: n.p.), and I would emphasise that this 'previously unthinkable' formation of trans is growing in cultural representation and acceptability in many parts of the world, which progressively allows for greater cultural acceptance of this trans identity. This can be seen, for example, in the growing number of trans – in this sense of gender at odds with sex – characters in many popular TV series from the minority world[2] such as *Glee* (Wolf & Schweisberger 2013). The trans characters in *Glee* are paradigmatic of the appeal to a gender 'essence' that is a psychological or mental identity, and at odds with biological sex.

This particular form of trans identity politics has indeed allowed a powerful challenge to cisgender[3] privilege. This is the case in so far as it presents a challenge to the determining power of perceived biological sex for one's identity in the popular imagination, in the same way that the sex/gender divide served feminism to this end, as I will discuss below. As well as the shift in social perceptions, this approach to trans identity politics that places the 'true' gender identity of an individual apart from biological sex has also resulted in some important pragmatic institutional gains for those who identify in this manner, such as the ability to change legal documents and access desired surgery (Spade 2003).

However, discussion around this invocation of trans also characterises the debates around minority identity politics more broadly. Some queer thinkers with more complex ontological understandings of sex/gender outline the limits of a sexual and gender politics premised on binary essentialist formations of identity, even those where the 'essence' derives from a psychological subjectivity and not a material body as in this case (Campisi 2013; Hausman 1999; Wolf & Schweisberger 2013). Indeed, 'isn't each of those concepts very limiting?' (Feinberg 1998: 9), and does 'exploding the belief that gender expression is linked to birth sex' (Feinberg 1998: 9), that is, the sex/gender divide, really constitute an ultimately gender disruptive act? Continuing the case study of youth media representations of trans represented in just this way as an essentialist gender identity opposite to biological sex, Campisi (2013), for example, presents the issue that such media representations may ultimately result in a normalisation of certain types of trans identities to the exclusion or further marginalisation of other more troublesome gender identities.

In the context of legal recognition, this formation of trans premised on the separation of sex and gender is now enshrined in the UK's most progressive gender law, the Gender Recognition Act 2004. This Act embraces gender rather than sex as the true marker of selfhood, and allows for an 'adopted' gender identity at odds with the birth sex of the individual and which is not dependent on surgery to adjust biological sex. However, as with the above critiques of this sex/gender divide, Cowan (2004; 2005) and Sandland (2005) point out that within this seemingly progressive law regarding gender identity, there is an element of (re) disciplining potentially disruptive, *non-binary*, sexes and genders. This again occurs through the maintenance of the binaries *within* sex and gender while enabling only variation *between* sex and gender, as well again as the assumption that real gender identity is a result of subjectivity, regardless of the fixed sex of the body. Hausman calls this tendency 're-gendering' (Hausman 1999: 199) and suggests it relies on the assumption of a '"real world" of gender' (Hausman 1999: 191) that opposes itself to the non-determining, but biologically fixed, world of bodily sex. In the queer and trans literature this same essentialising impulse can indeed be seen in Halberstam's vision that in an ideal world there would be a 'coming out' (Halberstam 1998: 27), wherein one's true gender would be revealed, drawing on essentialist notions of a 'true' repressive gender resultant from a gendered subjectivity and regardless of, and not necessarily continuous with, morphology. Likewise, while refuting that gender is an aspect of essential biology, Feinberg makes references to the importance of being free to 'find' one's own true gender by exploring 'the path of self-expression' (Feinberg 1998: 6).

In these same texts, and elsewhere in trans literature, there is also an implicit and sometimes contradictory invocation of an individual voluntarism that assumes complete agency in choosing a gender from a more expanded model of gender (not sex) identities. This is apparent in the following quote, which also assumes that it would be possible to obtain equal validity for all categories in this new proliferated model of gender, despite the continued existence of the poles: 'Each person should have the right to *choose* between pink or blue tinted gender categories, as well as other hues of the palette' (Feinberg 1998: 1). Halberstam uses the voluntaristic language of 'gender preference' (Halberstam 1998: 27) alongside the more essentialist language of coming out, cited above.

Other attempts at expanded models of gender that do attempt to challenge the binarism have seen portrayals of its nature as a 'continuum' (Halberstam 1998), and Bornstein's (1994) 'spectrum'. Trans activists have drawn on metaphors of gender as a 'rainbow' (Hubbard 1996: 165), 'a gender galaxy – an infinite number of different beautiful genders' (Vade n.d.) or invoked the term 'pan-gender' (Ettling 2005). However, like Feinberg, many of these formulations retain the poles and categories at either end of these spectrums, and only rearrange *between* them – e.g. 'pan refers to the concept of there being an infinite number of gender and sexuality *combinations*' (Ettling 2005: n.p., my emphasis) – such that this multiplying can easily retain the spectre of binarism or bigenderism.

What these ideas still retain is the assumption that morphological sex is immutable, although not necessarily congruent with 'gender display', and that both sex and gender are binary, with occasional anomalies lying somewhere between these two binaries. Also, such an aim of the freedom either to express one's *true* gender identity, or choose one at will, while understandable, and having pragmatic benefits for many gender-variant individuals (Campisi 2013; Spade 2003), is destined to logical and practical failure through the re-essentialisation of gender and reinscription of the binaries such that further exclusions are ultimately produced. These models tacitly reproduce the premise that sex/gender is a real and essential thing and that *some kind of* sex/gender identity is essential, desirable and imperative to selfhood, and reassert a truth claim regarding what they think that identity should be like.

It is this inability to conceive of the self *without* some kind of gender identity to attach to that I challenge in depth by drawing on ontological formulations from new-materialists who propose that our notions of gender and sexual difference are a mischaracterisation of 'nature'.

This will allow me to go on in later chapters to propose an alternative way of being that both transcends sex/gender with an androgynous impulse, and allows for a proliferation of ways of being that does not reinforce gender and sexual difference as essential to understanding ourselves and others.

In the next chapter, I will account for the limits of the above strategies on the following grounds. Firstly, sex, gender and sexuality are co-constitutive, and to deconstruct one without the others is to destine a project to logical failure because they will always appeal back to and define each other in the popular imagination. Secondly, these categories are co-constitutive on the basis of oppositional binary difference, such that to assume that gender can be separated from sex and thus proliferated neglects the extent to which sex is assumed to be dimorphic and gender, being oppositional in nature, is co-constitutive of this dimorphism. Thus I will argue for considering *sexual difference* as the mode of thought at the root of sex, gender and sexuality, which renders attempts to multiply or alter impotent. Thirdly, these differences are intersubjectively constituted and maintained (i.e. in relations between people) and to assume a voluntaristic level of individual agency and choice belies the historical and cultural weight of sexual difference, so that 'while it is plausible to contend that gender displays – construed as conventionalised expressions – are optional, it does not seem plausible to say that we have the option of being seen by others as female or male' (West & Zimmerman 1987: 130). While some theorists derive from this historical and cultural weight a sense of the inevitability of difference, and seek through their ethical and political projects to strategically revalue the hierarchical imbalance that is inherent to this difference, I will use the premises developed in this chapter to make the more utopian normative argument in Chapter 2 that the social assumption of oppositional difference *can* and *must* itself be eradicated or transcended in order to undermine the hierarchy at the root of sex, gender and sexuality as currently understood.

2
Diagnosing and Transcending Sexual Difference

In Chapter 1, I presented the problem that has inspired this book, that of the persistence of compulsory, oppositional gender. In this chapter I will offer an account of the ontology of gender that explains this persistence even in the face of significant attempts to challenge it. This 'explanatory-diagnostic analysis' (Benhabib 1985: 405), that is, the attempt to determine what causes this persistence, has significant political and practical implications for the 'anticipatory-utopian critique' (Benhabib 1985: 405) that will make up the bulk of this book. I will argue that gender is so resilient because the sexual difference with which it is co-constituted has tended to remain bracketed off and unchecked, thus the problem shifts to this very sexual difference. I will offer an ontological account of bodies as developmental rather than fixed in their dimorphic characterisations, and argue that the sexual difference that appears so immutable is in fact intersubjectively constituted and maintained. This analysis allows for sexual difference to be denaturalised, and thus justifies the argument that it could be transcended. By then presenting the ways in which this oppositional sexual difference constitutes a symbolic violence in terms of identity, these ontological and normative accounts coalesce into the premise of the rest of the book: sexual difference *need not* be the mode through which we see ourselves and each other, and it is also not the best or most just way of seeing ourselves and each other. The rest of the chapters in this book will then explore what better, more enabling, more androgynous, modes of being and sociality might replace it.

'Explanatory–diagnostic analysis'

This first section of the chapter presents a literature review of sorts of contemporary trajectories in gender studies and biology, which are sometimes called 'new materialism' (Hird 2004b), 'feminist corpomate-rialism' (Lykke 2010a) or 'post-constructionism' (Lykke 2010b), which offer effective diagnoses for why oppositional and essentialist under-standings of gender remain so resilient, as well as accounts of how sex and gender may be better understood. Beyond this explanatory function, I am most interested in these formulations of the 'nature' of bodies for their corollary implications as ontological foundations for possible alternative modes of thinking about the self and others, and thus being, beyond sexual difference. These analyses pose a challenge to the sex/gender divide, and explain why this divide has been limited in its uses for expanding gender.

The limits of the sex/gender divide

Many approaches that seek to, or appear to, challenge the restrictions of binary gender are limited for a real transcendence of gender. This was illustrated in the previous chapter by the limits of the optimistic early predictions for the virtual, queer proposals for the proliferation of gender and the separation of sex and gender in the Gender Recognition Act and elsewhere. They share not only an adherence to the principle that some kind of gender is central to selfhood, but also that, while gender should be and can be challenged, 'sex' (or rather sexual differ-ence) is essential and immutable, while not necessarily determining of gender. The sex/gender divide has gained salience in medicine, the legal context in many countries and in the popular imagination, and gained particular popularity in feminist thought after Ann Oakley's *Sex, Gender and Society* in 1972, and this conceptualisation has undoubtedly helped feminists to further the notion that women are not restricted in behav-iour by biology. As outlined in the Introduction, this divide allows for biological sex (which places one as male/female) to be 'bracketed off' and separated from too much determining power over 'gender', which is thought to be behavioural characteristics (masculine/feminine). Like Lykke (2010b: 106), who proposes that feminists return to considering biological sex, I am keen that this aspect of my 'diagnosis' does not 'diminish the invaluable contribution' of the 'radical interrogation of gender conservative, biologically determinist and culturally essentialist perceptions of gender' that the sex/gender divide has allowed.

Similarly, for some gender-variant individuals, the appeal to a subjec-tive gender identity separated from notions of fixed biological sex often makes life more liveable when the new subject positions fit (Butler 2004). For example, the extra identities offered by trans identity politics discussed in greater depth in Chapter 1, wherein 'males' can identify as 'females' and vice versa, allows for some more diversity of identity. Additionally, appealing to a subjective source of gender identity can be strategically useful for transgender individuals to gain social and legal approval for more diverse expressions of selfhood, as well as desired surgery (Butler 2004; Cowan 2004; 2005; Sandland 2005; Spade 2003), and indeed does provide some new cultural resources.

While there were always those theorists who retained their conceptualisations of the social nature of biological sex *and* gender (e.g. Kessler & McKenna 1978; Stanley 1984), the sex/gender divide has remained the accepted sociological account of gender in much gender research and in most sociology textbooks until the very recent past. This way of thinking allowed theorists to 'see gender as the content with sex as the container. The content may vary ... but the container is considered to be invariable because it is part of nature' (Delphy 1993: 3).

Cowan identifies the limits of paradigms that invoke the sex/gender divide in order to allow incongruence between sex and gender, referring specifically to the UK Gender Recognition Act 2004: 'developing legal discourse on transsexuality, while ostensibly offering a challenge to natural biological and linear understandings of sex and gender, does not engage with the idea that sex is a construct' (Cowan 2005: 72). Additionally, the Gender Recognition Act, while conceding that gender may be divergent from sex, restabilises binary gender through not issuing a birth certificate with the new 'adopted' gender to an individual until they have been considered sufficiently a member of their 'adopted' gender by a 'Gender Recognition Panel' (Cowan 2005: 75). Thus, even if the correspondence between sex and gender is adjusted (itself of course an inherent confrontation to dominant normative notions of sex/gender), as in the second definition of transgender as 'crossing' (Kessler & McKenna 2000) – adjusting one's gender but not one's physical sex – there are still assumed to be only two of each. Halberstam's model of non-biologically determined gender in *Female Masculinities* (1998) is paradigmatic of the trans identity politics that I discussed above. Ze proposes that there should be the possibility to identify with feminine and masculine genders regardless of sex. Such models thus contain four options – masculine male, feminine female, masculine female, feminine male. However, one can only be considered a 'masculine female' if one's sex category is stable. By retaining such a marked adherence to an at basis essential binary biological sex, the aims of multiplicity are doomed to failure because superimposed on to a morphology understood in binary terms: 'There are not limitless numbers of genders precisely because gender is a system that refers back to the body as its a priori counterpart' (Hausman 1999: 197). As a result of such bracketing off, corporeal feminists such as Grosz diagnose that gender deconstructionist approaches that remain at the sociocultural level to the neglect of considering how we understand biological sex draw on 'Western philosophy and its problematic binary oppositions of mind/body and culture/nature' (Lykke 2010b: 111).

The queer models that seek to rearrange gender discussed in Chapter 1 are therefore unable to offer a premise for a post-gender ethos or sociality and are destined to (however unintentionally) reify binary gender, as they negate that gender is constituted by an assumed sexual difference, just as it constitutes this sexual difference in a feedback loop, a process on which I will elaborate below. In their desire to 'abolish hierarchy and even sex roles, but not difference itself', many of the above queer and transgender approaches consequently 'abolish the contents but not the container' (Delphy 1993: 6). By envisioning the ultimate solution as only a more multiplicitous notion of *gender*, they leave intact and immutable the *sexual difference* from which this is derived, with the consequence that this type of queer theory that brackets off the biological 'may be able to produce interesting cakes, but it uses the same ingredients every time' (Hird 2000: 359).

Danish gender theorist Widerberg (1998), whose first language does not have separate terms for sex and gender, expresses frustration with the extent to which the canonised status of the sex/gender divide in much gender research limits the premises of much of feminist and gender studies:

> sex is just as socially constructed as gender; what is nature or not nature is decided beforehand, a fact which this very dichotomy makes invisible. ... Although all this has been debated and critiqued for quite some time now (by Haraway as early as 1991), I cannot see that there has been any change of praxis. The term 'gender' is still used in feminist writing in English and thanks to the expansion of feminist research, to such an extent that it has become an institution. (Widerberg 1998: 134)

However, as noted there has been consistent scholarship on this matter of extending social analysis to biological sex since at least the 1980s. Theorists who incorporate bodily sexual difference in their social analysis are now consistently included in add-on paragraphs in 'Gender' chapters in Sociology textbooks, as in Giddens' *Sociology*

(2009). This is limited, however, because, as Widerberg emphasises, this addition remains as lip-service to these theoretical positions, and this incorporation is rarely operationalised as *a priori* in empirical research. The biological categories of man and woman are still often taken for granted as research premises, such that the use of sex categories 'already assumes differences between them and similarities among them' so that researchers 'end up finding what we looked for' (Lorber 1993: 578). While there are useful historical genealogies of the way that biological sex has been understood over time and how it came to be understood as a 'two-sex' model (Hsueh-Hao Chiang 2007; Laqueur 2003), as well as sociological accounts of how sex is constructed (Connell 2003), there is still a pressing need for practical elaboration of more accurate understandings of biology to be applied more broadly to empirical gender theory, and consideration of the corollaries of this for gender research and social life.

The alternative 'diagnosis': the sex/gender/desire continuum

Approaches that attempt to sever sex from gender fail to take into account the extent to which the meanings of gendered traits are inextricably linked to the sex of the person enacting them, and that there are therefore limits in reconstructive praxis that attempts to revalue 'gendered' traits without paying attention to their variability contingent on – and their co-constitution with – 'sex'. Frosh, Phoenix & Pattman's (2002) empirical research into boys' constructions of masculinity beautifully illustrates this process in action. These researchers simply asked school-aged boys to talk about girls and boys. As well as being able to evidence the oppositional and relational nature of constructions of masculinity and femininity, their findings de-essentialise the 'contents' of supposedly 'masculine' and 'feminine' traits, demonstrating that the same characteristics are often described in both girls and boys, but crucially are understood quite divergently according to the perceived sex (container) of the actor. For example, when enacted by girls, an attention to appearance is understood by most boys in this study to be demonstrative of the feminine traits of frivolity and silliness, while the trait is understood in one particular boy by most of the participants quite differently: 'he could get away with the "eccentricity" of keeping his friends waiting while he concentrated on his appearance, having it defined positively as "individualism" – itself an important goal for boys' (Frosh et al. 2002: 102). There is also a hierarchical element to this dualising according to the (assumed) biological sex of the person. While 'the capacity not to take things seriously was usually presented as characterising *boys*' (Frosh et al. 2002: 105), when girls used humour, boys 'constructed them not as funny, like boys, but as pathetic and childish' (Frosh et al. 2002: 105).

Alternative ontological diagnoses to those of the sex/gender divide are more able to account for examples like this and the impasses discussed above, with Gatens suggesting that the divide represents 'confused terminology and conceptualizing' (Gatens 1994: 144). This example demonstrates that gendered characteristics are not arbitrary, but are inextricably linked to social notions of biological sexual difference. Thus utopian 'gender play' (Hausman 1999) analyses that suggest that subjective gender can be limitlessly varied do not account enough for the persistence and the historical weight of the always already sexed 'imaginary body' (Gatens 1994) through which gendered characteristics are understood. Some theorists have therefore suggested that, instead of focusing on the 'contents' of gender, a better way to understand the mechanism of gender is through a conceptual shift to considering how bodies are understood and how they are sexed *and* gendered. While importantly rejecting essential or *a priori* understandings of the body, Gatens wishes, through a formulation of 'the imaginary body', to draw attention to 'the active process of signification' (Gatens 1994: 145), which lends different significance to gendered characteristics in different 'sexed' bodies. Many theorists both before and after Gatens (Butler 1990; Delphy 1993; Fausto-Sterling 2003; Gatens 1994; Hird 2000, 2004a & 2004b; Hood-Williams 1996; Hubbard 1996; Kessler & McKenna 1978; Lorber 1993; Stanley 1984) therefore reverse the diagnosis, theorising that it is gender that precedes sex:

> There is no recourse to a body that has not always already been interpreted by cultural meanings; hence, sex could not qualify as a prediscursive anatomical facticity. Indeed, sex, by definition, will be shown to have been gender all along. (Butler 1990: 12)

Exemplary here in charting how bodies have been represented in an always already gendered manner is Hird who, extending the influential account of Martin (2006), asserts that the relationship between 'nature' and 'culture' is circular in that the social informs or constructs the natural, which is then reused to justify the social (Hird 2004a: 36–38). To illustrate this Hird contrasts traditional scientific and popular conceptions of gametes (sex cells, i.e. sperm and eggs) to per understanding of them. Ze undermines the traditional conception of eggs as immobile and passive in contrast to active mobile sperm, a notion that is extended to men and women, and used to 'gender' those features taken to be markers of 'sex'. Additionally, this gendered dichotomisation of gametes is co-constitutive with a heteronormative narrative of hierarchical complementarity. This helps to explain the inextricability of (hetero) sexuality with sex/gender. Both Hird and Martin (2006) explicate how bodies, especially those aspects considered to be 'sex cells', are perceived through a cultural framework based on a heterosexual fairytale. Further, Martin effectively demonstrates how this complementary binarism is inherently hierarchical and devaluing of the feminine, illustrating how historically scientists have tended to frame the sperm and the egg along the lines of 'male/female, productive/destructive' (2006: 10), such that negative traits are feminised, and the feminine devalued.

Gatens likewise emphasises the extent to which these assumed characteristics of sex cells have been extended allegorically to rejustify gender attributes, pointing out that Freud asserted that 'the psychology of masculinity and femininity ... "mirrors"' (Gatens 1994: 150) this relation. Hird reinterprets gamete behaviour and emphasises instead that 'recent research on sperm activity has found that contrary to the image of sperm as forceful seekers of eggs, the forward thrust of sperm is actually extremely weak' (Hird 2004a: 38). Hird's particularly thorough handling of all traits considered to be sexed similarly undermines assumptions about the determining roles of hormones by emphasising the arbitrariness of naming and gendering hormones 'male' or 'female' when both are present in 'men' and 'women' (Hird 2004a: 40). This leads Hird to accept Martin's summary of this process: that 'the implanting of social imagery on representations of nature ... lay[s] a firm base for re-importing that exact same imagery as natural explanations of social phenomena' (Martin 1991, cited in Hird 2004a: 38). Hird's analysis of this superimposition of heterosexual complementary difference onto bodies relates it to broader cultural values, suggesting that current dominant ethics of competition and dominance inevitably inform our understandings of the body, ourselves and others, and I would add that concurrently and reciprocally this naturalised characterisation of the nature of being informs our understandings of society. This is the crux of a post-constructionist diagnosis of the process by which binary and hierarchical sex/gender reinforces itself through circular co-constitution.

The co-constitution of sex/gender and (hetero)sexuality is neatly summarised as correspondence theory (Stanley 1984: 15) or the 'sex-gender-desire continuum' (Allen 1999: 67; Butler 1990: 17). This conflation of sexuality with sex/gender and the hierarchical nature of the categories that results in heterosexism is further illustrated in the social world by the ways that Pascoe (2007) demonstrates that the epithet 'fag' is used as a gendered insult, a catch-all for un-masculine behaviour, and is the worst possible insult for a boy: 'Becoming a fag has as much to do with failing at the masculine tasks of competence, heterosexual prowess, and strength, or in any way revealing weakness or femininity as it does with a sexual identity' (Pascoe 2007: 54). In masculinity studies, this correspondence has been identified as an effective explanation for the mechanisms of masculinity. Thinkers have pointed to the extent to which masculinity is constructed oppositionally, as *not* femininity, as well as in correspondence or co-constitution with a notion of embodied manhood, and in turn that this masculine manhood is vehemently heterosexual (Kimmel 2007).

The assumed correspondence of gender with bodily sex is also apparent in the examples of internet use noted above, wherein people assumed a participant's bodily sex from their gender display and felt cheated when a participant's sex did not match their gender presentation, which demonstrates the 'resilience [of materiality] within popular culture to explain sexual difference' (Hird 2004b: 2). This, then, calls for more emphasis on deconstructing the oppositional hierarchies that shape how we understand bodily materiality (i.e. sex), and considering the process by which biological sex becomes gendered, with both co-constitutive with sexual difference. The analysis of this process will be enlightening for considering the extent to which this might be changed, and by what means.

The accounts that I have outlined so far argue that the body is an effect of social understandings of gender, often a heteronormative gender. This diagnoses the direction of influence as culture to biology. However, some thinkers posit that the risk of approaches that characterise the body as an effect of the social (i.e. the argument that gender *precedes* sex) is a linguistic or cultural determinism that is still unable or afraid to account for the pre-discursive or the material. This is the claim made by Colebrook (2000: 78), who suggests that Butler's approach to incorporating bodily sex in cultural analysis serves to intensify the material/cultural divide by over-privileging the linguistic and conceptualising the 'body as effect', thus leaving the body still inert. I will demonstrate below that Butler's ideas can be used to understand sex or the body in a manner that does not do this, and I will elaborate on Butler's later ontological ideas in Chapter 4. However, the thinkers I will outline in the next section do not shy from explicit ontological theorisations about the *nature* of the material, and are not afraid 'to question ... *what it is* that gender re-presents' (Colebrook 2000: 83), and neither do they reify sexual difference. How, then, can the social and the material be re-'collapsed' without further bracketing off the material or reifying them both with a return to a biologically determined sex/gender?

The nature of sex: beyond sexual dimorphism and beyond the cultural vs. the material

Gatens' notion of the *imaginary* body is a particularly important premise here as it demonstrates the extent to which incorporating the corporeal in an analysis of sex/gender's persistence does not imply a capitulation to the naturalness of oppositionally sexed bodies and thus binary gender, and does not necessarily result in accepting an 'air of inevitability' (Gatens 1994: 146) regarding sexual difference and gender identity. After discussing alternative conceptualisations of the 'nature' of sex, which form an ontological premise for arguing that sexual difference is not inevitable, in this section, however, I will argue that however imaginary, owing to their intersubjective compulsarity and mainte-nance, conceptions of sexual difference are still hugely hegemonic. This chapter, then, forms the ontological premises of the reconstructive aims of the rest of this project by presenting the case that, while the nature of bodies is both more similar and complex (i.e. less dimorphic) than sex/gender allows for, this does not imply that the difference through which they are currently constituted can be rejected and replaced at will. I will clarify these delimitations at the end of this chapter.

Recent accounts, then, interrogate this proposition of the gendering and subsequent naturalising of the material that better explains the persistence of binary gender, and offer sophisticated accounts of the *co-constitution* of the social and material (cf. Alaimo 2008; Barad 2003; Carlson 2010; Dreger 1998; Fausto-Sterling 2012; Hird 2004; Lykke 2010).

Many of these thinkers articulate the true 'nature' of sex as more accurately characterised not by oppositional difference or dimorphism, but by an overarching similarity with more internal proliferation and potentiality than currently accounted for in our cultural categories. Feminist sociologist Lorber has argued that the ideology of difference imposed on to biological sex has hidden the reality, which is that 'the basic bodily material is the same for females and males' (1993: 569). Likewise Myra Hird (2000; 2004a; 2004b), in per close critique of the social gendering of biological traits considered to be markers of sex, has argued that the traits that are taken to be sexed are actually not so easily fitted to dimorphic categories, and that most of these traits can be understood better in a more multiplicitous model: 'Nature ... offers shades of difference and similarity much more than clear opposites, and it is rather a modern ideology that imposes the current template of sexual difference' (Hird 2000: 348).

Indeed, many of the studies characterised as corpomaterialist draw on the historical variability of understandings of 'sex' through some level of genealogy of the concept, often thus positing the arbitrariness or 'underdetermination' (Marinucci 2010) of current markers of sex (cf. Hsueh-Hao Chiang 2007; Laqueur 2003). In *Sex, Gender and Science*, for example, Hird explores the pre-Enlightenment conception of sex as determined by quite different criterion from those used today: by 'heat, strength and rationality' (Hird 2004a: 19) for males, against 'colder, weak and emotional' (Hird 2004a: 19) women. Ze then goes on to analyse those aspects of morphology contemporaneously taken to be classifiers of sex (skeletons, gametes, hormones and genes) in terms of their similarity rather than their difference. What this argument adds up to is that the social conception of difference superimposes oppositionality on to the more complex reality of bodies, but that however it is justified, this oppositionality holds great historical and social weight.

The undermining of dimorphic, hierarchical, complementary and difference-based interpretations or constructions of 'sex' leads Hird to per conclusion, already stated above, about the 'nature' of sex: that 'the human body is intersexed since all cells, except those that make up sperm and eggs, have "female" and "male" chromosomes' (Hird 2004a: 15), such that 'the differences which we hold so dear ... and on which so much of our social organization is based ... are minuscule in comparison with our biological similarities' (Hird 2000: 354). What can be concluded from this analysis is that sex is already gendered, and that gender is already sexed, so that 'science and culture often work conterminously to reinscribe sexual difference on to the human body' (Hird 2004a: 5). This has led many theorists to conclude that the 'dichotomization into two and only two sexes or genders gets superimposed in a heterogeneous mix of bodies, feelings and minds' (Hubbard 1996: 164). By avoiding deterministic reduction to either the material or the social, the above-cited thinkers and other contemporary ontological accounts from gender studies and feminist natural science hold exciting potential, with their possibility for 'heterogeneity' as just the ontological foundations required for a post-gender ethic and sociality.

Taking this further, the 'developmental' (Fausto-Sterling 2003; 2012) characterisations of bodies made by many of these thinkers (to be elaborated below) that are premised on natural scientific research can be used to explain how sexual difference has become so reified without capitulating to fatalism, and how it could be different and thus how it may be challenged and replaced, without resorting to simplistic voluntarism.

Reconstruction: the malleability of matter

Having effectively argued that sexual difference is a cultural imposition, and for an understanding of humyn biology as heterogeneously intersexed, some of these thinkers offer promising premises for reconstruction. These approaches characterise the processes of biological development to allow for both a sophisticated analysis of reification of difference that appears so fixed, as well as a potentiality or capacity for other formations or development.

In many of these accounts, there are possibilities for reconstruction on other terms, with Hird's and others' perspectives providing alternative ways of understanding the body and evolution, emphasising the non-functionality, contingency and chance that frequently make up 'nature'. This undermines some of the naturalising and evolutionary functionalism of the gendered 'heterosexual fairytale' (Martin 2006) of gametes. By unravelling functional accounts of anatomy and evolution, new materialism is able to emphasise 'non-linear emergent properties' (Hird 2004b: 230) and 'superabundant diversity' (Hird 2004a: 13), and thus to undermine the evolutionary justification for complementary accounts of sexual difference. Martin is keen to emphasise those characteristics of 'sex cells' that are often sidelined in these cultural narratives, 'evolution over time, and changing response to the environment' and interaction 'on more mutual terms' (2006: 12), that is, a less determined, oppositional and hierarchical picture.

In particular, a developmental analysis, wherein the co-constitutive relationship between the environmental and the material is taken seriously, radically de-essentialises the immutability of the material, and offers a point of departure for thinking reconstruction on different terms from those of sexual difference. Such developmental analyses de-universalise the biological categories of dimorphism and, even more importantly, paint an ontological picture wherein what appears so fixed is more contingent on use and environment and thus much more emergent and developmental. For Hird, for example, the determining role of genes is challenged by demonstrating the extent to which 'developmental information develops from the *contingent* relationship between genes and the environment' (Hird 2004a: 47). However, it is Fausto-Sterling's (2003; 2007) application of the notion of 'Developmental Systems Theory' (DST) to understanding the circular and reifying causality between environment, culture and 'biology' that offers both a comprehensive diagnosis of the persistence of sexual difference *and*, crucially, the potential for reconstruction. Fausto-Sterling's diagnosis is that 'biological' differences, such as supposed brain differences, that are used to justify the immutability and foundational nature of apparently fixed classifications of people based on sexual difference, develop in conjunction with experience in social contexts. An example ze uses to illustrate this developmental process is the interpretation of differences in the corpus callosum, which has been exhaustively used to argue that there are inherent sexually differentiated divergences in spatial abilities. For Fausto-Sterling, echoing the ideas of neuroplasticity and extending them to the formation of gendered differences, 'the interesting question is how the differences develop in the first place. For example, this possible difference in the adult corpus callosum is not present in the brains of small children' such that ze hypothesises that 'different experience leads to a divergence in brain development. Instead of asking how anatomy limits function, one asks how function shapes anatomy' (2003: 125).

By returning to the biological with such a dynamic analysis, Fausto-Sterling does not capitulate to functionally determinist heteronormative corollaries. Such an account does not lead to the inevitability or the preferability of sexual difference. Quoting Susan Oyama to the effect that DST gives 'fewer conclusions about what is inherently desirable, healthy, natural or inevitable' (in Fausto-Sterling 2007: n.p.), ze takes the risk of appealing to a new kind of *developmental* ontological functionalism in order to combine it with a social and ethical argument that sexual difference is *not* the most functional or most just way to develop our selves. This informs my argument here in that I will argue that there is the need for cultural resources that are less sexually differentiated such that identity, subjectivity and hence materiality may develop in contexts that do not impose sexual difference but allow for different potentialities.

In terms of malleability and potential for different ways of being, Fausto-Sterling's application of DST to sexual difference is an extension of Judith Butler's notion of performativity to the 'biological'. Understanding what we take for fixed identity and being to be an ongoing practice means that we can posit that 'relatively stable states of being emerge from a process of repetitive trial and error' (Fausto-Sterling 2003: 126). A performative ontology (as distinct from role theory, which posits identity as a voluntaristic role), not just of representations of biology but of biology itself, then offers a delimited ground for agency and change, some potential for interruption in this mutual reconstitution and reification of sexual difference, sex and gender. The key outcome for this is that it presents sexual difference as not fixed or inevitable because 'since these things ... have been made, they can be unmade, as long as we know how it was they were made' (Foucault 1988, in Cooper & Blair 2002: 517). If use shapes the biological, then different use can reshape it. However, the notion of performativity also presents a picture where the use of our bodies in sexually differentiated ways is socially compulsory such that 'socially induced difference does not necessarily imply malleability' (Fausto-Sterling 2003: 125), as I will discuss in the next section.

To summarise the implications of these emergent, developmental notions of the material, this ontological picture, where 'being is not a substance or ground but only the active becoming of qualities' (Colebrook 2000: 85) means that the question can now become, not whether sex is indeed difference-based, or should take some other form, but whether 'sex' need become *at all* an aspect of identity, and whether we can become subjects and social participants in a non-sexually differentiated, more similar but at once more proliferated way. Indeed, in terms of extending this ontological work to the ethical, Fausto-Sterling (2007: n.p.) suggests that 'our labels of homosexual, heterosexual, bisexual and transgender are really not good categories at all, and are best understood only in terms of unique developmental events affecting particular individuals'.

These new materialist and post-constructionist accounts therefore allow for the possibility of different understandings of biology and therefore the gender and sexuality identity with which it is co-constitutive. Thus, the problem or the root that preserves the persistence of gender and the related restrictive models of sexuality shifts to the production and maintenance of the *perceived reality* of sexual difference. The following section will offer an account of how this oppositional and hierarchical difference-based mode of perception at the root of sex, gender and (hetero)sexuality is produced and reproduced intersubjectively and environmentally in order to develop and become reified in seeming biological differences in the manner described by Fausto-Sterling above. This will complete my ontological justification for seeking out alternative socialities and alternative ways of being and relating.

The intersubjectivity of sexual difference: cultural genitals

While post-constructionists propose that sexual difference is not a 'natural' or inevitable mode of perceiving selves and others or of developing bodies, their accounts still emphasise the weight, persistence and consequences of the pre-existence of cultural categories. It is the resultant environments that these categories provide within which bodies become intelligible, develop, interact and reify. This section will chart how this aspect of the reification occurs, and thus what must be borne in mind when considering if and how sexual difference might be deconstructed and identity subsequently reconstructed. It will do this by presenting an account of ideas from sociology and social theory that have explicitly engaged with this sexual difference aspect of selfhood and society, and which theorise this intersubjective, cultural or social level of identity formation and perpetuation, and what they propose in terms of possibilities for transformation. Alongside the developmental diagnosis of sexual difference posited above, this section will thus result in another ontological delimitation (but also potentiality), which must be borne in mind for the rest of the book when developing reconstructive visions for androgynous ethos or queer socialities that do not reinforce sexual difference.

I follow the lead in this aspect of my diagnosis of theories that view gender (gender understood in my case as sex/gender) as in some sense a verb, rather than a noun. For example, ethnomethodologist Harold Garfinkel suggests that identity 'consists of an endless, ongoing, contingent accomplishment' (Garfinkel 1967: 1). In a study of the achievement of 'the ascribed status of a natural female' (Garfinkel 1967: 165) by a transgendered individual, Agnes, Garfinkel states that 'it would be incorrect to say of Agnes that she has passed. The active mode is needed: she is passing' (Garfinkel 1967: 167). More recently, Butler has also conceived of gender (in per definition of sex/gender) as a practice, a doing rather than a noun:

> If gender is something that one becomes – but can never be – then gender is itself a kind of becoming or activity, and that gender ought not to be conceived as a noun or a substantial thing or a static cultural marker, but rather as an incessant and repeated action of some sort. (Butler 2007: 152)

In terms similar to Garfinkel's, then, Butler articulates gender as 'performative' and this performativity as an ongoing process: 'performativity is not a singular act, but a repetition and a ritual, which achieves its effects through its naturalization in the context of a body' (Butler 2007: xv). While these accounts offer yet more fuel for the argument that the 'difference' aspect of sex/gender is not eternal and natural but is, rather, an ongoing accomplishment or a *fabrication* 'manufactured and sustained through corporeal signs and other discursive means' (Butler 2007: 185), these accounts are also careful to emphasise that this accomplishment is not a simple, voluntaristic game (in the words of Garfinkel). Performativity is not to be understood as a temporal performance, but actually constitutes the most permanent and least malleable aspect of sex/gender. Butler is keen to emphasise that our very intelligibility as humans relies on our being constituted in existing 'discourses':

> to understand identity as a practice, and as a signifying practice, is to understand culturally intelligible subjects as the resulting effects of a rule-bound discourse that inserts itself in to the pervasive and mundane signifying acts of linguistic life. (Butler 2007: 198)

In the context of Fausto-Sterling's extension of performativity to physiological development above, despite not being inevitable or pre-determined (that is, foundational), this 'naturalization in the context of a body' (Butler 2007: xv) appears even less malleable.

As emphasised in Chapter 1, many of the queer and trans theorists who call for a different model of gender fall short in their prescriptions for the process of this change because they not only neglect the weight of the imaginary body, but also assume the 'gender-play' they posit to be achievable on an individual, voluntary level. The work of both Martine Rothblatt (1995) and Kate Bornstein (1994; 1998) in formulating uto-pian trans visions is paradigmatic of voluntaristic so-called 'gender-play' accounts (Hausman 1999). While including the commonly perceived biological character of 'sex' under the social term 'gender', Bornstein nonetheless assumes that the revelation of this sociality alone would mean a subjective understanding of gender and the ability to treat it as 'performance' and to transcend it. This negation of the social, of the weight of the historical and cultural, and under-recognition of the extent to which sex and gender rely on assumptions about natural pre-existing bodily sexual difference, is apparent in the transformative emphasis given by per to 'the virtual': 'We have the opportunity to play with gender in much the same way that we get to play with other forms of identity – through performance in any virtual medium' (Bornstein 1994: 139). However, as noted earlier, interaction in 'the virtual' tends to rely on, and perhaps even reify, the same oppositional, sexed and gendered assumptions as in all other spheres of social interaction:

> Cultural fascination with transgendering does not erase gender categorisation, it underscores the dichotomy. The presence of gender 'deviates' [in the virtual] constitutes a boundary event (cf. Barthes) in which the collective norms for differentiating self and others are made visibly, viscerally apparent. Rather than being nullified or erased, boundary transgressions etch the boundaries deeper into the collective conscience. (O'Brien 1999: 84)

The failure of individual acts of gender transgression, and the persistence of interaction according to sex/gender, leads O'Brien to conclude that 'Gender as a primary category for sorting self/other is not likely to be erased in the near future of cyberspace' (1999: 88). The above accounts tend to reduce these more complex formulations of gender/ identity such as those of performativity, gender as an achievement and 'doing' gender to the simple idea of a subjective and voluntaristic 'performance'.

Ethnomethodology, conversely, while taking a radically social constructionist perspective that sex/gender is an achievement, qualifies this by emphasising the structured limits that come from it being a compulsory part of *social* life: 'the "doing" of gender is undertaken by women and men whose competence as members of society is hostage to its production' (West & Zimmerman 1987: 126). Fenstermaker & West (2002) explicitly distinguish between 'role theory', which was popularly applied to gender in the 1970s, and their more ontologically refined, and hence delimiting, ethnomethodological notion of 'doing'. They emphasise that role theory implies that one can choose whether or not to play one's 'gender role', whereas their account of doing sex/ gender, like that of West & Zimmerman in 1987, emphasises its 'ominrelevance' in all social situations, so that 'placement in a sex category is both relevant and enforced, [such that] doing gender is unavoidable' (Fenstermaker & West 2002: 13).

Butler later theorises this as intelligibility, such that the doing of gender is a matter of 'the viability of our individual personhood' (2004: 2). These socially situated limits explain why individualised resistance is largely destined to failure, and offer a starting point for considering how conditions more conducive to deconstructing the difference at the root of sex and gender, and reconstructing an alternative sociality and ethos within which individuals may develop, could be fostered.

'Gender play' accounts and models in characterising 'performance' of sex/gender often neglect the restrictions of the 'stage' upon which these performances take place and the 'audience' to whom they are performed as well as the extent to which the performances reify, most radically theorised by Fausto-Sterling's DST diagnosis of sexual difference. 'Performance' is a thoroughly agentic approach, and assumes an agent who pre-exists the role and can exist outside of it, as distinct from Judith Butler's conception of 'performativity', especially as ze began to present it in per later work and as Fausto-Sterling engages it:

> ... *gender* is not a noun, but neither is it a set of free-floating attributes, for we have seen that the substantive effect of gender is performatively produced and compelled by the regulatory practices of gender coherence. Hence, within the inherited discourse of the metaphysics of substance, gender proves to be performative – that is, constituting the identity it is purported to be. In this sense gender is always a doing, though not a doing by a subject who might be said to preexist the deed. (Butler 2007: 34)

Despite per use of the terminology of 'performance', Goffman's (1956) analysis of the mechanism and maintenance of selfhood and gender is not reductively agentic and subjective but incorporates the extent to which an actant relies on their 'audience'. Hence sex/gender develops, perpetuates and reifies in conjunction with others. Goffman's analysis suggests that incongruences will be recuperated, because the pre-existence of categories and expected behaviours means that transgressions will be covered up by other participants in interaction through 'prompting'. In developing an analysis of the self as 'performed,' Goffman points out that, due to performances of the self being socially situated (1956: 44), 'the performer can rely upon his [sic] audience to accept minor cues as a sign of something important about his performance' (Goffman 1956: 59). Likewise, while asserting that 'sexed persons ... [are] cultural events that members make happen' (Garfinkel 1967: 181), Garfinkel radically qualifies the agency of particular sexed members in making sex/gender 'happen' by emphasising the extent to which there is a pre-existent set of categories according to which other members attribute sex. Garfinkel demonstrates this tendency for assumptions and attributions to be made based on certain 'cues' in per study of Agnes, who represented perself as a 'natural' woman, and the methodological ways that Agnes was able to 'pass' as a 'true' member of the female sex, despite not having all the biological signifiers of 'sex'. In developing an account that is neither reductive to volition nor to structure as constitutive of gendered identity, Garfinkel asserts that there always already exists 'culturally provided sexual statuses' (Garfinkel 1967: 117) that allow for, or demand, binary readings of people's genders. Garfinkel refers to a pre-existing '"community of understandings" by and about sexed persons treating each other's sex as known in common and taken for granted by them' (Garfinkel 1967: 126). However, like the distinction between 'role-theory' and 'doing' that West & Zimmerman draw, Garfinkel is adamant in distinguishing per account of 'passing' as an ongoing personal but still situated and reified accomplishment from the idea of passing as a game (Garfinkel 1967: 140). Per account, then, while demonstrating that sex/gender is a non-foundational achievement, also emphasises the *compulsarity* of doing gender and the extent to which, for most trans people, gender is not a matter of 'play':

> When I say that Agnes achieved her claims to the ascribed status of a natural female by the successful management of situations ... I do not mean thereby that Agnes was involved in a game, or that it was for her an intellectual matter, or that ego control for her extended to the point where she was able to switch with any success, let alone with any ease, from one sex role to the other. (Garfinkel 1967: 165)

This helps to explains why an incongruence between sex and gender is not inherently subversive. Gagne & Tewkesbury, like phenomenologists and ethnomethodologists before them (Garfinkel 1967; Kessler & McKenna 1978; West & Zimmerman 1987), suggest that this is because, in passing, transgender people 'rely on assumptions that gender is indicative of sex ... [and] socially construct, in the minds of others, the presence of appropriately sexed bodies' (Gagne & Tewkesbury 1998: 95). Kessler & McKenna paradigmatically call these signs 'cultural genitals' (Kessler & McKenna 1978: 154). This strength of the social is beautifully illustrated by reference to a trans person undergoing 'gender reassignment' surgery, in the comment that 'all the changing comes prior to the surgery' (*Sex Change Hospital* 2007).

This also explains why assuming that ambiguous sex, that is, intersex, is inherently subversive (as suggested by Fausto-Sterling's early work in 1993a) is ill-fated, because this ignores that 'in the everyday world gender attributions are made without access to genital inspection' (Kessler 1993: 3). Both of these assertions are illustrated by accounts of butch lesbians being attributed not as ambiguously gendered, but as male, in female toilets (Browne 2004; Halberstam 1998). Thus in all of these cases it is the *attributions* made that are significant and take precedence, and these attributions tend to rely on an assumed fixed, natural *sexual difference*. Indeed, Gagne & Tewkesbury point out that, for the trans people in their study, 'the expression of self was limited by the constraints of relationships, self-preservation, and the social categories available to them' (Gagne & Tewkesbury 1998: 86). Both in Fausto-Sterling's later return to this topic (2003), and in Hubbard's (1996) account, it was concluded that 'supposed biological factors *are* often easier to manipulate than are the forces thought to reflect cultural institutions and traditions or deeply held beliefs' (Hubbard 1996: 158, my emphasis).

This also provides an explanation as to why gender-neutral pro-nouns, discussed above, have been criticised as 'ineffective markers of a futile resistance to the prevailing gender order' (Park 2006: 45). That is because cultural resources for understanding people outside of male and female do not widely exist, and so gender-neutral pronouns are signifiers of something that cannot exist. Owing to the compulsory nature of sexual difference, participants in interaction will look for cues that reveal a position in binary sex/gender and make an attribution as best they can. The people attempting to 'read' Hill-Meyer, discussed earlier, lacked the cultural resources for understanding an individual situating themselves outside of sex/gender binaries, but rather drew on the only existing resources for understanding people, those based on sexual difference and on the correspondence of sex-gender-desire. In emphasising the pre-existence of a sexed and gendered way of under-standing ourselves and others, Butler emphasises that 'limits are always set within the terms of a hegemonic cultural discourse predicated on binary structures that appear as the language of universal rationality' (Butler 2007: 12). Thus, the individual choices we make are only effec-tive in enabling social contexts, with participants who share our per-spective. Likewise, Margaret Archer complicates the simple structure/ agency binary by introducing the delimitations of culture to the scene of agency, and emphasising how the availability and accessibility of cultural resources, what ze calls the 'fund of ideas', can be so crucially limiting to agency:

> There is the same tension to be resolved both theoretically and expe-rientially between the fund of ideas which in a real sense we feel free to accept or reject, and the fact (sometimes known but sometimes happening behind our backs) that the pool itself has been restricted

or contaminated and that our sensed freedoms can be more a matter of manipulated feelings than of genuine liberty. (Archer 1996: xiii)

I have already demonstrated above how Fausto-Sterling extends and links the pre-existing limits of this hegemonic cultural discourse to the ways that our constantly becoming embodied selves become seemingly fixed in sexual difference. That is, ze proposes that the fund of ideas in fact shapes our biology. Approaches that take into account that 'cultural resources', limited by the pre-existing 'hegemonic cultural discourse', play an important role in maintaining binary sexual difference will help with diagnosing the problem and developing strategies for overcoming it. Such an analysis shifts the focus and the 'source' of sex/gender from the embodied individual to the embodied individual situated and developing in a particular historical and cultural position. In turn, this complicates the agency that understanding gender as a 'doing' seems, in a simplistic reading, to offer. Despite this careful diagnosis of the persistence and reification of sexual difference, and the conclusion of some 'openness to resignification and recontextualization' (Butler 2007: 188), we are still, like Judith Butler, left asking:

What performances where [sic] will invert the inner/outer distinction and compel a radical rethinking of the psychological presuppositions of gender identity and sexuality? What performances where will compel a reconsideration of the *place* and stability of the masculine and the feminine? And what kind of gender performance will enact and reveal the performativity of gender itself in a way that destabilizes the naturalized categories of identity and desire[?]. (Butler 1990: 139)

In departing from the delimiting precepts that this ontological diagnosis has left us with (to be reiterated at the conclusion of this chapter), it will be the aim of the rest of this book to attempt an answer to this. However, first it is necessary to make the case that this destabalisation is indeed ethically desirable at all.

Refining the problem and the aim: doing and un-doing difference

The key premise of this book is that *oppositional sexual difference* is a central performative aspect of selfhood that is 'done' in order for individuals to define their own positions in contrast to what they are not, and that this naturalises and reifies. One cannot *be* without doing sex/gender, and the doing of sex/gender is the doing of sexual difference. This approach is able to account for different *types* of difference, and the varying contents of that difference in varying contexts, as well as the mechanism and mode of thought that unites them, and the hierarchy and notion of value that result from this way of thinking. Thinking about the mechanisms of gender in this way can also avoid the 'totalising gestures' that Butler has critiqued in some feminist approaches, which blame particular groups for the oppression of women: 'The effort to identify the enemy as singular in form is a reverse-discourse that uncritically mimics the strategy of the oppressor instead of offering a different set of terms' (Butler 2007: 18), shifting it instead to a mode of thought. To drive this point home, Kathryn Woodward emphasises the extent to which identity is almost always defined by difference, polarisation, inclusion/exclusion, and opposition (Woodward 1997: 2). This is especially true in the case of gender.

An important and useful aspect of this 'doing gender' lineage is that it tends to conclude that this doing of gender is done according to a doing of hierarchical, oppositional difference. This is useful for the social 'diagnosis' aspect of this book for ascertaining the mechanisms that underpin gender, and is supported by the literature that demonstrates the social framing of biological sex according to oppositional, difference impulses. Here I follow the lead of ethnomethodologists Fenstermaker, West and Zimmerman, whose vocabulary and focus explicitly and tellingly shifted from 'doing gender' to 'doing difference' (Fenstermaker & West 2002; West & Zimmerman 1987) as their analysis of the real 'causes' of gender developed. Thus, like me, they conclude that it is the doing of *difference* that is the underlying 'mechanism ... for producing social inequality' (Fenstermaker & West 2002: 96; cf. Risman 2004: 432).

Combining this interactional approach with a more 'structural' analysis, Risman proposes that the power of pre-existing oppositional categorisation, and hierarchisation, of difference, is the spectre that maintains gender inequality. Echoing the agentic limits posited by Butler and others, Risman asserts that this very difference cannot help but delimit choices:

> As long as women and men see themselves as different kinds of people, then women will be unlikely to compare their life options to those of men. Therein lies the power of gender. In a world where sexual anatomy is used to dichotomize human beings into types, the differentiation itself diffuses both claims to and expectations for gender equality. (Risman 2004: 432)

Having presented this ontological account of sexual difference as intersubjectively constituted and maintained along with a recharacterisation of humyn bodies that offers the ontological potentiality of a different way of being, this potentiality does not necessitate any particular normative prescription. There needs to be an explicit reasoned and ethical case for why the transcendence of sexual difference is preferable to other possible corollaries. I will begin this work below in outlining the symbolic violences of sexual difference, followed by a normative defence of the transcendence of sexual difference as a preferable mode of being and relating.

Opposition(s) and hierarchy(s): the symbolic violence of gender

Even if these claims regarding the social basis of sexual difference are conceded, the ethico-political corollary is still not necessarily and obviously that the overcoming of this sexual difference is the inevitable solution. The same premises could be – and have been – used to support divergent normative ends. Indeed, Van Lenning (2000) makes the claim that, despite the social or constitutive basis of sex articulated by Hird, the best strategy is not an overcoming of sexual difference but rather a revaluation. Van Lenning proposes that it would be possible to maintain the categories themselves, but still overcome the limits to claims for equality outlined by Risman above. However, Hird's own conclusion is that, given per recharacterisation of the nature of bodies, feminists will need to offer compelling normative, political and strategic arguments for the value of continued emphasis on sexual difference (Hird 2000: 360).

I will thus foreground my normative defence of transcending sexual difference as the only lasting, and most effective, method for social change by presenting compelling evidence that sexual difference can be understood to inherently constitute symbolic violence and as such its reification will always have unintended consequences. That gender constitutes a symbolic violence can be argued using Bourdieu's characterisation of symbolic violence as one that is done when there are limited, or not freely chosen, 'cognitive instruments' for people to understand themselves and others:

> Symbolic violence is instituted through the adherence that the dominated cannot fail to grant to the dominant ... when, to shape her thought of him, and herself, or, rather, her thought of her relation with him, she has only cognitive instruments that she shares

with him and which, being no more than the embodied form of the relation of domination, cause that relation to appear as natural. (Bourdieu 2004: 339)

This is apparent in many of the examples discussed in Chapter 1 and above, wherein individuals' identities are not freely chosen but are, rather, shaped by the dominant cognitive instruments of oppositional dualisms in a co-constitutive manner with intersubjective attribution, which Browne (2004: 332) describes as genderism, the: 'often unnamed instances of discrimination based on the discontinuity between the sex/ gender with which an individual identifies, and how others, in a variety of spaces, read their sex/gender'. Similarly, Lombardi et al. (2001: 91), who research both physical and more symbolic violence against trans folk, use the term 'gender fundamentalism', which they suggest 'operates by denying and stigmatizing any form of gender nonconformity, in the same manner heterosexism denigrates nonheterosexual relationships'.

As well as the symbolically violent results of bigenderism for intersex and trans folk discussed in depth in Chapter 1, this inter/subjective work of doing oppositional gender has also been well established in gender literature as inhering cognitive pre-limits and negative impacts for those whose sex assigned at birth and gender display can be understood in binary or normative terms, and/or who are cisgendered. Some of the concepts developed to the end of theorising this include hegemonic masculinities, which notes the strictly hierarchical nature of masculinities, its violent enforcement and the unobtainability of the ideal for most men (Connell 1995); other masculinity studies that focus on the subjective and intersubjective violence inherent to masculinity, which I will discuss below; Connell's associated concept of emphasised femininity (Connell 1995); classic feminist analyses of patriarchy and alterity (e.g. Beauvoir 1997; Daly 1979; Irigaray 1985; Wolf 1998); research into the gendered nature and negatively impacting work of maintaining heterosexuality (Frosh et al. 2002; Gagnon & Simon 1974; Pascoe 2007); and psychological studies that highlight the negative psychological impacts of strictly hierarchised binary gender (Baumrind 1982; Bem 1975; 1995; Woodhill & Samuels 2004).

It has now been widely acknowledged that gender as it currently stands is a hierarchical way of thinking that privileges the male over the female and, through the specific content of femininity, negatively impacts on girls and women. Frosh et al.'s (2002) study of school children's perception of boys' and girls' behaviour, discussed above, effectively illustrated this. Carol Gilligan's psychological studies offer empirical evidence for the conclusion that an over-emphasis for women on 'selflessness, which is associated with care and connection ... [leads to] a loss of psychological vitality and courage' for girls (Gilligan 2003: 158–159; also Gilligan 1982). Additionally, in psychological tests that quantified 'situationally effective behavior', Sandra Bem found that while all gender-polarised individuals had some behavioural deficits, 'the feminine females show[ed] ... perhaps the greatest deficit of all' (Bem 1975: 634). Bem concludes that:

> ... feminine females failed to display masculine independence in the face of pressure to conform, but ... they failed to display feminine playfulness when given the opportunity. ... Thus, across the two experimental situations, the feminine females can be said to have 'flunked' both critical tasks, and consequently, it is they who seem to have the most serious behavioural deficit. This result ... is not inconsistent with previous findings ... that femininity in females is generally associated with high anxiety and poor social adjustment. (Bem 1975: 642)

Studies of social and cultural norms and ideals for women at different times have also argued that feminine ideals are unachievable and damaging for most women (see e.g. Friedan 1965; Wolf 1998). These analyses can be used and still hold if we assume that the 'contents' of the sex/gender categories – i.e. masculinity and femininity – are culturally and historically variable, as it is the mechanisms of difference and hierarchy that are universal to these categories that are perpetuating the damaging effects. Feminist theories such as 'patriarchy', 'abjection' or 'othering', 'objectification' and sexism all attempt to account for the hierarchy inherent to this difference in varying ways. Feminist thinkers such as Luce Irigaray have emphasised the extent to which, owing to (what is widely held as) the masculine having been held as the universal, as the subject and the reference point for male *and* female sexuality, the libidinous impulses of the 'feminine' have not even had a chance to exist (Irigaray 1985). Woman is the object, man the subject:

> Woman, in this sexual imaginary, is only a more or less obliging prop for the enactment of man's fantasies. That she may find pleasure there in that role, by proxy, is possible, even certain. But such pleasure is above all a masochistic prostitution of her body to a desire that is not her own, and it leaves her in a familiar state of dependency upon man. (Irigaray 1985: 25)

Woodhill & Samuels (2004), while acknowledging greater freedom for non-stereotypically gendered behaviours for both men and women in 'the west' (the minority world) than in the past, neatly summarise the extent to which a dominant, and specifically a *negative*, masculinity still shapes social life and has negative effects on women as well as men themselves:

> on a global level, many societies still suffer under the offence of undesirable masculinity and ... an unmitigated or overdeveloped masculinity can be destructive. Negative femininity on the other hand mostly effects just the individual who displays it. (Woodhill & Samuels 2004: 20)

The damaging aspects of femininity can, to a great extent, then, be understood by their oppositional and subordinate role in relation to masculinity. This is illustrated in Ursula Le Guin's sci-fi novel *The Dispossessed* by a character who visits from another planet:

> This matter of superiority and inferiority must be a central one in ... social life. If to respect himself ... [men] had to consider half the human race as inferior to him, how then did women manage to respect themselves – did they consider men inferior? (Le Guin 1974: 15)

The severity of being considered un-masculine demonstrates not only the congruence of sex, gender and sexuality in the popular imagination, but also the devaluing of feminine traits. Connell's (1995) concept of 'hegemonic masculinity' explains the ways that men are placed in a social hierarchy depending on the extent to which they can achieve certain ideals associated with masculinities (which vary across cultures). This has led to a popular idea in masculinity studies that the un-achievability of hegemonic masculinity results in negative outcomes for most men as well as for women: 'The way we [men] have set up that world of power causes immense pain, isolation, and alienation not only for women, but also for men' (Kaufman 1999: 59). As well as emphasising how few men can achieve dominant masculinities and how disempowering that is for the majority of men, Kaufman (1999) and Kimmel (2007) lament the poverty of access to (those traits considered to be) 'feminine' traits for men: 'men come to suppress a range of emotions, needs, and possibilities, such as nurturing, receptivity, empathy, and compassion' (Kaufman 1999: 65; see also Woodhill & Samuels 2004). Thus, many academics and activists have shifted to include men and boys more centrally in the analysis of gender's undesirable effects:

> For every girl who is tired of acting weak when she is strong, there is a boy tired of appearing strong when he feels vulnerable. For every boy who is burdened with the constant expectation of knowing everything, there is a girl tired of people not trusting her intelligence. For every girl who is tired of being called over-sensitive, there is a boy who fears to be gentle, to weep. For every boy for whom competition is the only way to prove his masculinity, there is a girl who is called unfeminine when she competes. For every girl who throws out her E-Z-Bake Oven, there is a boy who wishes to find one. For every boy struggling not to let advertising dictate his desires, there is a girl facing the ad industry's attacks on her self-esteem. For every girl who takes a step towards her liberation, there is a boy who finds the way to freedom a little easier. (CrimethInc. n.d.[b]: n.p.)

This version of this poem is from a poster distributed by US anarcho-punk collective CrimethInc. and has reached international notoriety in the punk scene. The poem itself is adapted from a poem by Nancy Smith that was popular in the women's movement and demonstrates that feminism has always been mindful of gender's universally negative effects.

Kaufman theorises the process of masculine domination as one in which the un-achievability of hegemonic masculinity results in fear and homophobia, with it being this that perpetuates the dominating behaviour of men in a cyclical fashion. Like Connell, Kaufman and Kimmel emphasise the hierarchies *among* men. Research undertaken by C.J. Pascoe (2007) in an American high school, to which I referred earlier, highlights the hard work of maintaining masculinity and the pain caused by failing to do so, charting the use and power of the gendered insult 'fag' as demonstrative of the negative connotations still so strongly associated with a boy being considered un-masculine: 'To call someone *gay* or *fag* is like the lowest thing you can call someone. Because that's like saying you're nothing' (interviewee in Pascoe 2007: 55).

The discussion in these two chapters indicates the need for an 'explanatory-diagnostic analysis' (Benhabib 1985: 405) of sex/gender that can account for these impacts of sex/gender upon cisgendered and normative women and men, as well as sex and gender non-conformists. Additionally, I have demonstrated the necessity of an 'anticipatory-utopian critique' (Benhabib 1985: 405) and creation of alternative ethics, and developing this will be the job of subsequent chapters.

'Anticipatory-utopian critique': transcending sexual difference

These characterisations of the oppositional, restrictive and hierarchical nature and negative impacts of sex/gender, then, underpin my position that a lasting solution is its eradication. This is a political position shared by other thinkers who have charted the non-essential nature of sexual difference:

> If our understandings of nature continue to reveal the focus on sexual difference as politically derived, feminist theory will need to ascertain that the artificial emphasis on sexual difference, contra nature, is better able to effect social change than conjoined efforts to expose 'sex' as a construction intended to ground divisions. (Hird 2000: 360)

Not all thinkers reach the same conclusion given this same evidence. Appealing to pragmatism, Van Lenning's (2004) response to Hird's (2000) assertion of the social and mutually constitutive nature of sex *and* gender and the intersexuality of most humyn cells, in fact goes on to defend difference as a basis for feminist ethics that 'is better able to effect social change' (Hird 2000: 360). Like Gilligan (2003), Irigaray (1985) and Whitbeck (1989), Van Lenning suggests that, owing to the pervasiveness of people considering sex/gender to be a real and essential part of the self, the best strategy for overcoming the hierarchy of patriarchy that would benefit women would be to work on the valuing of those characteristics traditionally associated with women. Following Irigaray, Van Lenning (2004) suggests that the real root cause of the hierarchies of the gender binary is that the feminine is still not valued, and that a better aim would be that of 'some change from the extension of the categories of masculinity and femininity, rather than from attempts to break free from them altogether' (Van Lenning 2004: 25). This particular argument for more modest aims stems not from an ontological reassertion of the realness of the dimorphic categories, but from a pragmatic, but explicitly feminist, position that accepts the resilience of gender. Likewise, Gatens, whose arguments are so important to feminists' deconstructions of the fixity of biological sexual difference, follows this same line of reasoning. After asserting the social origins of the imaginary sexed body, ze still concludes that 'to suggest the degendering of society as political strategy is hopelessly utopian, ahistorical, and functions theoretically and practically as a diversionary tactic' (Gatens 1994: 150). Instead of extending this 'degendering' to eradicating the sexual difference at its root, Gatens capitulates to the historical weight of sexual difference and supports a 'tactical shift from equality to difference' (Gatens 1994: 153). Gatens argues that owing to the patriarchal nature of society, it is always the case that 'neutrality is not neutrality at all but a "masculinisation" or "normalization" (in a society where men are seen as the norm, the standard) of women – a making of "woman" into "man"' (Gatens 1994: 154). I am going to depart from the position, instead, that it is possible to propose 'degendering' or a post-gender ethic, so long as this is done with the hierarchically gendered context from which this reconstruction begins in mind. In other words, with an awareness of the contaminated context of an already gendered society.

I am choosing here instead to take another of Gatens' premises to its logical corollary: that owing to the co-constitution of sex, gender and sexual difference, to reify it through basing a political strategy on difference negates a more long-term strategy and 'can only lead to the reproduction, at another site, of these relations [of difference]' (Gatens 1994: 149). Owing to the negative effects of the persistence of understanding gender as inevitably bound up with ideas of difference, outlined above, and the extent to which this diminishes autonomy of identity for people of all 'genders', a more lasting, universal and effective strategy for a political project that seeks to overcome the symbolic violences imposed by gender is the overcoming, eradication or 'transcendence' of sexual difference. As critiques of identity politics have long argued, by drawing on the category of women, it is *re*-ified: 'the category of "women" is normative and exclusionary' (Butler 2007: 19).[1] Gender hierarchy cannot be escaped through the categories that create that hierarchy, and neither can it be escaped by attempting to alter ideas about gender and not sex, as gender is always already oppositionally difference-based, and this will only exacerbate the subordination of women. Following Risman's diagnosis of how the difference inherent to gender means that gender's very existence cannot help but to internalise unequal life expectations of men and women, 'indirectly by shaping actors' perceptions of their interests and directly by constraining choice' (2004:432), ze goes on to normatively argue that 'because the gender structure so defines the category woman as subordinate, the deconstruction of the category itself is the best, indeed the only sure way, to end gender subordination' (2004: 446; cf. Risman, Lorber & Sherwood 2012). Likewise, de Lauretis (1987) posits that the 'relative power' afforded to women in hierarchical, relational sexual difference underpins resistance to more radical challenges to sex/gender itself. This is similar to Connell's 'patriarchal dividend' (1996) for non-hegemonic men, which is a trade-off for not being at the top of the hierarchy and is, if you will, better than nothing. However, de Lauretis's prognosis is that

> Any changes that may result therein ... are likely to be changes in 'gender difference,' precisely, rather than changes in the social relations of gender: changes, in short, in the direction of more or less 'equality' of women *to men*. (de Lauretis 1987: 17)

Further, it is my argument that we can only overcome the gender hierarchy by eradicating the ideas of gender, sex *and* sexual difference completely, as they have an inseparability and a fundamental association with this heterosexualised oppositional difference. Attempting to alter only one aspect of sex/gender/sexual difference 'will keep us – a collective, inclusive us – from tackling systematic discrimination of women and of those persons whose gender presentation is at odds with cultural norms' (Hausman 1999: 192).

But what most of these accounts fall short of is a serious consideration of how this is to be done, and how it can be done without unwittingly strengthening or reinforcing gender subordination. A degendering project or a project of sex/gender transcendence requires the elaboration of an alternative way of being that overcomes the androcentrism of universalist accounts of equality but also does not reify difference. This is the project of post-gender ethics.

Conclusion: the task ahead

Delphy (1993) asserts that hierarchical and oppositional difference is not a universal mode of thought that applies to all humyn thinking, highlighting that there are some things that are considered through other modes of differentiation: 'Alongside cabbages and carrots, which are not "opposites" of each other, there are courgettes, melons, and potatoes ... distinctions are not necessarily hierarchical: vegetables are not placed on a scale of value' (Delphy 1993: 4).

In conclusion, then, and to reiterate the implications of this diagnosis for the remainder of this project, I have argued that to develop a mode of being and relating where 'hierarchy [is not] ... a constitutive element' (Delphy 1993: 5), a truly androgynous ethic and queer sociality would need to include the following precepts:

- Sex/gender/sexuality are co-constitutive, and thus one of these cannot be eradicated or varied without the others;
- Oppositional difference-based modes of thought are at the root of these, and it is this that should be the locus of change;
- The intersubjective and cultural aspects of identity are key terrains for maintenance and change, and thus an effective strategy for change must include the subjective, the intersubjective and social/cultural terrains;
- A truly androgynous ethic must not collapse difference in to either homogeny (i.e. sameness) or a neutrality that is really 'masculinisation' (Gatens 1994: 154) but needs mechanisms to ensure it remains truly heterogenous.

I will go on to argue that an effective alternative to this hierarchical opposition inherent to sex/gender *identity* is a certain *ethos* and congruent ethic of reciprocity, which can be fostered and maintained through developing new ways of reading self/others (reading practices), collective cultural resources for doing so, and new modes of interacting and communicating with others intersubjectively and socially.

In shifting the focus to political change, Chapter 3 will explore current ethico-political paradigms in order to demonstrate their insufficiency for a qualitative post-gender politics as a result of departing from or naturalising some aspect of self/other or difference-based thinking. This will help me to refine what a truly post-gender ethic would need to consider.

3
Gender Justice

Chapter 2 argued that one of the key explanations of the resilience of gender and the endurance of its hierarchical binarism is the assumption and construction of oppositional sexual difference. After proposing that bodies and subjectivity need not be framed and constituted in this way, I went on to propose that, owing to the way that sex/gender is constituted and maintained through how we see ourselves, how others see us and how we see them (i.e. subjectively *and* intersubjectively), the problem is the 'fund of ideas' (Archer 1996: xiii) from which we draw to do this constituting and understanding of identity. It is my position that the metaphysical foundation of this problem is that the prevalent mode of perception inheres an *oppositional* mode of perceiving the other – that is, the presumption of an antagonistic self/other relationship – which is co-constitutive with how we understand bodies, and subsequently each other and society. Foucault makes the normative claim that such hierarchical opposition, which ze characterises as 'dissymmetry, exclusion of the other ... a kind of threat of being dispossessed of your own energy, and so on. All that is quite disgusting!' (Foucault 1984: 346). The question is, then, what would a less oppositional, less exclusionary, more symmetrical and more reciprocal ethic look like?

The 'recognition debates' (McNay 2008; Nussbaum 1996; Okin 1999; Taylor 1992) are an attempt to consider how people may best be 'recognised' to do a justice to them. The recognition debates can construct this as a choice between two options: that of a universalistic, equal right to individual recognition, or one premised on recognition of a minority identity, of which identity politics is a kind. This debate can perpetuate the oppositions between sameness/difference or individual/collective in considering ideal recognition, and both options can maintain some 'othering'. The issue of recognition thus becomes central to the next few chapters, and throughout Chapters 3, 4 and 5 I will traverse this ground, where I will consider how we may be recognised, and recognise. I will consider the possibility of recognition that transcends this dualistic impasse, and by truly transcending (not just nullifying) identity, can underpin a less oppositionally gendered but simultaneously less homogenous and more proliferated way of recognising, according instead to *differences*.

In positing a normative ideal of what constitutes 'justice', ethico-political paradigms inherently depart from an assumption about humyn nature and what is consequently possible, and relatedly, a prescription for the ideal mode of being, and the ideal way of seeing and treating others. Thus, given the diagnosis of sexual difference as intersubjectively constituted, much of the ontological and ethical questioning in this part of the book is about what is both *possible* and *desirable* in terms of how we perceive ourselves and others, which has often been framed as an issue of recognition and how we can be recognised and recognise others in the most just way possible. I call this development of a more positive relation *to* the self and a more positive relation *between* self and other 'ethics', and I do so because moral thinking entails considering the principles that ground how best to conduct oneself. Foucault conceptualises ethics as the relationship you have to yourself:

> ...there is another side to the moral prescriptions, which most of the time is not isolated as such but is, I think, very important: the kind of relationship you ought to have with yourself, *rapport à soi*, which I call ethics, and which determines how the individual is supposed to constitute himself as a moral subject of his own actions. (Foucault 1984: 352)

This chapter will consider existing ethico-political paradigms to conclude why they are insufficient for developing a code of conduct (an ethics) that could suitably overcome or transcend the problems, what I argue are symbolic violences, of sexual difference. This symbolic violence is one of limiting resources for understanding oneself and others (i.e. identity) and corollary outcomes of othering, negation or other forms of subordination or domination. Given this, I will argue here that many existing models that have been applied to gender continue to have unjust ends, that is, do not fully overcome the injustice caused by the pervasiveness and resultant compulsarity of sexual difference. I will implicitly argue that the modes of recognition made possible or idealised by the following paradigms are insufficient for transcending the ontological problem diagnosed in the first two chapters, and that in different ways these approaches re-establish some of the problems inherent to sexual difference. In particular, individualistic liberalism, which is the dominant mode of thought in the minority world, cannot account for the 'unfreedoms' or 'symbolic violences' of sex/gender, as it denies, to differing extents, social and non-institutional inequality. By maintaining the metaphysical spectre of an 'oppositional epistemo-logical frame' (Butler 2007: 195), they cannot underpin true *androgyny* because they accept as given the foundationalism of oppositional selves, and thus do not challenge the real terrain of on which gender inequal-ity is perpetuated.

By demonstrating what is lacking, this discussion will foreground the next chapter where the aim is to develop an ontological ethics of reciprocity that attempts to evade these shortfalls. This alternative will try to take seriously both the individual *and* their intersubjective situatedness.

There are various assumptions underpinning this chapter. First, that presumptions of sex/gender as an essential and compulsory aspect of selfhood limit freedom by limiting the cultural resources or 'fund of ideas' (Archer 1996: xiii) from which we can perceive ourselves and others. Second, that sex/gender is premised on an assumption of difference and an oppositional self/other mode of perception. Third, that sexual difference and this oppositional mode of perception are intersubjectively/socially constructed and maintained. Fourth, that othering and difference-based identity restrict freedom and create hierarchy. Fifth, that 'neutrality' can disguise a norm that assumes sameness according to the norms of the dominant. And finally, that gender does currently socially exist and constitutes a hierarchy of value that devalues women and the sex/gender non-normative while also having negative impacts on men and the sex/gender normative.

Limits to liberal justice and freedom

Liberal ethico-political ideas posit maximum possible 'freedom' as their telos, which they characterise as individual 'liberty and equality' (Fukuyama 1992: xi; see also Berlin 1969; Nozick 1974; Rawls 1973), and these constitute the dominant ethos of most of the contemporary world, the 'remarkable consensus concerning the legitimacy of liberal democracy' that Fukuyama posits (1992: xi). An important assumption of such an ethos is a dedication to individualism as both a premise and an aim, and a principle of equal *opportunity*. I will argue that the gender-*blinkeredness* (not transcendence), which is the corollary of liberal premises and notions of freedom, does not nullify sex/gender, but rather negates the real terrain of injustice, valorises dominant masculinist values and negates what has been traditionally associated with 'the feminine', *intensifying* gendered distinctions. This is because liberal equality of opportunity discourses that argue for the freedom of equal opportunity regardless of background and characteristics cannot account appropriately for the endurance of unequal social relations, in particular the social endurance of sexual difference. Such perspectives negate the *constitutive* impact of the social and intersubjective on subjectivity and 'autonomy.' Such a mode of thought is not conducive to my aim of developing a way of perceiving the self and others, and of acting, that truly transcends difference, that is, an androgynous ethics.

Following many before me, I argue that, while liberal ethics claim to be deontological in their principle of 'justice as fairness', the very claim to equal opportunity and idealisation of an atomised autonomy actually departs from assumptions about the self as selfishly rational, as subjectively autonomous and inherently opposed to the other. Their ontological premises tend to dictate a model of recognition that collapses back into a naturalisation of individualism, dualism and negation of the other. Consequently, I propose, they limit analyses and strategies for challenging the hierarchy at the root of sex/gender, and thus do not offer a way for fostering real freedom of identity. Various critiques of the vaunted impartial and rational liberal ethics of justice have been levelled, and I find these a useful starting point for considering what a more situated ethics that takes the precepts of my first two chapters into account would entail.

As I will expand below, while liberal feminism offers many qualifications and developments to liberal ethics, it also fails to satisfactorily account for the social maintenance of sexual difference and gender inequality because it continues to idealise atomised, pre-existing selves in the political sphere. Liberalism cannot be extended to argue for the eradication of gender identity, as this would constitute a reduction in the ostensible personal choice that it idealises – it can only be extended to argue for the eradication of the political and institutional significance of gender.

The veil of ignorance

In its aim of equal *opportunity*, liberalism perhaps best represents the atomised, antagonistic, individualistic perspective on humyn nature, assuming it to be both ontologically inevitable and, to differing extents, desirable. From Thomas Hobbes' assertion (originally made in 1651) of humyn 'nature' as war of 'every man against every man' (Hobbes 1994: 84) to John Rawls' assumption that all humyns are 'concerned to further their own interests' (Rawls 1973: 10), within this way of perceiving the ontological state of nature, mutual disinterest becomes the ideal model of tolerance and freedom. To differing extents liberalism tends to negate the importance of the social and intersubjective, and denies these realms any effective power, idealising individuals who can transcend them.

Tellingly, Rawls' paradigmatic liberal theory of justice contains a set of ontological assumptions that are necessary for per principles of liberalism to apply, assumptions that I argue in Chapters 1 and 2 are problematic when considered in the light of the precepts. Rawls states that per principles of justice 'are the principles that free and rational persons concerned to further their own interests would accept in an initial position of equality' (Rawls 1973: 10). There are various taken-for-granted points of departure inherent in this statement that would need to be true for Rawls' arguments to hold. These are that:

- people are free and rational,
- people are self-interested,
- people are in an initial position of equality.

This position of equality ('the original position') is the necessary assumption underpinning this impartial ethic of justice, so that 'The principles of justice are chosen behind a veil of ignorance' (Rawls 1973: 11) – that is, in order to be applicable this ethic must be applied by pretending that people have no context particular to them, that there is a level playing field: 'Among the features of this situation are that no one knows his place in society, his class position or social status, nor does any one know his fortune in the distribution of natural assets and abilities, his intelligence, strength, and the like' (Rawls 1973: 11). What prevents freedom in this formulation is *partiality*, that is, treating people *differently*. What maximises it is freedom of choice for everyone on equal terms, that is, equal rights. Criticisms have been levelled at this on several levels. Liberal feminists such as Susan Moller Okin (1987; 1989) point out that the list of features that are to be irrelevant to justice does not include gender. Approaches such as Okin's seek to extend the ethic of liberal justice to be really universal and so to include women. More critically, other feminists and communitarians have argued that the idealised impartiality necessary for justice is an impossibility, as well as being undesirable. I will discuss these perspectives below.

At its most atomised and autonomous there are liberal approaches that depart from entirely 'negative' conceptions of liberty that understand freedom as merely the absence of explicit coercion. This takes for granted a repressed but ever-present autonomous self that, without said coercion, could flourish. For example, Isaiah Berlin states that

> Coercion implies the deliberate interference of other human beings within the area in which I could otherwise act. You lack political liberty or freedom only if you are prevented from attaining a goal by other human beings. (Berlin 1969: 122)

In stating that freedom is the absence of deliberate coercion by others, this conception characterises freedom as thoroughly agentic. According to this analysis, sexual difference does not represent a limit to liberty, because it is not a deliberate interference by particular humyn beings in a goal.

The typical liberal approach allows that government's minimal function consists of ensuring that this type of domination or coercion by other individuals does not exist (Nozick 1974). Regarding sexual difference, this would mean that government would be justified in preventing discrimination, in the sense of equality of opportunity, based on gender identity. This does not account for possible non-intentional coercion due to social and cultural forces or dominant discourses, such as that of sexual difference. Indeed, it does not locate any effective power in culture or discourse, assuming differences in culture to be irrelevant to liberty and choice. Barry Hindess argues that to attribute the status of 'actors' to abstract entities can be:

> ... an obstacle to serious and informed political discussion. This occurs when the concept of actor is extended to aggregates that have no identifiable means of formulating decisions, let alone acting on them – societies, communities, classes, racial or gender categories, bureaucracy, or whatever. (1986: 124)

However, per formulation of the concept of 'spurious unities' for understanding such aggregates is useful for analysing entities or discourses such as sexual difference in abstract terms and understanding them to have an effect, but without losing sight of the problems of assigning independent agency to them. Applying this understanding to sexual difference will help me later to understand the complicated process by which sexual difference is maintained and thus how it may best be altered, but without seeing this as an 'it', with agency in its own right.

As outlined in Chapter 2, due to the social imperative of attribution, the 'choice' of identity is not simply a subjective decision and is fundamentally social and *inter*subjective. Difference feminism warns that difference *does* exist, and so the 'initial position of equality' in Rawlsian liberalism does not and cannot exist, and mutual disinterest is an impossible illusion. Many recent formulations of selfhood or subjecthood would concede that there is no 'pre-cultural' ideal self and that humyn subjects are 'always already' understood according to prevailing cultural discourses (Butler 1993a; 2005; 2007). Indeed, whether synchronically understood (as in the case of structuralism, which considers structures fairly statically) or diachronically understood (as with poststructuralism, which considers structures more historically), the pre-existing power of the social and intersubjective has been greatly emphasised, as well as the delimiting function of the cultural (Archer 1996), all of which have effects on the equality of choice so vaunted by liberalism. Consequently, theoretical equality of opportunity cannot ensure actual qualitative 'equality' if intersubjectively maintained social and cultural conditions make some opportunities more easy than others, as well as some being impossible (for example, Chapter 1 emphasised the practical impossibility of gender ambiguity). This greatly complicates the ontological assumption of autonomous choice at the root of liberal ethics, and in Chapter 4 I will develop a more nuanced account of autonomy with an explicit ontological basis.

Liberalism as androcentric androgyny

In analysing the points of departure of this theory of justice, it becomes apparent that rather than being a useful gender-blinkered or gender-transcendent ethic, it is inherently what Rosinsky would call an 'androcentric androgyny' (Rosinsky 1984: x) because, in acting as though gender does not affect equality of opportunity, it neglects to account for the social and cultural effects of gender at all (Okin 1997). Likewise, Benhabib emphasises that this supposedly universal ontological perspective is actually a polarised and inherently masculinist perspective applicable only to the public sphere and which omits many other ways of being and relating that exist: 'contemporary universalist moral theory has inherited this dichotomy between autonomy and nurturance, independence and bonding, the sphere of justice and the domestic, personal realm' (Benhabib 1985: 410). While the moral principles of freedom, autonomy and equality of opportunity are theoretically useful to my project of maximising freedom of identity, in reality they rely on and idealise as the most 'just' a self-interested and atomised conception of humyn 'nature' that belies how sexual difference is maintained, and thus is limited in offering means of developing an alternative way of being.

Critiques of the vaunted impartial and rational liberal ethics of justice are a useful starting point for considering what a more situated ethics that takes the precepts of Chapter 2 into account would entail. These include its negation of the current *social* reality of sex/gender and its negative effects for 'freedom'; its related inability to account for the effects on 'freedom' of the social, intersubjectivity and cultural discourses; its limited definition of 'the political' and as a corollary its limited analysis of how to foster greater 'freedom'; its claims to irreducible ontological impartiality and autonomy and the assumption of power to be repressive of this primary freedom.

Critiques from liberal feminism, feminine ethics, feminist ethics, communitarianism and anarchism all offer ontological and ethical challenges to liberalism. Liberal feminism challenges the neglect of aspects of the 'private sphere' for considering how impartiality may be fostered and applied to gender, but maintains this telos of impartiality. Communitarianism and feminine ethics both dispute the very possibility of impartiality and of the atomised autonomous subject, and emphasise more positive humyn traits and the possibility of other ways of being, although communitarianism can be critiqued for the possibility of value-free relativism. Feminine ethics seek to give value to the non-institutional ethics of the private sphere and as such challenge the very borders of what has been considered to be the political. Anarchism also emphasises benevolent traits and is useful for suggesting that legislative and institutional change may limit the scope of resistance; and, finally, poststructuralism can add to anarchism's normative aim a way of understanding freedom that does not rely on power as repressive of a primary autonomous subject.

Liberal feminism

Some liberal feminists, in dealing with the injustices presented by sex/gender, posit their aim as 'a world without gender' (Enslin & Tijattas 2006; Korsgaard 1995; Okin 1989), but what they mean by this is an end to the significance of gender in the public sphere, and a better elaboration of Rawls' original position to include gender. This argument is for a 'gender-blindness', implying that to some extent liberal feminists hold that gender itself does not have to inhere negation or hierarchy, and does not necessarily have effective power, and that it does not necessarily limit autonomy. Thus they are reluctant to assert that this eradication would extend to the eradication of *identifying* with a gender, and definitions of gender here are strictly separated from the perceived natural difference of 'sex'.

The liberal feminist corrective to liberalism is one of including gender inequality as a possible limit to the initial position, and attempting to minimise its effects for equal *opportunity*. Thus liberal feminists have sought to demonstrate the extent to which the gender-blinkeredness of liberalism negates a social and cultural reality of gender inequality, asserting that 'more than formal legal equality of the sexes is required if justice is to be done' (Okin 1987: 65). These approaches do to a certain extent propose the existence of something more socially embedded that is not entirely determined by choice. For example, Nussbaum posits the possibility of 'diseased preferences' (1999b: 130–153), which demonstrates a more complex notion of autonomy and the possibility of skewed choices, and Susan Moller Okin emphasises the extent to which the family is a private institution but does influence our 'choices': 'The family in which each of us grows up has a deeply formative influence on us – on the kind of persons we want to be as well as the kind of persons we are', which affects our 'equality of opportunity to become what we want to be' (Okin 1989: 184). As such, liberal feminists do often concern themselves to differing extents with modes of thought as well as institutions.

Additionally, liberal feminists have offered the ontological challenge that thinking 'as if' in the Rawlsian original position (Okin 1989: 248), in necessitating an impartiality towards your own position in society, would require an empathy towards other possible positions in society. In emphasising this, Okin challenges that complete atomised selfish rationality is, in fact, the most conducive ontology for the liberal aim of 'justice as fairness'. Liberal feminists Benhabib (1996) and Nussbaum (1999b; Nussbaum 1996; Nussbaum & Glover 1995), in furthering the project of liberalism, also attempt to evade this binary thinking, considering the importance of self/other modes of perception, for maintaining inequalities. As such, liberal feminists go some way to challenging the universalisation of the ontology of selfish rationality in Rawls' 'original position', but they still suggest that this mind-set of empathy, and better self/other relations, should be used in the process of liberal democracy towards the *ends* of impartial justice and free autonomous subjects in the public sphere.

Essentially, while crediting some power to social and cultural spheres, then, liberal feminists do still hold to an *ideal* or telos of an autonomous self, and to do so recommend extending the remit of justice to what has been traditionally considered the private sphere in order to foster this liberal ideal of autonomy for all people, not just men. Okin explicates per telos, for example, as ensuring that everyone has the capacity to 'think as if in the original position' (Okin 1989: 248). Enslin & Tijattas (2006), in explicitly referring to developing 'a world without gender', are concerned with fostering autonomous individuals capable of this thinking 'as if' – that is, capable of thinking impartially and 'as if' not aware of the position of the self and other in society, but also, in Okin's refined version of the original position, with empathy for this possible other. Likewise, Nussbaum's exploration of 'diseased preferences', to which I referred earlier, while taking in to account forces outside of the individual, is still in the service of fostering '*individual* choice and self-determination' (Nussbaum 1999b: 153, my emphasis). Indeed, liberal feminist Christine M. Korsgaard states that Enlightenment ideals of individual autonomy have 'not been tried and found too difficult, but rather ... been found too difficult and so not tried' (Korsgaard 1995: 402). Korsgaard (1995) thus imagines that the problems of gender can be 'transcended' through individual freedom of impartiality, that is, the structures of gender can be made to have no effective power through fostering individual autonomy.

As such, liberal feminists still tend to hold that liberal democracy is the ideal model for justice, and that it can be made just for women given enough refining from feminists. Benhabib states per

> ... assumption that the institutions and culture of liberal democracies are sufficiently complex, supple and decentred so as to allow the expression of difference without fracturing the identity of the body politic or subverting existing forms of political sovereignty. (Benhabib 1996: 5)

Liberal feminist approaches like this that idealise atomised autonomy remain very much rooted in the ontological assumption of a separation between self and other, with an over-emphasis on the 'self' pole. They assume that freedom in the sense of complete autonomy can be gained by legislating for impartiality and equality of opportunity, simply extending this legislation more into what has been traditionally considered the private sphere. The ontology of autonomy and rationality, then, even if understood in this refined way that takes account of social limits to it, still informs an ethics of individual freedom and choice that denies the ongoing existence of sexual difference *in itself* to be a limit to this autonomy.

Demonstrably, while Okin has argued that the family is a gendered social institution, the validity and justice of which needs to be considered in terms of its *internal* dynamics, gender itself is not considered in such terms. Okin states that owing to the assumption that 'the "individual" who is the basic subject of liberal theories is the male head of a patriarchal household', for them 'the application of principles of justice to relations between the sexes, or within the household, has frequently been ruled out from the start' (Okin 1987: 43). Okin, then, argues for a consideration of *gendered institutions* such as the monogamous traditional family in terms of their justness (Okin 1987; 1989), but does not frame gender or sexual difference itself in this way. That is, ze does not consider whether *sex/gender itself* is a just social institution, a 'spurious unity' (Hindess 1986) with some resultant effective power. Most liberal feminists aim for, and assume possible, an end to the political significance of gender. This means that the maintenance of the compulsarity of identifying with a gender is not seen to be an obstacle to a nullification of its effects, and the explicit aim is merely a 'diminishment of gender-identification' (Korsgaard 1995: 403).

However, along with other critiques of liberal gender and sexuality identity politics and rights discourses (Butler 2007 [1990]; Kollman & Waites 2009; Waites 2009), it is my position that in demarcating rights for particular categories, the liberal discourse is (re)constitutive of the categories that it evokes, and thus, in seeking equality, it succeeds in laying the ground for differences and boundaries, which, as I argue throughout, are the basis of *in*equalities. As deconstruction emphasises, making claims to identity is always done through opposition and always constitutes an other, a 'constitutive outside'. This has led Butler to claim that 'feminist goals risk failure by refusing to take account of the constitutive powers of their own representational claims' (Butler 2007 [1990]: 6). The UK's Gender Recognition Act discussed in Chapter 1 is exemplary of this. Indeed, Cowan (2004; 2005) and Sandland (2005) argue that this Act, in attempting to extend the liberal rights discourse to encompass trans experience, serves not to extend the definitions of gender by refuting its biological basis, but (re)constitute its subjective basis, reifying a subjective binary gender. In this way the Act offers recognition and therefore rights only to certain specific trans experiences. This (re)construction of difference owing to an unwillingness to challenge the identity aspect of sex/gender explains the ineffectiveness of institutional change in making real social change and demonstrates the 'necessary limits of identity politics' (Butler 2007 [1990]: 6) for more permanent and long-term challenge to *all* negative aspects of sex/gender. This point will be significant in considering limits to and sources of agency in Chapter 7, when considering strategies for eradicating sexual difference.

Queer theory has been vocal in critiquing these limits to rights discourses, suggesting that while life has been made more liveable because of identity or liberation politics, the constitution of categories that identity politics produces or draws upon has resulted in further homogenisation and exclusion, or ghettoisation (Butler 2007 [1990]; Travers Scott 1997). Many liberal feminists can be characterised as 'uncritically mimic[ing] the strategy of the oppressor instead of offering a different set of terms' (Butler 1990: 13), by retaining a telos of atomised autonomy that negates and devalues what it sublimates as the less evolved ways of being. Other thinkers (CrimethInc. n.d.[a] & [b]; Friedman 1993; Gilligan 1982; 2003; Sandel 1982; Whitbeck 1989) suggest that the direction of influence can be usefully reversed. Instead of liberal feminist ideas that empathy is merely necessary to the ends of impartial individualism, other thinkers consider whether partial and interest*ed* ways of being, such as those within families or among friends, can instead be extended to the public sphere and made the ends rather than the means.

What is required from an ethics that transcends sexual difference and its ontological assumptions, then, is an idea of freedom that truly acknowledges not just the sometimes limiting, but also the *constitutive* roles of intersubjectivity, cultural discourses and social situation. As well as being able to account for these constitutive and exclusionary aspects of power, however, it still needs to account for the repressive aspects of power that create this necessity for rights discourses. I will return to this need for strategic engagement with repressive power in Chapter 6, but for now I will address various ethical approaches that have made claims that the most just way of being is not the atomised impartiality of liberalism, and seek to challenge the over-emphasis on self and value the ways of being traditionally associated with women. This will foreground my development in the next chapter of an ethics premised explicitly on the basis that freedom cannot be conceived as a possession of the atomised self, but needs to be understood as contingent on, made possible by, and achievable only through, the social, cultural and intersubjective.

Ethics of benevolence and partiality

In this section I will consider existing challenges to the impartial and autonomous ontological and normative claims of liberalism to further justify and develop a reciprocal ethics as a truly androgynous replacement to sexual difference. I suggest that these ethical models are useful for demonstrating that impartiality is impossible and that to behave 'as if' may have negative consequences of neglecting the real terrain upon which inequality is perpetuated.

Communitarianism

Communitarianism is the most explicit challenge to liberalism's Rawlsian 'original position', and explicates that other, more partial ways of being both exist and are desirable. In particular, it is critical of liberalism's supposed deontological foundations, with communitarian ethics emphasising the extent to which humyn values are derived from social and communal attachments (MacIntyre 1985; Sandel 1982; Walzer 1985). Many communitarian approaches emphasise the impossibility of impartiality owing to the radically situated nature of existence, drawing attention to relationships where more positive benevolent relations exist between people. However, in idealising partiality some thinkers worry that they lose the ability to make any universal normative claims or distinctions (Gutmann 1985; Okin 1987), which might be able to formulate an ethical response to the violences of sexual difference.

The primary critique of the supposedly deontological premises of liberalism by communitarians is the rejection of the indefensible claim for the isolated self or the autonomous subject, what Sandel calls 'the primacy of the subject' (1982: 7), which is the foundation required by liberalism and its vision of atomised autonomy. Communitarian critiques of the self/other divide depart instead from the assumption that 'The vaunted independence of the deontological subject is a liberal illusion' (Sandel 1982: 11), and their alternative visions tend instead to proceed from an ontological assumption of the interconnectedness of self and others, and instead to valorise community. Additionally, in critiquing the supposed impartiality of liberal ethics of justice, communitarianism conversely idealises small-scale ethics of partiality and context, and it emphasises the characteristics of benevolence and mutual co-operation where liberalism would emphasise mutual disinterest. However, communitarians do not necessarily propose extension of the partial benevolence offered to relatives or friends, or any other localised group, to all humyns.

Michael Sandel's critique of liberalism is a paradigmatic here, where ze emphasises the collaborative elements of self that liberalism neglects: 'to see ourselves as deontology would see us is to deprive us of those qualities of character, reflectiveness, and friendship that depend on the possibility of constitutive projects and attachments' (Sandel 1982: 181). Sandel theorises that the conditions of mutual disinterest and conflict upon which Rawls' theory of justice is predicated belie the actually existing 'solidaristic associations', such as the family, which make up the majority of our associations. The key argument of communitarianism is that 'we can readily imagine a range of more intimate or solidaristic associations in which the values and aims of the participants coincide closely enough that the circumstances of justice prevail to a relatively small degree' (Sandel 1982: 31).

While the emphasis on relations that are not premised on disinterest, selfishness and impartiality is useful for my project of finding an alternative ethic to that of opposition by demonstrating that ethico-political paradigms do not have to be premised on opposition or othering, communitarianism can too easily fall into conservatism and fail to draw normative lines by blithely perpetuating intra-group homogeny. Communitarians have emphasised the impossibility of imposing universal principles of any kind, and so have trouble formulating normative values of a kind that would be useful to my end of greater freedom of identity. This perspective, then, represents the perspective of complete partiality, the corollary of which is, according to some, that 'the good society of the new critics [of liberalism] is one of settled traditions and established identities' (Gutmann 1985: 309). Feminist ethics and some non-foundational approaches to care ethics go some way towards challenging atomised impartiality as foundation and ideal, without necessarily conceding that the only alternative to oppositional difference is sameness.

Feminine/feminist ethics

Feminine ethics, and some approaches to feminist ethics, also tend to emphasise the fundamental interdependence of existence, alongside the valorisation of non-institutional, positive relations between people. While they have been criticised for re-essentialising care traits with women (Sargisson 1996), they offer fruitful ways of thinking non-dominating self/other relations that do not rely on the depersonalised and impartial institutional realm.

Thinkers associated with feminine ethics, care ethics and feminist ethics note, like liberal feminists, that the theory of justice has tended to negate the broader value of the private sphere and therefore much of women's experiences. But feminists associated with 'feminine ethics' have reached different conclusions for action from those of liberal feminists by suggesting that altering traditional conceptions and visions of justice to extend to and include women is a self-effacing project. Proponents of these alternative ethical models all draw attention to the unachievability (and undesirability) of Rawls' original position (which, as I demonstrated above, Okin and other liberal feminists still maintain is ultimately ideal) and instead they depart from 'the *original condition* – dependency and group or family-defined identity' (Noddings 2006: 12). Thinkers such as feminist psychologist Carol Gilligan (1982; 2003), feminist ethicist and education theorist Nel Noddings (2003; 2006) and feminist philosophers Sara Ruddick (1980) and Caroline Whitbeck (1989) choose instead to privilege these (traditionally) feminine values, emphasising the value of the informal and partial ways of being that often characterise the private sphere. These writers suggest or imagine that the way that we perceive and behave towards others in these informal, partial and situated connections or relations could perhaps be a better basis for *all* social relations.

Thus, unlike some approaches to communitarianism, feminine care ethics do not have to concede to complete conservatism or relativism, and seek codes of conduct that might foster greater freedom and tolerance alongside their partial ontological point of departure. In this way, they are sometimes able to evade the impasse of requiring a disinterested impartiality for tolerance, as with liberalism, or of conceding to intra-group homogeny and conservatism, as some critics have argued is the corollary of communitarianism.

In illustrating 'feminine' ways of being and of conducting oneself, in per studies of the different moral development of boys and girls, Carol Gilligan undermined the traditional universalised and taken-for-granted masculinist definitions in developmental psychology of what is valuable in moral development. Ze suggests that women often express a 'different voice' – one of being socially situated and mutually caring – and seeks to revalue this way of being and relating, claiming anyway that the 'rational' public world of men has always relied on this 'labour of caring' in the private sphere in order to be able to function in a purportedly impersonal, disinterested way (Gilligan 2003: 157; see also Gilligan 1982 for the original formulation of this idea). One consequence has been that the '*privatization* of women's experience ... [has led] to the exclusion of its consideration from a moral point of view' (Benhabib 1985: 405). A result is that this neglected mutually co-operative and nurturing way of being, traditionally associated with women, is the hidden other upon which the public sphere relies in order to operate.

An important aspect of 'feminine' ethics is, then, the valuing of this 'other' pole in contrast to the atomised Selfhood of traditional ethics, and the positing of the fundamental interconnectedness of self and others as the ideal. The male way of being in the public sphere is not only valued over partiality and care, but becomes the universal story of development of subjectivity: 'The story of the autonomous male ego is the saga of this initial sense of *loss* in confrontation with the other' (Benhabib 1985: 409). These approaches de-essentialise this antagonistic self/other relation as the basis of humyn relations and development, and the related assumption of the inevitability of domination in non-regulated humyn relations.

One formulation of this feminine ideal is Whitbeck's (1989) exemplification of the maternal relation as exemplary of an unregulated, selfless, partial relation between self and other. This makes an explicit link to the masculinism of impartial ethics, and suggests that an ethics more rooted in the 'other' end of the self/other polarity as represented either literally or metaphorically by maternity is possible and desirable. Gilligan further emphasises that women have been excluded from traditional androcentric ethics owing to their more informal experiences of 'a sense of connection' and 'a web of relationships' (Gilligan 2003: 156), rather than the atomised self idealised by androcentric modernist ethics.

In considering the usefulness of feminine ethics to my aim of transcending sexual difference, however, it is important to note that there is a tendency or possibility in some approaches to essentialise the situated, nurturing ethic, associating it with a conception of women's fundamentally different 'nature'. Indeed, while seeking to invert the hierarchy, Gilligan perself notes that 'it is difficult to say "different" without saying "better" or "worse"' (Gilligan 1982: 14). In valorising as ideal the non-institutional, voluntarily nurturing *maternal* relation, Whitbeck (1989) does, in particular, tend to (re)associate this way of being in some essential way with women as mothers. This also makes it less useful for extending to broader social relations between individuals who do not have any biological or even cultural common-ality. Additionally, in critiquing the male emphasis on the self and the antagonism between self and other, Whitbeck's feminine/ist ethics of care and nurturing valorise the values of the 'private sphere' to the extent, not of the eradication of the dualisms of sex/gender and self/other, but rather the over-valuing of the feminine principle of selfless-ness. The danger of valuing selfless care for others is that it may be to the detriment of a more balanced *reciprocity* (Hoagland 1990), which, as I have already mentioned, Gilligan charts as having negative outcomes for girls: 'selflessness, which is associated with care and connection ... [can lead to] a loss of psychological vitality and courage' (Gilligan 2003: 158–159). However, while critiquing even feminist psychologists for a binary thinking that postulates that 'energy is *either* directed toward the self *or* directed toward an other' and claiming per model to be one of 'the-self-in-relation-to-others' (Whitbeck 1989: 59), approaches such as Whitbeck's do not emblematise an androgynous approach to ethics, lying rather on the opposite side of the 'difference' pole. As well as over-emphasising the other, Whitbeck claims special access to the ethics of care for women, suggesting that men can reach it but in different (and perhaps less valuable) ways. Whitbeck claims that this ethic is avail-able to men as well as women and that 'people may become convinced of the superiority of a particular ontology and seek the relationships and practices consistent with that view. (Theory may guide practice!)' (Whitbeck 1989: 60). However, ze maintains a special access to it for women, in stating that men's 'ways of acquisition are necessarily dif-ferent from ours' (Whitbeck 1989: 60). Likewise, Noddings states that

> ... there is reason to believe that women are somewhat better equipped for caring than men are. This is partly a result of the construction of psychological deep structures in the mother–child relationship. A girl can identify with the one caring for her and thus maintain relation while establishing identity. (Noddings 2003: 97)

McLaren (2001: 105) argues that this gendering of virtue will ulti-mately solidify women's oppression. Implicit valuing of 'natural' sources of partial benevolence, such as maternal relations, over social and chosen relations, does *not* necessarily hold the corollary extension of these relations to the social. Indeed, a possible corollary is that non-institutionalised co-operation between people who are *not* biologically or institutionally linked is less effective. What both communitarian-ism and feminine ethics risk, then, is the possibility of their ideal of benevolence not being extendable to all social relations, but being restricted to the specific contexts that they have drawn upon. Below I will discuss care ethics that valorise similar characteristics as feminine/ feminist ethics, but in less gendered terms.

To be clear, because of this historical devaluing of women's prac- tices, an androgynous ethics beyond sexual difference *does* need to be able to account for the social fact of the current existence of gender categories and hierarchies, and the oppressive 'power over' (Holloway 2002) that develops from this, and not downplay, negate or deny them as does liberalism. Additionally, however, it needs to acknowledge that these hierarchies may not necessarily have the posi- tive outcomes for men (for example) that a simple characterisation of gender hierarchy may assume. This was illustrated in Chapter 2 in reference to hegemonic masculinity and the work of performing normative masculine roles.

Care ethics

Speaking to this danger of reassociating care with 'womanhood' and following some charges of essentialism levelled at *In A Different Voice*, Carol Gilligan was careful in per later work to emphasise the extent to which current sex-polarised moral development negatively impacts on both boys *and* girls, men *and* women (Gilligan 2003). The over-emphasis on the self and competition for men means that it is less acceptable for men to form nurturing relations, and the over-emphasis on care results in a loss of sense of self and independence for women (Gilligan 1982), thus ethical models that universalise either are not ideal. This was also a concern for Noddings (2003), who emphasised the extent to which boys find it hard to make connection. The obvious corollary of this is a mode of perception that is not just gender-blinkered, but truly gender- transcendent, in that it rejects dualisms, rejects gendered associations with different modes of being, and emphasises an androgynous balance of all of these values and ways of being, freeing 'the voices of women *and* men ... from patriarchal strictures' (Gilligan 2003: 160, my emphasis). To this end, after per diagnosis of the sometimes gendered nature of caring above, Noddings (2003) goes on to make the distinc- tion between 'natural caring' and 'ethical caring', asserting that caring is in fact only ethical when it is a *choice* to care, suggesting that we can, and should, *learn* to care.

This might best be explicated by a semantic distinction between feminine ethics and feminist ethics, separating the ethical compo- nent from the biological. McLaren argues that while it is possible that 'the feminine virtues and care ethics are dangerous for women ... I conclude that care may indeed be a *feminist* virtue worth cultivating' (McLaren 2001: 105). Marilyn Freidman (1993) attempts to distance *per*self from such regendering accounts of feminine ethics, and the possible heteronormatising of the idealisation of the traditionally gendered family by communitarianism (Sandel 1982), by basing *per* ideal for unregulated and partial self/other relations, not on anything biological as with the maternal, but on the metaphor of friendship. It is in friendship that Friedman finds this balance between the self/other poles in a way that does not reify masculinity or femininity: 'friendship [is] ... a relationship that is based on approximate equality ... and a mutuality of affection, interest, and benevolence' (Friedman 1993: 189). Ze views friendship as exemplary of particular and partial relations of reciprocity that do not homogenise the other:

> ... commitment to a person in her unique particularity, a friend, for example, takes as its primary focus the unique concatenation of wants, desires, identity, history, and so on of a particular person. It is specific to that person and not generalizable to others. It acknowledges the uniqueness of the friend and can be said to honor or celebrate that uniqueness. ... Just how we care for a particular friend depends on her specific needs, interests, and values. (Friedman 1993: 190–191)

These non-institutional characterisations of humyn qualities and codes of conduct challenge the liberal assumption that 'the cultivation of moral sentiments is but a way-station on the road to full rationality when all feeling can safely be set aside' (Noddings 2006: 10) in Noddings' reading of Rawls' theory of justice. As such, as well as presenting moral ideals, *ontological ethical* approaches like this have implications for considering strategies for change. They indicate that legislation is not the only, nor indeed the best, way to ensure maximum freedom, especially considering the force of the social and intersubjective such that legislation will never ensure real equality.

While a corollary of this is that modes of perception or 'moral sentiments' are potentially more resilient than legislation can account for, what feminine, feminist and care ethics offer is the idea that alternative, and just, non-institutional relations are possible and already exist. This is a fruitful and practicable insight for thinking a reconstructive ontological ethic, and provides identification of more effective political terrain for fostering real change. It indicates that androgynous ethics needs to consider how change can be instigated at the level of social interaction. This extension of the political is something shared by feminism and anarchism, and Ursula Le Guin has identified this relationship between the feminine ethic, or 'female principle' in per words, and anarchist ethos: 'To me the "female principle" is, or at least historically has been, basically anarchic. It values order without constraint, rule by custom not by force' (Le Guin 1976: 134). I will elaborate on this below in a discussion of the implications of poststructuralist anarchist insights about the workings of power and domination for the nature and terrain of an androgynous and reciprocal ontological ethic.

(Poststructuralist) anarchism: ontological ethics

Like queer theory, anarchism is often understood as a negative, antiposition of critique. Indeed, its bare principle of anti-authoritarianism has been extended to wildly divergent ends, from anarcho-syndicalism to anarcho-capitalism, which is an extreme form of free-market liberalism. However, I argue that a particular approach to anarchism as a nonfoundational ethos concerned with minimising all forms of qualitative domination is a very useful way of thinking and approaching positive, reconstructive politics and ethics in a manner that is able to take account of the precepts developed in the book so far.

Poststructuralist anarchism is a paradigmatic model of an ontological ethics in that it combines the normative principles of anarchism – critique of domination – with a more nuanced, productive ontology of power such that it has much more potential to qualitatively intervene in the real terrain of domination. Additionally, there are some imaginative solutions to impasses of appealing to either minority identity politics *or* universalism that marginalises difference developed by anarchists thinking through the problems of recognition and the real roots of domination (e.g. Heckert 2002; 2010). These are paradigmatic for an ethos that transcends some of the problems identified in recognition politics (cf. Fraser 2000), and offer an excellent foundation on which to build a reconstructive, androgynous ethos.

Anarchism emphasises benevolence and non-legislative co-operation, and poststructuralism can offer anarchism a way of thinking about the subject that does not rely on essences or the assumption of autonomy, and expands the normative aim of mutual aid and a positive relation between people to all aspects of social and political life. It can also offer a refined definition of agency that takes heed of the premise of intersubjectivity without this precluding a particular formulation of freedom and agency. Contemporary approaches to anarchism that take off from a non-foundational conception of the subject and maintain a normative stance of freedom (Bey n.d.; CrimethInc. n.d.[a]; Heckert 2002; 2010; Holloway 2002; May 1994; Newman 2001) demonstrate that a constructivist ontology does not obviate a value-stance.

Anarchism, literally meaning 'without rule', obviously includes a support for a 'freedom *from-*' (Holloway 2002: 213, emphasis added) that is a repressive understanding of power as domination, and has always been associated with an anti-state stance. In some ways this is a principle as an end in itself, and can be related to the concern with 'the right' in liberalism. However, without a reconstructive norm *or* an appeal to an ontological essence, anarchism understood as the bare principle of freedom 'without rule' lacks the normative capacity to differentiate between freedoms and to make value claims about freedoms that delimit other freedoms, a charge that has also been levelled at deconstruction. It is undeniable that for many 'classical anarchists' this bare principle was augmented by ontological premises of natural mutual aid as essentialising as the premise of liberal theories of justice, merely with inverse claims. Kropotkin's (2007) point of departure, for example, expressed in *Mutual Aid*, first published in 1902, was the assumption of an innate humyn *sociability*: 'Sociability and need of mutual aid and support are ... inherent parts of human nature' (Kropotkin 2007 [1902]: 125). Per work in *Mutual Aid* was the emphasis of behaviour in the animal kingdom that demonstrates mutual aid in order to generalise this to humyn behaviour and refute the competitive premise of liberalism and social Darwinism. Likewise, Proudhon's foundational point of departure in *What is Property?*, first published in 1840, was the assumption of an inherent and natural sense of justice apparent in per reference to 'the social instinct which governs us' (Proudhon 1994 [1840]: 174) such that 'the selfish man ... sins against nature' (Proudhon 1994: 174). Thus most classical anarchist discourses rely on the concepts of humyn nature, a natural order and a natural law to allay the charge that anarchism would result in chaos (Woodcock 1980: 16). This conception of humyn nature taken as a point of departure by anarchism is diametrically opposed to the Hobbesian 'fear and self-interest' or Rawlsian 'mutually disinterested' conception of humyn nature, which is the point of departure for liberal theories of the social contract. While liberalism asserts that life in a state of anarchy would be 'nasty, brutish and short', both liberalism and classical anarchism share the Enlightenment assumption of a foundational humyn nature as a premise for their political assertions.

However, an element of anarchist thought has always also been concerned with 'power *to-*' (Holloway 2002: 213, emphasis added) and a reconstructive and normatively argued-for *principle* of anarchism. I will call this element 'autonomist' to distinguish it from essentialist ideas that assume a repressive power of the state, which, once eradicated, would reveal a pre-cultural free humyn nature. This use of autonomist is distinct, however, from the use of autonomy as an atomised state as used in liberal discourses. This 'power to-' is related to ideas of 'the good' that are concerned with outcome rather than principle, and tends to extend the political to the cultural terrain. The strategy of prefiguration of alternative, preferable ways of being, for example, has always been an element of anarchism (Franks 2006: 97), and marks one of its major differences from Marxism, along with a general suspicion of the state and all forms of authority and power over-, leading to the split of the first Internationale (Woodcock 2004: 100–101). Emma Goldman's concern in 1910 with 'the internal tyrants, far more harmful to life and growth ... [of] ethical and social conventions' (Goldman 1969 [1910]: 227) demonstrates the emphasis ze placed on the internalisation of power, and 'ethical and social conventions' rather than either essence or abstract principle. More recently, this characterisation of power has seen contemporary anarchist thinker Heckert (2002: 7) posit subjects as 'both products and producers of systems'. This points towards an analysis of power beyond the state as in some classical anarchist approaches, or class and economics as with Marxism, that is compatible with, and can be helpfully elaborated with, various theories of subjectivity and poststructuralism, as I will argue below. Benjamin Franks suggests that

> The anarchist ideal extends the notion further by not tying oppression to an objectively knowable singular power, but realises that different forces operate in different contexts. As such, it shares important characteristics with the politically-engaged poststructuralisms of the likes of Jacques Derrida, Michel Foucault, Jean-François Lyotard, Gilles Deleuze and Felix Guattari. (Franks 2006: 154)

This, then, is the useful core of poststructuralist anarchism: a dual analysis that considers freedom from- and power to-. This can be helpfully applied to theorising sexual difference as a form of power over- or negative power, as well as more insipidly hindering autonomy in the sense of capacity, power to-, or positive power by limiting the 'fund of ideas' (Archer 1996: xiii) through its very compulsory (but inessential) existence. This impacts on how the subject, power, freedom, agency and 'resistance' are understood by extending the analysis to the intersubjective and social mechanisms of power. The focus here is on more abstract hierarchies and authoritarian modes of thought, such as the 'discursive regimes' that Saul Newman theorises as constitutive of subjects:

> I employ a deliberately broad definition of *authority*: it refers not only to institutions like the state and the prison etc.; it also refers to authoritarian discursive structures like rational truth, essence, and the subjectifying norms they produce. (Newman 2001: 12–13)

Clearly influenced by Foucault, Newman emphasises that for post-structuralist anarchists there are not determining structures, but rather constitutive 'power, discursive regimes, and practices' (Newman 2001: 14), or 'intersections of power rather than emanations from a source' (May 1994: 52). These constitutive elements are 'dispersed and unstable' (Newman 2001: 14), and therefore, while constitutive, still open to resistance. The non-foundational ontology of much contemporary anarchism tends to emphasise the *potential* for non-legislative benevolent co-operation, and recognise the diverse terrain that perpetuates the current dominant ethos. In the next chapter I will build on this ontology of potentiality outlined here and in my ontological characterisation of sexual difference in Chapter 2, emphasising further how it can underpin a normatively argued-for androgynous, reciprocal ethics. This potential for an ethos whereby the other is not viewed as an oppositional threat is illustrated in contemporary anarchist literature by emphasising and extending contexts where such modes of interaction already exist and work, but without reducing this co-operation to an essential characteristic. Hakim Bey, for example, reasons that the dinner party is an ideal co-operative social situation that does not require official rules (Bey n.d.: n.p.), and DIY anarcho-punk collective CrimethInc. make a similar point:

> It's true. If your idea of healthy human relations is a dinner with friends, where everyone enjoys everyone else's company, responsibilities are divided up voluntarily and informally, and no one gives orders or sells anything, then you are an anarchist, plain and simple. The only question that remains is how you can arrange for more of your interactions to resemble this model. (CrimethInc. n.d.[a]: 4)

Such a perspective therefore augments the examples of feminine ethics by idealising *chosen*, non-foundational co-operative relations.

Similarly to the performative ontology (Butler 1990), then, subjects, in being constituted by discursive power regimes as opposed to being pre-cultural entities (May 1994; Newman 2001), can be understood as having no proclivity towards either mutual disinterest *or* mutual aid, but rather as having *capacities* that are shaped by discursive context that is constantly being (re)constituted. Thus it is possible to posit humyn nature as a situated potentiality that has the *possibility* of being fostered according to anarchist principles. Bearing this in mind as a precursor, in the next chapter I will draw on Beauvoir and Butler to develop a more detailed ontological ethics of a similar sort, wherein I emphasise the possibility of subjects being fostered with androgynous, reciprocal principles.

The unique contribution of poststructuralist anarchism for thinking a truly androgynous reciprocal ethics, then, is in arguing for a more benevolent way of being and relating to others as a *chosen* and explicated ethos, an 'ideal' rather than an essential ontological or normative characteristic. This is what has allowed it to transcend the binary of sameness or difference that characterises the crux of the recognition debates (McNay 2008), and which I will tease out in the following two chapters using a different, but compatible, set of conceptual tools.

Conclusion

The ethics outlined in this chapter all hold a normative ideal of how the self and the other *should* be perceived or related to for maximum justice to prevail, derived from what they consider ontologically possible or potential. This all prompts *explicit* consideration of exactly how the other *could* be seen in a manner that is truly androgynous by not relying on reified identities, and truly does not privilege or do a violence to either end of the self/other pole.

In the next chapter, I will formulate an ontological ethics that can justify and underpin a theory and practice of real, qualitative androgyny, understood as actual transcendence of sexual difference and its related exclusions. I will propose this ethical telos or ideal from an ontology of potentiality (as detailed in Chapter 2) that does not re-essentialise its traits as in some feminine ethics, but rather emphasises how it can be *fostered*. In this way, the ontological ethics of reciprocity that I will outline in Chapter 4 share this ontological/normative balance with poststructuralist anarchism. I will argue premises about the nature of being, and normative or ethical reasoning for a reconstructive mode of being and relating that does not collapse into the exclusionary mechanisms that many posit as inherent to identity politics and some formulations of recognition (Fraser 2000; McNay 2008; Young 1995), but also does not fall into the exclusionary trap of universalism, which neglects differences, a charge of other formulations of recognition such as impartiality.

4
Philosophical Arguments for Post-Gender Ontological Ethics

In Chapter 3 I outlined the limits to the dominant, liberal ethico-political paradigm. Its formulations of the nature of being, and its congruent solutions for the problems of sex/gender are insufficient for analysing the realities of sex/gender and for overcoming its effects. This chapter seeks a more effective 'ontological ethical' (Stanley 1996) theory to constitute the key philosophical argument and justification for post-gender ethics. It uses metaphysical and ethical reasoning to argue that getting rid of sex/gender is both possible and desirable, and to propose more positive ways of being in the world. I will draw on the ethical philosophy of 'philosopher manqué' (Stanley 2001) Simone de Beauvoir, alongside some of the ideas of Michel Foucault and Judith Butler, to present an 'ontological ethics' that can account for the problems from which this book departs and underpin an argument for a more enabling mode of being. Beauvoir's ontological ethics can be used as a foundation for arguing that freedom is the purposive enactment of existence, that sexual difference prevents this, and given that our subjectivity is fundamentally situated, that purposive existence can only be enacted in wilful concert with others.

These thinkers allow me to build a more realistic account of the nature of being (ontology) that takes seriously all aspects of subjectivity: the self, the other, the social and the cultural, to account for the resilience of sexual difference, and to develop a qualified account of 'freedom' as capacity as indicated in Chapter 3. This allows for the assertion that there is possible agency for (re)constituting the ways that we understand ourselves and others. This informs the way that I will go on to develop the principles and characteristics of 'post-gender ethics', and I will use Beauvoir's ideal of 'reciprocity' as a starting point that demonstrates the possibility of what a more positive way of being in the world might be like. Beauvoir argues normatively (normative in the sense of 'ethical justification' (Butler 2007: xxi)) for, and illustrates in per fictional work, the preference of reciprocal, non-objectifying relations between self and other. But the justification is not hidden in ontological assumptions, it is explicated.

I have chosen in this metaphysical and ethical portion of my project to draw on Beauvoir's entire oeuvre of ethical work that is both explicit, in political essays or ethical philosophy books, and implicit in novels and autobiography, de-emphasising per oft-cited work *The Second Sex*. This follows Stanley's (2001) project of attempting to revalue Beauvoir as a significant philosopher of existentialist ethics, whose work often predated the malestream existentialists in terms of ideas (Fullbrook & Fullbrook 1994) and also exceeded them in terms of nuance and sophistication, particularly in per picture of the nature of being, which I will outline in detail below. In particular, Beauvoir evaded the pessimistic solipsism that plagued much existentialism, which tended to posit that there is 'only self' and held a hostile assumption about the other and their relation to yourself (Simons 2001: 231). Beauvoir instead emphasises our fundamental intersubjectivity as humyns, that is, the un-deniability of our relatedness to other humyns, and posits that this both shapes (and thus to some extent delimits) but also enables our existence. This has clear implications for thinking about how our sense of self (including but not restricted to sexed/gendered sense of self) is made, how it may be otherwise and how it ought to be, which I will elaborate. Sharing with other existentialists a concern with freedom and how to maximise this, Beauvoir's main ethical argument was that, given that existence is fundamentally collective or intersubjective, the most ethical way of living is to attempt to make this collectively as purposive as possible, a process that must necessarily be social or intersubjective. This makes Beauvoir's thinking immensely practicable for reconstructive ethics of freedom. Thus Beauvoir's importance has been highlighted not only for challenging the 'problem' of solipsism (Simons 2001), but also for the creation of a non-foundational ethics of freedom, that is, one not premised on essences, but an ethics that is still practical and positive (Simons 1999).

Butler famously departed from and to some extent rejected the hugely influential ideas of Beauvoir's *Second Sex* (written in 1949) in per own *Gender Trouble* (1990). In Butler's reading, Beauvoir's germinal phrase 'one is not born a woman, but rather becomes one' ties Beauvoir's analysis to the sex/gender distinction (Butler 2007 [1990]: 151), that is, with an essentialist analysis of a biological sex that precedes the 'becoming' of a gender. Butler posits that Beauvoir's argument there holds the implication that that while gender is achieved and variable, sex is a fixed given. However, read contemporaneously in the light of new materialist deconstructions of biological sexual difference (charted in Chapter 2), as I will demonstrate, Beauvoir's ontological ideas do not have to be applied according to the sex/gender divide. Per notion of becoming can complement new materialist ideas about bodily potentiality and be extended easily and productively to biological sex, or sexual difference itself. This is another reason for returning specifically to a rereading and reapplication of the earlier, purely ontological ethical works of Beauvoir over sticking to *The Second Sex* and demonstrates per ongoing usefulness for contemporary queer concerns.

The timeliness of a reconsideration of Beauvoir's ontologically nuanced ethics of freedom for social change is profound given the trajectory of Butler's oeuvre, which charts a move from 'explanatory-diagnostic' work about sex/gender to more ethical, normative and practicable concerns – from ontological concerns in problematising the sex/gender divide (1990), to more materially grounded ontological formulations (1993), to a concern with power (1997), to an ethical account and concern with justice (2005), and finally to some gestures towards social practices and social change (2011a; 2011b). Butler has most recently explicitly called for positive, ethical, reconstructive accounts of social relationships on 'queer' terms (2011c). Thus I want to apply Beauvoir's ethical philosophy quite separately from the trajectory that *The Second Sex* has been taken down. Instead of dwelling on per ontological diagnosis of sex/gender, I will draw on per ontological *ethics* that do not rely on essences, as an ethical reconstructive counterpart compatible with sex/gender deconstruction. In this vein, Beauvoir commentator Vintges emphasises Beauvoir's preoccupation with 'Ethics as Art of Living' (2001), directly connecting this project with Foucault's later work around purposive and moral existence, hence my use also of Foucault's work, particularly per later work, which was concerned with 'The Ethics of the Concern of the Self as a Practice of Freedom' (Foucault 1997). This work, like that of Beauvoir, is concerned with developing an ethics or code of conduct without appealing to essentialist foundations. Read in this way, the ethical work of Beauvoir and Foucault can be reconceptualised as containing just the normative ideas that Butler seems to be looking for in the wake of such radical sex/gender deconstruction.

It is my position, then, that Butler's – and other queer theorists' – desire for the 'variable construction of identity' (1990: 5) and 'undo[ing of] restrictively normative conceptions of sexual and gendered life'

(Butler 2004: 1) can be lent considerable argumentative and practicable power using Beauvoir's ethical works, in particular per ethical ideal of reciprocity. The politics of queer studies have been accused of 'amounting to a revolution of subtraction, eroding existing norms and verities, rather than a revolution of addition, creating new values. What passes for reinventing is merely disinventing' (Dynes 1995: 37). Reciprocity is a principle for existence that is compatible with the post-identity, or non-foundational, ontology and politics of queer theory, but also extends this such that it underpins positive, reconstructive ethics and does not leave this position with the negativity – or even value-free relativism – with which it has been charged. In this way, I posit that the ontological insights of poststructuralist ideas such as Butler's and other queer theorists' and more normative ideas are not mutually exclusive, and that 'Feminists need both deconstruction *and* reconstruction, destabilization of meaning *and* projection of utopian hope' (Fraser 1995: 71).

McNay (2008) found robust ontological explication lacking or inconsistent in many accounts concerned with similar aims of finding the most enabling 'way of being' and way of recognising others in an intersubjective existence, for example, in accounts about recognition politics. Thus I deem such explication necessary for my project of a reconstructive androgynous queer ethics/mode of being. This reciprocal mode of relating to the self and other, hence of 'recognition', would ideally stay true to the ethos of deconstruction and evade the reductions of much recognition politics, which has been critiqued for undertheorising the social and power in subject formation:

> Far from resulting in a more embodied, dialogical account of subjectivity, most of the thinkers [of contemporary recognition politics] ... end up invoking relatively abstract and disembodied conceptions that are closer than they might care to acknowledge to the monological concepts they oppose. (McNay 2008: 2)

It is notable that, in a brief mention, McNay does concede that Beauvoir's work on recognition departs from 'a more nuanced understanding' of ontology than identity-based recognition politics (2008: 3, 5). As such, this chapter will outline Beauvoir's account of the possibility of transcending the self/other oppositional difference, which I have already argued is the dominant mode of thought that underpins sexual difference. I will also outline how, in per particular formulation of freedom, sexual difference can be understood to constitute the unfreedom of 'immanence': 'subjection to given conditions' (Beauvoir 1997: 29).

Finally, I will present the argument for reciprocity as a better alternative for a mode of being that, as far as possible, attempts to enable the 'transcendence of immanence'. This moral reasoning about what is 'the good life' based on explication of the nature of being is, then, what is meant by ontological ethics (Stanley 1996).

The ontological: the ambiguous existence of others

Beauvoir and Butler both, rather differently but in my opinion complimentarily, develop explanations of subjectivity that account for the resilience of sex/gender in the popular imagination, account for the failure of purely subjective, individual attempts to eschew it, and therefore deliver substantial qualifications for understanding what constitutes 'freedom' and how alternatives to sexual difference could be fostered. Beauvoir asserts a fundamental co-constitution between the self, the other (that is, intersubjective relations), the social and cultural discourses. The 'ambiguity' that ze posits is a situatedness that both enables and delimits our agency (Beauvoir 1976a). This way of thinking evades the analytic limits of the overly agentic self in the impartial Rawlsian liberal 'veil of ignorance', which imagines that situation does not shape us. It also, as I have already outlined, avoids the solipsism of some existentialism. However, staying true to the basis of existentialism, it also does not reduce to a social determinism that loses the 'self' pole in self/other polarisations. What it leaves is an ontology of situated potentiality, with the potential that relations between people (between self and other) *could* be more positive and enabling, rather than negating. Applied to sexual difference, it can explain why sexual difference is persistent and difficult to resist individually, being as it is a social resource for interaction and understanding others. It also lends the possibility that this constitution may be otherwise.

Beauvoir's account of the self/other relation was greatly influenced by Hegel (Le Doeuff 1995: 63), but the basic ontological situation of intersubjectivity ze posited did not contain any particular inevitable negative *or* positive relations between self and other. Per definitive statement is perhaps that 'I concern others and they concern me. There we have an irreducible truth' (Beauvoir 1976a: 72). Beauvoir is persistently keen however, to emphasise this facticity (that is, absolute given-ness) of the extent to which the other exists and influences subjectivity. In her fiction work *The Blood of Others*, originally published in 1945, Beauvoir illustrates the extent to which the other demands an account: 'Hélène's eyes were asking questions, weighing up, demanding an account. Who was this other personality who dared to be there, confronting me?' (Beauvoir 1978: 55). Likewise, the opening chapter of Beauvoir's earlier novel *She Came to Stay*, originally published in 1943, is an early existentialist musing on the nature of situated existence and uses the character of Gerbert as representing the possibility of a solipsistic corollary of this demand for an account. Gerbert assumes the relation to the other to be that of competition and negation: 'I find it so unpleasant to listen to people talking to me about myself. ... I feel they're gaining some sort of an advantage over me' (Beauvoir 2006: 7). This is illustrative of the Hegelian consciousness that 'seeks the death of the other' (Beauvoir 1976a: 70), which Beauvoir considers 'naïve' (1976a: 71). The character of Françoise represents an alternative corollary, emphasising the way in which the other is indeed always implicated in one's subjectivity, but not necessarily negatively, by coming to think of herself through the perspective of Gerbert. This is the necessary realisation of the subjecthood of the other, but Beauvoir emphasises the ambiguity of this, that this does not necessarily devalue existence or autonomy and this underpins per formulation of *The Ethics of Ambiguity* (Beauvoir 1976a [1947]):

> It's almost impossible to believe that other people are conscious beings, aware of their own inward feelings, as we ourselves are aware of our own. ... To me, it's terrifying when we grasp that. We get the impression of no longer being anything but a figment of someone else's mind. But that hardly ever happens, and never completely. (Beauvoir 2006: 6–7)

This discovery that others possess subjectivity, just as I do, is what demarcates the transition from the irresponsibility of what Beauvoir characterises as the child-like stage of subjectivity in terms of assuming an atomised selfish rationality, to the realisation that the self is implicated in the other and vice versa. Such an account of selfhood as developed with an awareness of the other and their understandings of you has been pursued more empirically elsewhere in symbolic interactionism, ethnomethodology and other sociology, gender and social theory, as I discussed in Chapter 2 (see Garfinkel 1967; Goffman 1956; Mead 1934). The next step is to consider what this means for ethical conduct. As I have charted, this explains why individual attempts to transcend gender are ultimately recuperated and ineffective.

This allegory of the immaturity of individualism, and the social and moral implications or responsibilities of our collective nature, is illustrated by the character of Hélène in *The Blood of Others* (Beauvoir 1978). Initially, Hélène behaves like a child who has not yet internalised social values, and represents the selfishly rational perspective: '"we always seek to further our own interests," said Hélène. "And I think we're quite right," she added challengingly. "After all, we only have ourselves"' (Beauvoir 1978: 49). Hélène is representative of the ostensible impartiality of liberalism, stating that 'I don't care a rap for people I don't know' (Beauvoir 1978: 50). Hélène, then, can be understood as what Beauvoir described in *The Ethics of Ambiguity* as the child who, in assuming that the world is a given, an absolute, is 'allowed to play, to expend his existence freely' and who is 'happily irresponsible' (Beauvoir 1976a: 35).

However, Hélène then becomes the allegory for how intersubjectivity *can* provoke responsibility. Upon seeing a woman with a child who is in a worse situation than Hélène herself,[1] both having fled Paris in response to the German occupation, Hélène hears 'a voice from the past, "The others exist. You must be blind not to see them"' (Beauvoir 1978: 202). This provokes empathy and a generosity wherein she sacrifices her place in a car to the woman and child. Beauvoir, then, did not posit any *necessary* ethical implications as the corollary of this ambiguous subjectivity, but does make the reasoned case for them on normative terms, which will be elaborated below. Significantly, this ambiguity means that Beauvoir makes an argument for ethical intersubjectivity without foundations such as essential co-operation or essential selfishness. This allegory prefigures Beauvoir's more positive corollary of this inevitable intersubjectivity, that of a reciprocal relation that realises that 'to will that there be being is also to will that there be men by and for whom the world is endowed with human significations' (Beauvoir 1976a: 71), which I will elaborate below. A reciprocal approach to intersubjectivity represents an enabling and positive means of subjectivation more in line with the ethics of queer theory and gender deconstruction.

In contemplating this same issue of the self/other relation and coming to subjectivity, there are clear parallels in Butler's use of similar language of 'giving an account' in per later work (see *Giving an Account of Oneself* 2005). This account retains a certain amount of negativity in the self/other relation in stating that there is 'a primary *vulnerability* to the Other in order to be' (Butler 1997: 21, my emphasis), and that we are 'beings who are formed in relations of dependency' (Butler 2005: 20). This situated 'ambivalent' (Butler 1997: 15) condition of existence explains for Butler how oppression can exist, and why subordinating identities or norms – of which sex/gender is paradigmatic – are so persistent. However, Butler's aim in unpacking the process of giving an account and the extent to which this relies on gender norms, is to consider the nature of agency and what more positive, what I call purposive, intersubjectivity might look like. While Judith Butler's *Gender Trouble* (published in 1990) appeared to offer a potential agency in the subversive repetitions of hegemonic ways of being (such as the doing of gender), *The Psychic Life of Power* (published in 1997) emphasised the power of social discourses such as sex/gender and appeared more pessimistic about the pre-existing and more constitutive nature of power and norms. However, *Giving an Account of Oneself* (2005) to some extent transcends this structure/agency bind by echoing Beauvoir's ambiguity in settling on the idea that the facticity that there is no 'I' that is not a set of relations does not preclude a 'ground for moral agency and moral accountability' (Butler 2005: 8).

The conditions of agency: situated capacity

I have established that Beauvoir and Butler reject individualism and concede that subjectivity and thus freedom is shaped, to some extent, by relations with others and by situation, which is invaluable for explaining sex/gender. While Beauvoir does account for pre-existing structures (which ze characterises as situation), it is notable that ze – as an existentialist thinker – also evades the reduction to social determinism that is a threat of some identity-based models of recognition politics (McNay 2008). These models over-state the power of social positioning and subsume the interests of the individual to the collective. Beauvoir's account allows for a nuanced agency that can underpin the possibilities for intervening in and reconstituting the becoming of subjectivity. I will go on to consider Beauvoir's formulation of what is morally good in order to consider how we can think about a more ethical process of coming to subjectivity. However, first I want to dwell briefly on the extent to which, and how, 'critical desubjectivation' (Butler 1997: 130) is possible and whether, in turn, a different process of 'subjectivation' is possible. That is, I want to clarify what agency consists of in this picture.

In *The Blood of Others*, Beauvoir illustrates the political futility of over-privileging the collective and downplaying individual agency through Communism and the character of Blomart. This character becomes a dedicated communist, and comes to represent the subsuming of the self to the collective: '"Our petty personal desires don't seem to be very interesting to me. ... I can't see what's to be gained by satisfying them"' (Beauvoir 1978: 49). Blomart becomes a communist as a polarised reaction to individualism, because he experiences the futility of being a self who attempts to negate situation and responsibility, but Beauvoir frames this attempt to resolve the self/other bind as just as naïve as Hélène's individualism. The character of Paul Perrier goes on to articulate the ethical problems of subsuming the self under the collective through communism: 'Communists treat human beings like pawns on a chessboard, the game must be won at all costs; the pawns themselves are unimportant' (Beauvoir 1978: 59).

Beauvoir, then, resists reduction to either side of the self/other or individual/collective binarism. Ze states that 'the meaning of the situation does not impose itself on the consciousness of a passive subject' (Beauvoir 1976a: 20), giving the example that the act of choosing to enrol in a political party or undertake a political action is in itself an act of autonomous agency. For Beauvoir as an existentialist the self is still a key source of all things and the source of freedom, and the world, or situation, is always perceived by the self. This is made apparent in the opening chapter of *She Came to Stay*, characterised as the key articulation of Beauvoir's existentialist ontology (Fullbrook 2004), where Françoise realises that all things are perceived through per: 'When she was not there, the smell of dust, the half light, and that forlorn solitude did not exist for anyone; they did not exist at all' (Beauvoir 2006: 1).

This ontological position of a truly co-constitutive relationship between self, others and situation, and the picture of agency it paints, is best characterised as *situated capacity*. Beauvoir's 'ambiguous' ontology is then that 'the existence of others as a freedom defines my situation and is even the condition of my own freedom' (Beauvoir 1976a: 91). This renders the 'fundamental ambiguity' (Beauvoir 1976a: 9) of situatedness of selfhood and the need for pre-existing discourses to attach to as a positive diagnosis. The situated self has an agency, but this agency is still delimited, what Kruks has called 'living on rails' (Kruks 2005). This is echoed in the 'ambivalent scene of agency' (Butler 1997: 15) in Butler's notion of ontology. Butler's conception of 'opacity' is the condition that the self is never fully transparent to the self, but that simultaneously, and ethically, 'there is a desire for norms that might let one live' (Butler 2004: 3). This leaves important limits for agency as, in narrating one's own subjectivity, the 'self is already implicated in a social temporality that exceeds its own capacities for narration' (Butler 2005: 8). However, importantly, these pre-existing norms are conditions that can be perceived, not as the omission of, but rather the *condition* of, agency: 'This struggle with the unchosen conditions of one's life, a struggle – an agency – is also made possible, paradoxically, by the persistence of this primary condition of un-freedom' (Butler 2005: 19). Butler articulates a co-constitutive relationship between self, other and situation, but crucially, like Beauvoir, retains that the norms and rules are negotiated by a subject 'in a living and reflective way' (Butler 2005: 10). My interest is in how this negotiation of norms may be as enabling as possible. This is compatible with the notion of 'freedom to-' as a positive aspect of power outlined in Chapter 3.

Being situated capacity, unlike some accounts that Fraser describes as 'vulgar culturalism' (2000), these formulations are still able to account for material inequalities in agency in a way that is useful to feminist analyses of sex/gender. In *The Blood of Others* (Beauvoir 1978), for example, this capacity to 'fend for oneself' is referred to as being 'armed', and there needs to be an acknowledgement that, owing to situation, all are not armed equally. For example, in response to Hélène's assertion (allegorical to liberal ontology) that, for justice to prevail, all one must do is fend for oneself, is met by the response from Blomart: 'I think you were born fully armed' (Beauvoir 1978: 50). This illustrates how Beauvoir, while valorising freedom, is aware of the difference that social situation can make. Subjects can, then, 'exercise their freedom, but only within this universe which has been set up before them, without them' (Beauvoir 1976a: 37). This accounts for the extent to which sexual difference is a collective cultural resource that both allows and delimits purposive, self-willed subjectivity, and that these capacities are differently distributed. It also allows that it might be possible for subjects to collectively create other cultural resources. However, this ontological picture requires ethical reasoning to posit what constitutes more or less desirable or preferable norms.

Despite what Beauvoir obviously considers to be the more valuable *ethical* corollary of this self/other/situation characterisation, the only definitive and certain ontological conclusion that can be drawn is that 'I concern others and they concern me. There we have an irreducible truth. The me–others relationship is as indissoluble as the subject–object relationship' (Beauvoir 1976a: 72). What is needed is a normative first principle that is able to posit what 'freedom' would look like, and thus morally evaluate different ways of relating, and thus coming to subjectivity. I will now use Beauvoir's characterisation of freedom as the purposive undertaking of existence to argue that sex/gender is a collectively perpetuated cultural resource that renders the other to an object – rather than a subject – and thus prevents their freedom. This will underpin an ethico-political argument for an alternative in the form of a reciprocal and benevolent interrelation that allows the subject maximum participation in this process of subjectivation. Given the ontological premise that 'the subject is *neither* fully determined by power *nor* fully determining of power (but significantly and partially both)' (Butler 1997: 17), it is logical that the enactment of this ideal should be collective.

The ethical: transcendence through self creation

I have outlined a situated and intersubjective account of subjectivity that is able to account for the resilience of attachment to and attribution of sexual difference and sex/gender identity, and the self/other dualisms with which they are co-constitutive. It also presents a qualified account of agency that could allow for the constitution of a different way of being. I need to consider not only what this thin ontology of a radically situated capacity *could* allow, but also clarify the normative principles I am departing from that could underpin an alternative ethic for what *should* replace this current way of being. While stating that 'otherness is a fundamental category of human thought' (Beauvoir 1997: 17), Beauvoir also later makes the non-foundational claim that 'the nature of things is no more immutably given, once for all, than is historical reality' (Beauvoir 1997: 19). Thus, this ontological premise that I have developed from Beauvoir and Butler lacks inherent value and normative claims because, while claiming that we are situated beings, Beauvoir also states that 'no pre-established harmony exists between men' (Beauvoir 1987: 139). If we are always already self/other/situation, then the question of whether the self *should* be impacted by other and situation becomes un-askable, and must shift to how this collective subjectivation should best play out. Using the moral arguments of Beauvoir, Foucault and Butler, then, my argument for a reciprocal ethics to replace oppositional ethics departs from the 'rejection of any extrinsic justification' (Beauvoir 1976a: 15). As such, the ontological points of departure have been stated *a priori*, and, by combining them with the normative valorisation of freedom as doing, I will make a reasoned case for an alternative.

The value-based principle that Beauvoir openly departs from is that, given that existence is a doing not a being (as exhaustively argued in Chapter 2), existence is fulfilled only by freedom or 'liberty' in this doing. This is inherent in Beauvoir's rejection of a more relativist notion of the pursuit of happiness as the ultimate principle, normatively claiming that 'those who are condemned to stagnation are often pronounced happy on the pretext that happiness consists in being at rest' (Beauvoir 1997: 28). For example,

> Are not women of the harem more happy than women voters? Is not the house-keeper happier than the working woman? It is not too clear just what the word happy really means and still less what true values it may mask. There is no possibility of measuring the happiness of others, and it is always easy to describe as happy the situation in which one wishes to place them. (Beauvoir 1997: 28)

Beauvoir rejects the relative and indefinable principle of 'happiness' on the grounds that it is often concomitant with stagnation, but also because the happiness of one person can impact negatively on the happiness and freedom of others. Those who draw on it often do not take into account the situatedness of being and values. Hélène in *The Blood of Others* is representative of this way of existing that is concerned only with the pursuit of selfish happiness, and demonstrative of its ostensible folly. In the first scene in which Hélène appears, ze is stealing a bicycle only for the reason that ze desires it. In *The Second Sex* (1997 [1949]), Beauvoir elaborates on this articulation of existentialist ethics, stating that the ambiguous principle of happiness should be replaced with understanding freedom as the purposive 'transcendence of immanence' (immanence is defined as 'subjection to given conditions' (Beauvoir 1997: 29)): 'Every individual concerned to justify his [sic] existence feels that his existence involves an undefined need to transcend himself, to engage in freely chosen projects' (Beauvoir 1997: 29). For Beauvoir, then, 'Human freedom [is] ... the ultimate, the unique end to which man should destine himself' (Beauvoir 1976a: 49).

Freedom, in this sense of the transcendence of immanence, is defined by Beauvoir not as a static state or end-point in the way that happiness is often characterised, but as a constant striving or doing, a constant transcendence of immanence. Meaningful existence, then, is a continual becoming. Ze states that a person 'achieves liberty only through a continual reaching out towards other liberties' (Beauvoir 1997: 28). Beauvoir's existentialist notion of freedom is not a teleological end or a site of pure freedom. Instead it is rather a freedom without ends or absolutes, freedom in the *ability* for continual transcendence through projects without end, in and of themselves: 'With each step forward the horizon recedes a step; for man it is a matter of pursuing the expansion of his existence and of retrieving this very effort as an absolute' (Beauvoir 1976a: 79). This ideal of perpetuity is best summarised by Beauvoir as attempting to see 'the transitory as an absolute' (Beauvoir 1976a: 80), and I will return to this principle of inexhaustibility as a characteristic of an ideal reciprocal ethic in Chapter 5. Justifying this way of characterising freedom as an eternal doing, Beauvoir elaborates upon why this lack of closed and complete telos or end-point, the lack of a site or state of pure freedom, does not lend itself to inactivity, but rather is the only possible basis for projects of transcendence:

> Regardless of the staggering dimensions of the world about us, the density of our ignorance, the risks of catastrophes to come, and our individual weakness within the immense collectivity, the fact remains that we are absolutely free today if we choose to will our existence in its finiteness, a finiteness which is open on the infinite. (Beauvoir 1976a: 159)

Demonstrating how humyns can create values with only the thinnest ontological premises of potentiality and without extra-humyn justification, Beauvoir argues 'it is a matter of reconquering freedom on the contingent facticity of existence, that is, of taking the given, which, at the start, *is there* without any reason, as something willed by man' (Beauvoir 1976a: 156). Existence is fulfilled by creating, by undertaking projects. In the aptly titled volume of per autobiography, *The Force of Circumstance*, Beauvoir often expresses the necessity of keeping going in the face of facticity or circumstance. For example, with the knowledge of then contemporary events in Algiers, ze asks 'How [people] can ... continue to live normally, to write?' (Beauvoir 1968: 610–611), but ze always returns to the idea that it 'seemed to me important again to take plaster, or words, and create something' (Beauvoir 1968: 625), that is, to transcend through creation. This is because '*one does not exist without doing something*' (Beauvoir 1976a: 156, my emphasis).

Likewise, Foucault, by seeing the self as something to be worked on or a project in per later work, which outlined 'The Ethics of the Concern of the Self as a Practice of Freedom', applies a parallel principle to subjectivity. Foucault inherently valorises this purposive ideal of the ability, or freedom, to work on the self. Per definitive statement with regard to ethics is perhaps that 'for what is ethics, if not the practice of freedom, the conscious practice of freedom?' (Foucault 1997: 284), which echoes

Beauvoir's conception of freedom as a *doing* and inheres a valorisation of the capacity to consciously practice this, that is, to transcend. Indeed, discussing existentialism explicitly and departing from Sartre's avoidance of 'the idea of the self as something which is given to us' (Foucault 1984: 351), Foucault

> Link[s] his theoretical insight to the practice of creativity – and not of authenticity. From the idea that the self is not given to us, I think that there is only one practical consequence: we have to create ourselves as a work of art. (Foucault 1984: 351)

Sexual difference as oppression and immanence

Given this moral position, subjectivity should then be a 'freely chosen project' (Beauvoir 1997: 29) without end, so the most free subjectivity is that which is undertaken as purposively as possible. According to this definition, by its very nature as a pre-existing and compulsory precondition for intelligibility, sexual difference is not such a 'freely chosen project'. I illustrated this empirically in Chapter 1, with the persistence and 'omnirelevance' (Garfinkel 1967) of 'bigenderism' (Gilbert 2009) that shapes and limits everyone's existence. Its pervasive characterisation in the social imaginary as an essential and *static* element of selfhood forecloses agency and does not allow for selfhood as a constant transcending of immanence, a constant becoming. In Butler's terms, it operates as 'a precondition for the production and maintenance of legible humanity' (2004: 11).

'Oppression' in this ontological ethical perspective can be understood as something that prevents the *capacity* for transcendence, as opposed to repressive understandings of power that view oppression and power as synonymous and as preventing *freedom itself*. Beauvoir calls this immanence. Situation can, then, allow some subjects almost no capacity for agency at all, rendering them to immanence, but as outlined above, situation is also the Janus-faced enabler of agency, the 'paradoxical condition for moral deliberation' (Butler 2005: 10). In *The Ethics of Ambiguity* (1976a), for example, Beauvoir diverges from Sartre by accounting for different levels of freedom and referring to circumstances that completely prevent transcendence, that is, situations of complete immanence. Ze makes reference to people who have 'been kept in a state of servitude and ignorance [and] have no means of breaking the ceiling which is stretched over their heads' (Beauvoir 1976a: 37). As examples of this, ze cites:

> The negro slave of the eighteenth century, the Mohammedan woman enclosed in a harem [who] have no instrument, be it in thought or by astonishment or anger, which permits them to attack the civilization which oppresses them. (Beauvoir 1976a: 38)

Similarly, Foucault's distinctions between the positive capacity of 'power to-' and oppressive 'power over-' – which have led to a more specific distinction between 'extractive' and 'developmental' power (Patton 1994) – clarify this distinction and have influenced the characterisation of Foucault as a 'post-existentialist' (Vintges 2001: 165). In a similar manner to Beauvoir, Foucault emphasises that undesirable situations of oppression are those where the conditions for freedom, the ability to practice freedom through 'creating ourselves as a work of art', are not present:

> one sometimes encounters what may be called situations or states of domination in which the power relations, instead of being mobile, allowing the various participants to adopt strategies modifying them, remain blocked, frozen. (Foucault 1997: 283)

Again, this ontological picture allows a similar distinction to that of the two complementary aspects of freedom identified in Chapter 3, of 'freedom from-' and 'power to-' (Holloway 2002).

Being rendered to immanence can therefore be a result of a situation that limits knowledge: 'Ignorance and error are facts as inescapable as prison walls' (Beauvoir 1976a: 38). Additionally, Beauvoir claims that 'woman may fail to lay claim to the status of subject because she lacks definite *resources*' (Beauvoir 1997: 21, my emphasis). Often, then, 'situation is imposed' (Beauvoir 1976a: 38), and Kruks emphasises the extent to which Beauvoir undermines the fundamental Sartrean existentialist assumption that 'I remain free to choose my own action in response to the other's transcendence; I always retain the possibility of turning the tables on the other' (Kruks 1987: 113), because there are situations where even this capacity is blocked. The constitutive role of intersubjectivity and the ontological compulsion for recognition by others means that 'my situation is always mediated for me by others' (Kruks 1987: 116), and sometimes dictated.

Sexual difference in this picture, then, can negate or minimise the possibility for this 'practice of freedom' characterised as the creativity of working on oneself. Indeed, Kruks asserts that Beauvoir's analysis allows that, along with 'direct personal relations of inequality and oppression', there are also 'what we might call a set of social institutions' (1987: 116–117), of which sex/gender can be understood to be exemplary. It is a social context or cultural resource that delimits agency or freedom (conceptualised above as capacity). In terms of the project of maximising freedom of identity for all people, then, I understand freedom to necessitate getting rid of the oppressive pre-existing and limiting discourse of compulsory sexual difference to which we *must* attach and perceive and which constitutes us, because it prevents interaction that grants participants full subjecthood.

Thus, the 'enemy' – the thing that needs to be challenged – that compels immanence needs to be rethought along with the means of challenging it. It should no longer be understood as an inherently selfish humyn nature that must be disciplined as in liberalism (as particular 'men' as in some difference feminism and thus the separation from them the solution), or a repressive state power as in some anarchism where the solution is its overthrow. The problem in this analysis is, rather, perceived as the 'oppositional epistemological frame' (Butler 2007: 195), that is the constitutive atomised and oppositional self/other mode of thought or ethos that currently prevails in social relations and constitutes all people's relationships with the world. This underpins and perpetuates sexual difference, and shapes people's capacities for purposive existence. While careful to emphasise that Beauvoir's analyses by no means collapse the problem of sex/gender into 'just power' (Stanley 2001: 218), Stanley does suggest that in Beauvoir's significantly ethical and political play *Les Bouches inutiles* (translated as 'The Useless Mouths', Naji & Stanley 2011), 'The philosophical move that de Beauvoir makes ... is one which denies sex/gender independent significance and treats the meanings attached to it as "really" the byproducts of power' (Stanley 2001: 217). In different terms, I think this is the shift that Butler is also making when ze posits the issue to be the 'epistemological paradigm' that mistakenly understands the terrain of politics to be the subject (as in identity politics), rather than the 'discourses' that constitute them. In per words:

If taken as the grounds of feminist theory or politics, these 'effects' of gender hierarchy and compulsory heterosexuality are not only misdescribed as foundations, but the signifying practices that enable this metaleptic misdescription remain outside the purview of a feminist critique of gender relations. (Butler 2007: 202)

Considered practically, the problem consequently becomes that of developing an alternative relation, an alternative set of norms or social discourses, 'alternative sources and modes of recognition' (Allen 2005: 207) that do not replicate this same foundationalism and present a viable alternative to this oppositional, identitarian way of being and relating. This is the central shift in the argument, from the problem of gender to its anterior problem of sexual difference and, anterior to that, constitutive oppositional difference and othering per se. The problem of 'can we understand our selves and others without gender?' has now become 'can we understand our selves and others, and can we even *become at all*, without oppositional difference?' Likewise, Heinamaa notes that Beauvoir's phenomenological perspective means that per central problem is that of why 'the sexual relation [is] experienced as a difference and an opposition ... [and] is this necessary?' (Heinamaa 1999: 115). Is there the possibility, as Butler poses, for a more reciprocal and self-aware mode of relation such that we can come to reflexivity, not as Hegel and Nietzsche would have it, through fear, aggression and punishment, but positively, in an enabling manner (Butler 2005: 14)?

Freedom as collective doing

The problem has then shifted to intervening in and transforming a constitutive mode of relationality. If we understand selfhood to be constituted in this situated way, then, as the relational maintenance of sex/gender demonstrates, and freedom to be purposive doing of selfhood as a 'freely chosen project' (Beauvoir 1997: 29), our freedom is contingent on others and, whether we choose it or not, intersubjectivity imposes responsibilities on us. Indeed, despite the absurdity and non-teleological nature of existence posited by existentialism (Camus 1983) as well as the radically situated non-foundational ontology that can lead to solipsism, Beauvoir still maintains that, as situated existents, 'There's nothing left to do but keep going' (Beauvoir 2005: 101). For Beauvoir, this ontological premise that being is doing means that we cannot choose to not be or do, not engage in intersubjectivity and impact on others so that even 'the rejection of existence is still another way of existing' (Beauvoir 1976a: 43), and this compels a 'moral responsibility' (Stanley 2001) for others and their freedom. Beauvoir illustrates this through the global examples of the French occupation of Algeria or the Nazi occupation of France, which illustrate that 'abstention is complicity' (Beauvoir 1976a: 86) and 'Indifference is also a stand' (Beauvoir 2005: 99). Echoing this, and substituting 'repeating' for 'existing', Butler posits that this inescapability of doing means that we cannot choose not to, and the repeated doing compels ethical reflection on how it is done: given that 'To enter into the repetitive practices of this terrain of signification is not a choice. ... The task is not whether to repeat, but how to repeat' (2007: 202).

Stone emphasises that in Beauvoir's account, a collective definition of freedom is not only ethically preferable, but ontologically necessary, because freedom is an intentional, collective and collaborative process and must be undertaken alongside equally free and purposive others: 'since our native freedom is thus other-oriented, electing to expand rather than to repress it – "to set freedom free" as she [Beauvoir] puts it – means electing a free world, a social space in which others do not repress one because they do not repress themselves' (Stone 1987: 125). This makes *enabling social space* and *enabling interpersonal or dyadic relations* key sites for the aim of purposive existence. In the second volume of per autobiography, Beauvoir describes per own shift of concern (allegorical to that of Hélène in *The Blood of Others*) from the irresponsible and individual pursuit of happiness (the value that she rejects as outlined above), to a subjectivity aware of situatedness and consequently aware of responsibility and with a more collectively concerned ethics of freedom. This occurred after writing *She Came to Stay* and as a result of the Nazi occupation, as follows:

> Little by little I had abandoned the quasi-solipsism and illusory autonomy I cherished as a girl of twenty; the I had come to recognize the fact of other people's existence, it was still my individual relationships with separate people that mattered most to me, and I still yearned fiercely for happiness. Then, suddenly, History burst over me, and I dissolved into fragments. I woke to find myself scattered over the four quarters of the globe, linked by every nerve in me to each and every other individual. (Beauvoir 1976b: 371)

Beauvoir's essay *Pyrrhus and Cineas* is key in outlining this responsibility to others, and here ze emphasises that, in requiring recognition to be validated, my self-created values must be accepted by other, equally free subjects, others to 'respond to my call' (Bergoffen 2004: 85). Again, this accounts for the way that self-identification that seeks to reject gender is futile. Stone (1987) emphasises that for Beauvoir recognition is only valid *if freely given* by the other – it cannot be forced, the other has to have the capacities to attribute it: 'In order for the project that I founded to appear as a good, the other must make it into his own good, and then I would have been justified for having created it' (Beauvoir 2004: 129), that is, if it is reciprocal. I will outline what this reciprocity might look like below. However, to reiterate freedom of these others who can validate my freedom is in turn contingent on 'political-material' conditions:

> Only equals, Beauvoir argues, can hear or respond to my call. Only those who are not consumed by the struggle for survival, only those who exist in the material conditions of freedom, health, leisure and security, can become my allies in the struggle against injustice. (Bergoffen 2004: 85)

Enabling subjectivity and interpersonal relations requires competencies that rely on pre-existing norms or discourses to act within or attach to. Crucially, this inclusion of the extent to which situation constitutes subjects and thus enables autonomy shifts the issue to one beyond structure/agency. I find particularly compelling in this vein the notion of 'cultural resources' or the 'fund of ideas' (Archer 1996: xiii), as this can speak to the sociological diagnoses of sex/gender as an attribution, and of agency as a situated capacity, without downplaying the individual. In thinking through similar problematics of how best people can be 'recognised' to maximise their autonomy, Fraser pushes home the power of 'social institutions' in providing the resources to which I referred earlier, the modes of recognition that allow us to be 'armed' appropriately in intersubjective life such that we can take 'the status of a full partner in social interaction' (Fraser 2000: 4).

Allen, who works from Butler's ontological premises, follows this same line of reasoning to reach the implication that 'If we resist the idea that subjection per se is subordinating, then this opens up the possibility of conceptualizing forms of dependency, attachment and recognition that are not subordinating' (Allen 2005: 210). This echoes the extent to which Butler's ideas about challenging sex/gender became increasingly socially and politically realistic, and helps us to apply this ontological ethics of a situated freedom to overcoming sex/gender. Concisely, Butler's position in *Gender Trouble* (1990) was that, if gender is a repetition, then exaggerated repetitions that parody its realness would subvert and undermine it, would 'expose the contingent acts that create the appearance of a naturalistic necessity' (Butler 2007 [1990]: 45). However, as critics outlined, in this picture, in order to subversively cite gender there would need to be not only a kind of agency or critical mode of thought in reference to the norms one is citing by the person doing the citing, but also some intervention at the level of the social rules or norms themselves, in order that the subjectively subversive performance would not be restabilised (Lorber 2000: 86) by people 'reading' it or attributing it within normative frames of reference. For such strategies to have real effect, then, the subject and their 'competency', their immediate others and their reading competencies (for 'one can tell an autobiography only to an other' (Butler 2005: 32)), *and* the cultural context that supplies these resources that social actors have to draw from for understanding themselves and each other, all have to be involved. Freedom, consequently, consists of collective reconstitution on non-subordinating terms of the cultural resources within which we become and behave:

> [individual] Criticism alone is no match for the deep-seated psychic needs for attachment and recognition ... [therefore] resistance to and transformation of subjection will require not only critical reflection on the legitimacy of prevailing norms of sex/gender, but also the cultivation of *alternative sources and modes of recognition.* (Allen 2005: 207, my emphasis)

Allen suggests that collective social movements may be able to provide some of these requisite spaces and resources for this, and this perspective that freedom must necessarily be a collective purposiveness (a freedom to- as in poststructuralist anarchism) is echoed by some social movements that incorporate purposive sexuality and gender in their analyses:

> So here it is in one sentence: When we speak of liberty, we mean the creation of our own cultural context for life, which is necessarily collective; when we speak of autonomy, we mean the opportunity to do that creating without interference. (CrimethInc. n.d.[a]: n.p.)

To this end, and in practicable terms directly applied to the problem of sex/gender, Lorber (1986; 2000; cf. Risman 2004; Risman, Lorber & Sherwood 2012) develops a multi-layered model for doing away with gendering and the dichotomised assumption of sexual difference at its root, similar in its 'integrative' approach to Risman's 'multidimensional structural model' (2004: 434). This underpins the proposal that a more enabling ethos (way of perceiving), and an ethic (mode of being) could be, and must be, applied to all of these levels. Below I will outline how the principle of reciprocity could serve the function of just this enabling 'alternative ... mode of recognition' (Allen 2005: 207).

Reciprocity as enabling alternative

Ideally, what form of recognition can enable the 'practices of freedom' (Foucault 1997: 283) and minimise 'dissymmetry [and] exclusion of the other' (Foucault 1984: 346)? Through what ethos can we come to subjectivity and come to understand our selves and others without oppositional difference? In considering whether we are 'able to have an ethics of acts and their pleasures which would be able to take into account the pleasure of the other' (Foucault 1984: 346), Foucault proposes that 'the practice of freedom' necessitates the virtues of 'reciprocity' and 'mutual recognition' (Foucault 1984: 345).

A central aspect of my argument is that a post-gender way of being, if it is to truly avoid the mistakes of gender, cannot be premised on or reconstitute an essential self as does identity. However, it must also acknowledge that sometimes people feel *mis*-recognised, which does them a symbolic violence. Reciprocity as conceptualised by Beauvoir, as 'a reciprocal recognition of freedoms' (Kruks 1987: 116), is a mode of recognition and cultural resource that is nonetheless not an identity. Reciprocity is presented by Beauvoir and Foucault as a principle-based ethos or collective norm that can in turn underpin a code of conduct (ethics) for how we relate to others that does not require the presumptions of identity. This, I argue, represents a truly queer (i.e. non-normalising) sociality. Like Beauvoir's definition of freedom above, reciprocity in being procedural is without closure – it represents a 'continual reaching out towards other liberties' (Beauvoir 1997: 28). Beauvoir and Stanley offer some examples of relations between people that illustrate this reciprocity, representing intersubjectivity that is not negating, but is, rather, mutually developmental, enabling and perpetually reciprocal. What these share is *form* rather than *content*, a specific way of approaching the self and other (ethos), which I will elaborate in the next chapter. Such ways of being are most fully illustrated in *The Ethics of Ambiguity* and in *The Blood of Others*.

In per fiction there are illustrations of 'social, mutual and collaborative' (Stanley 1996: 433) relations between subjects that share 'the same trajectory towards the same future' (Stanley 2001: 207). For example, when illustrating the various aspects of subjectivity in *She Came to Stay*, some of which I drew on above, Beauvoir presents a situation in which two selves share a 'touching though transitory intimacy' (Beauvoir 2006: 6). The characters of Françoise and Gerbert are collectively transcending facticity through the creation of a play, something that will carry their existence beyond them, as idealised by Beauvoir above as the ultimate enactment of freedom. This situation demonstrates two people collaboratively creating a situation wherein both of their capacities for transcendence may be enacted: 'The two of them were living within this circle of rosy light; for both of them, the same light, the same night' (Beauvoir 2006: 6).

Additionally, in *The Blood of Others*, Hélène, having already served as an illustration for a realisation of the other and the responsibility this entails, is not only the donor of generosity in offering per seat back to Paris to a woman with a baby, but is then the recipient of a positive interaction of benevolence with another stranger, who shares per bread with Hélène and helps Hélène get back to Paris, from where she had earlier fled (Beauvoir 1978: 204). This illustrates that the ideal corollary of this realisation of being situated and responsible for others is a reciprocal self/other relation.

What does this mean specifically for sexuality, for being sexual? What would an ethical queer sexuality based on principle, not identity, look like? Like being or conduct more broadly, it would mean sexual conduct organised around ethics and pleasure, not gendered identities. Gayle Rubin's important essay, 'Thinking Sex: Notes for a Radical Theory of the Politics of Sexuality' (1984) argues that the *content* of sexuality or eroticism needs to be understood as limitlessly variable, but morally assessed according to democratic principles or ethics, rather than deontological givens about the inherent value of certain acts. I understand this to be a vision of a reciprocal sexuality without identity, judged according to the principle of freedom as purposiveness doing:

> A democratic morality should judge sexual acts by the way partners treat one another, the level of mutual consideration, the presence or absence of coercion, and quantity and quality of the pleasures they provide. (Rubin 1984: 153)

Having theorised ontological and ethical premises to underpin a post-identity ethics of reciprocity, the following chapters will consider what an ethics of reciprocity (and a sexuality derived from this ethics) would look like: what qualities it would require, and how it may be fostered and, crucially, how it may be prevented from congealing into a new authoritative norm. This requires a brief reflection on the extent to which such an abstract ideal can be implemented given the ambiguous ontological context, and how it might be maximised.

Implications for post-gender politics: evaluating freedoms and maximising agency

The existence of alternative modes of recognition, such as reciprocity, does not in itself guarantee ethical behaviour that engages with the other in a responsible manner. The best that can be hoped for is to provide the most conducive context possible for developing the capacities for reciprocity. As I have been keen to emphasise, the constitution of selfhood cannot be reduced to self, others or material situation, for it is perpetually dialogical. However, in Beauvoir's terms, failing to lay claim to the status of subject and failing to strive to transcend immanence *if possible*, as well as *knowingly* rendering the other to facticity, returns the responsibility to the subject, so that 'a freedom which is interested only in denying freedom must be denied' (Beauvoir 1976a: 91). Beauvoir's position is that a person *can* be held fully responsible or culpable for their actions, that is, they can be assumed to be acting autonomously, but only if they are acting with full consciousness of all choices. Exploring how such ideal culpability or responsibility can be maximised will help me to articulate the ideal cultural or collective conditions for maximum agency, or purposive choices.

Beauvoir emphasises that the self is at fault if they still *choose* immanence given the possibility for transcendence: 'This downfall [of transcendence falling back into immanence] represents a moral fault if the subject consents to it ... it is an absolute evil' (Beauvoir 1997: 29). This is illustrated in Beauvoir's normative bottom line in per philosophical essay 'An Eye for an Eye' (in Beauvoir 2004). Here Beauvoir states that if a person knowingly and agentically, in 'complete freedom' (or the most freedom possible), chooses to negate another and render them immanent, punishment is justified. This essay was written as an explanation for Beauvoir's support of the execution of Robert Brasillach for his role in the execution of Jews in Nazi Germany, which may not appear readily to match with per picture of selves informed and restricted so much by situation. However, Beauvoir maintains the ability to make moral distinctions and rejects the relativism of complete social constructionism by distinguishing between 'those youthful sixteen-year-old followers of Hitler' (2004: 256) and those whose acts were 'willed by a freedom' (Beauvoir 2004: 255) as 'when a man deliberately tries to degrade a man by reducing him to a thing' (Beauvoir 2004: 257). The key is in creating a cultural resource that enables the choice not to reduce the other to a thing or an object but, rather, to approach them as a reciprocal subject.

In attempting to develop a model of justice, Beauvoir admits to these very complexities of holding an individual fully responsible or culpable for their negation of others in such an ambiguous ontological land-scape. Having moved beyond the radical Sartrean notion of existential freedom, Beauvoir explicates that the critical subjective state necessary for maximum freedom or culpability is socially contingent:

> ... the oppressor would not be so strong if he did not have accom-plices among the oppressed themselves; mystification is one of the forms of oppression; ignorance is a situation in which man may be enclosed as narrowly as in prison; as we have already said, every indi-vidual may practise his freedom inside his world, but not everybody has the means of rejecting, even by doubt, the values, taboos, and prescriptions by which he is surrounded. (Beauvoir 1976a: 98)

Thus, Beauvoir confesses to the impossibility of this ideal freedom in which it would be possible to be sure that a person 'freely recognize[s] its past faults, repent[s], and despair[s]' (Beauvoir 2004: 249). As Beauvoir states, it is a difficult or insuperable task to determine the level of responsibility:

> How can one measure the temptations a man could have faced? How can one appreciate the weight of the circumstances that give an act its real shape? One would have to bring his upbringing, complexes, failures, and entire past – the totality of his engagement in the world – into account. Then, without question, his conduct is explain-able. (Beauvoir 2004: 255)

This provokes a crucially refined and delimited democratic project. Given the inescapability of power the best that can be aimed for is 'to acquire the ... morality, the ethos, the practice of the self, that will allow ... *as little domination as possible*' (Foucault 1997: 298, my empha-sis). Foucault, like Beauvoir, holds that the self-consciousness that cul-pability requires is completely contingent, and perhaps unachievable in its purity, but at the same time advocates and considers it worthwhile and moral to strive for 'the maximum sense one can attain' and 'the most critical understanding' of the self possible (Coles 1992: 84).

How can we maximise the chances that acts, and allegorically, ways of being and relating to others, are 'willed by a freedom' (Beauvoir 2004: 255), that is, how can the ideal critical subject for reciprocity – the most culpable subject possible – be fostered? Given the ontological premise, it would be necessary to ensure that 'the totality of ... a person's engagement in the world' (Beauvoir 2004: 255) is enabling and reciprocal. Consequently attempts to apply or foster a reciprocal ethic premised on the telos of freedom must be fully informed by the co-dependence of 'autonomy', intersubjective reciprocity and social contexts of freedom. This will influence my triadic approach in considering the enactment of post-gender ethics, which considers equally the roles of the self, relationships with the other, and the social in the constitution and, thus, reconstitution of ways of being.

Conclusion

I have briefly outlined that a preferable way of seeing the self and others that takes into account all of the precepts outlined here, that maximises individual purposiveness but does not foreclose the agency of others to create the self as project, would be a reciprocal relation. Chapter 5 will be concerned with clarifying the internal characteristics of this alternative, reciprocal mode of recognition. It will consider how a queer sociality based on the principles outlined here can attempt to be explicitly developmental and reduce dominating aspects of relationality as far as possible. Chapter 5 will also be concerned with how far this responsibility for – and non-subordinating reciprocity with – others should and can practically extend, whether it can be universalised, and how.

5
Queer Futures and Queer Ethics: Sketching Inexhaustibly Reciprocal Androgyny

In proposing the eradication of gendered identity as I have thus far, there is a danger that, in challenging identity politics, one may inadvertently play into the conservative and negating impulses that many claims for recognition premised on foundational identity seek to challenge. This presents the ethical and political challenge 'to deal with marginalization without compromising ... political principles and the common good' (Hirvonen 2012: 113).

In Chapter 4 I outlined reciprocity as an ideal ethic of recognition (of oneself and of others) to transcend sexual difference and sex/gender identity. However, this chapter and the next are concerned with the reality of implementing reciprocity as a replacement to sex/gender identity in two different ways, and will elaborate on my specific usages of the notions of androgyny, recognition and reciprocity as well as their characteristics. This chapter will outline the possibility of the deconstructive problem of 'closure' (Critchley 1999) and elaborate some ideal internal characteristics of the ethic of reciprocity that I am advocating, and what this means for how one should perceive the self and other, to demonstrate more practically how these could prevent this reciprocal ideal from collapsing, congealing or reifying into the very problems of negation that it is intended to address and transcend. I will draw on thinkers who have thought their way beyond the dichotomising 'false antitheses' (Fraser 1995) of collective identity/individualism, self/other, same/different, and developed mechanisms for avoiding them. This includes some engagements in the 'recognition debates' in political theory that have sought to transcend the same/different impasse; notions of androgyny, 'utopia', and politics premised on principles or ethos rather than identity that likewise attempt to evade closure and fixed telos; and notions of an inexhaustible auto-critical impulse opera-tionalised in queer theory and politics.

The two related considerations in this chapter and the next are avoiding the negating 'violence' of imposed identity or homogenising sameness, and, in Chapter 6, of dealing with the seemingly inescapable engagement with strategic 'violence' that impure starting points of negation create – in order to refine the reciprocal ethics I am arguing for. In the first half of the chapter I will outline and exemplify the persistent problems of foun-dationalism and closure that a reciprocal ethic will need to evade, and go on in the second half to propose strategies and ways of thinking for transcending them. I consider the possibility of the congealment or solidi-fication of norms that could prevent reciprocity, and offer imaginative solutions to the problem of how exactly this reciprocity may be operation-alised and what it might 'look like', in the sense of how exactly one can really perceive the other *reciprocally*. If liberal ethics has tended to foster a disinterested impartiality and communitarianism a polar opposite, but still problematic, complete partiality, how exactly can reciprocity as ideal-ised by Beauvoir take seriously both, but not reduce to either, of the sides of this self/other, same/different divide? I will outline the potential foun-dationality of androgyny, and of queer understood or used as an identity, and of recognition if it inheres a reactionary, homogenising sameness. The fate of 'queer' as a discourse seems a fitting example of the difficulties in a mode of thought resisting congealment into a positive identity.

The violence of closure

Referring back to the definition of violence I earlier deployed will help me to elaborate on what this post-gender ethic is intended to replace, and thus better consider how it might do so. Traditional definitions of violence have over-emphasised intention by a person, and failed to account for injurious outcomes or 'violences' that may result from other processes. It is my argument that more contemporary redefinitions of violence, such as Bourdieu's notion of symbolic violence I outlined in Chapter 2, are useful to my analysis for understanding the way that impersonal forces may impact negatively on people. Mary Jackman (2002), for example, has emphasised the extent to which violence has been defined around inten-tion and physical injury. Ze cites the traditional definition of violence as paradigmatic of this focus on 'behavior by persons against persons that intentionally threatens, attempts or actually inflicts physical harm' (Reiss & Roth 1993, cited in Jackman 2002: 389). The alternative definition that

Jackman develops takes into account the different forms that violence can take and the different outcomes it can have:

> Actions that inflict, threaten, or cause injury.
> Actions may be corporal, written, or verbal.
> Injuries may be corporal, psychological, material, or social. (Jackman 2002: 405)

Jackman's above definition still retains some notion of violence having to be an action, but there is room in a definition that opens up violence from having a purely physical outcome and shifts the analysis to consider that certain discourses may be forms of violence, in that they result in injurious outcomes. Scheper-Hughes & Bourgois (2004), for example, suggest that 'violence can never be understood solely in terms of its physicality – force, assault, or the infliction of pain – alone. Violence also includes assaults on the personhood, dignity, sense of worth or value of the victim' (Scheper-Hughes & Bourgois 2004: 1). This is why Bourdieu's notion of the symbolic that considers that violence may be done when there are limited, or not freely chosen, 'cognitive instruments' for people to understand themselves and others has been so useful to my characterisation of the limits to existing paradigms for addressing the problems of gender (Bourdieu 2004: 339).

The closure of androgyny

Here I want to consider the obvious alternative to sexual difference: androgyny. Androgyny has been considered both as a utopian ideal or telos (Piercy 2001 [1979]) and as a pre-cultural, natural way of being that is repressed by dualistic culture (Foucault 1980). I will discuss whether an androgynous way of understanding the self and others is a mode of perception that could fulfil or exemplify the principles of reciprocity. I argue that contemporaneously androgyny often retains the universalising of male values that liberalism departs from, and that it is a model that contains the possibility of homogenising through the closure of sameness. Such an outcome of uncritical enforced equality and sameness is illustrated by science fiction author Le Guin, who demonstrates a preoccupation with challenging dualism:

> That was intolerable. That every soul on earth should have a body the color of a battleship: no! ... He could be born into any world. He had no character. He was a lump of clay, a block of uncarved wood. (Le Guin 1978: 112)

Additionally, I will consider whether utopian thinking more generally, but particularly regarding the eradication of sex/gender, must
always be premised on a pre-cultural essentialist ideal or a utopian
ideal/blueprint and whether it must always lead to totalising unity and
foreclosing difference. I will conclude, drawing on Andrews (2003), that
a certain understanding of androgyny from French romantic socialist
texts from the 1830s and 1840s is useful for the mode of thought that
I am proposing. I will also argue for a particular way of thinking about
the utopian that may be able to avoid what I argue is the 'violence' of
foreclosure. I suggest that these specific ways of thinking about androgyny and utopianism demonstrate a kind of universalised particularism,
which I will outline in the second half of this chapter, drawing primarily on the work of Seyla Benhabib, Martha Nussbaum, Nancy Fraser and
Nel Noddings, among others.

In much of the psychological literature, androgyny has been implicitly understood as a combination of what are considered to be masculine and feminine traits:

> The androgynous person can best be seen as one who can engage
> freely in both feminine *and* masculine behaviours and as one who is
> equally capable of both feminine *and* masculine tasks and does not
> prefer one above the other. (Woodhill & Samuels 2004: 16)

Additionally, Baumrind (1982) states that:

> As defined by Bem, by Spence, and by their colleagues, androgynes
> are individuals who, to a greater extent than is customarily the case,
> profess a self-concept that incorporates attributes considered to be
> socially desirable in men as well as those considered to be socially
> desirable in women. (47)

This is also the way that Marge Piercy depicts residents of the future
utopia in per science fiction novel *Woman on the Edge of Time* (2001
[1979]). Luciente from the future is unreadable by Connie, the protagonist from the present, owing to per combination of gender signifiers.
Initially Connie assumes Luciente is male owing to the lack of female
signifiers. However, this attribution is confused because 'He lacked the
macho presence of men in her own family, nor did he have Claud's mas-
sive strength, or Eddie's edgy combativeness' (Piercy 2001 [1979]: 36).
However, Luciente was 'too confident, too unselfconscious, too aggres-
sive and sure and graceful in the wrong kind of totally coordinated way
to be a woman' (Piercy 2001 [1979]: 99), and

she moved with that air of brisk unselfconscious authority Connie associated with men. Luciente sat down, taking up more space than women ever did. She squatted, she sprawled, she strolled, never thinking about how her body was displayed. (Piercy 2001 [1979]: 67)

Indeed, Luciente exhibited admirable male and female characteristics simultaneously in that 'He moved with grace but also with authority' (Piercy 2001 [1979]: 41). This depiction appears harmless, and Piercy's utopia does not depict homogeneity among those not defined by sexual difference, arguably presenting an image of a more *proliferated androgyny*, one premised on universal values applied to everyone in their particularity.

However, It is worth noting the dangers emphasised by Francette Pacteau (1986), who argues that owing to the current masculinist cultural context, or symbolic order, androgynous fantasies are usually 'a man-made fantasy, the virilisation of the woman, a means of oppression and alienation because emanating from a culture where the male principle dominates' (Pacteau 1986: 70). Like my premises from earlier chapters, this suggests that an alternative to sexual difference must not fall into the possibility of universalising on masculine terms and requires normative distinction among previously gendered principles. Indeed, Woodhill & Samuels (2004) distinguish between 'desirable and undesirable androgyny', arguing that more attention needs to be given to the fact that 'an unmitigated or overdeveloped masculinity can be destructive. Negative femininity on the other hand mostly effects just the individual who displays it' (Woodhill & Samuels 2004: 20). A perfectly androgynous humyn in this sense may have unintended consequences because of the possible negative aspects of masculinity. An androgyny premised on normative distinction among values thereby transcends rather than combines or collapses genders. This is a 'construct of androgyny [that] can be seen as incorporating but going theoretically beyond the unipolar, orthogonal view of masculinity and femininity' (Garnets & Pleck 1979: 273).

While I posit that the concept of androgyny is not inherently foundational or prone to closure, Judith Butler (1990) identifies a totalising impulse in some versions of it and uses it in *Gender Trouble* as illustrative of the totalising dangers of assuming any foundational or teleological identity. I concede that the assumption of an essential, foundational androgyny or the reification of androgyny as a privileged ideal identity would maintain the same essentialising violence as the assumption or idealisation of sexual difference. These criticisms have been made by Butler against both Michel Foucault (1980) and Monique Wittig (1993). Foucault is charged with the double crime of both teleological projection and foundational essentialism for per purported reliance on a pre-cultural intersexuality, as well as a totalising idealisation of this as a more ideal way of being, in per foreword to the diaries of *Herculine Barbin* (1980). The same holds true for Butler's critique of Monique Wittig because of per appeals to a seemingly pre-discursive 'polymorphous perversity', in 'One is Not Born a Woman' (Wittig 1993).

Butler argues that the implication of positing some kind of pre-cultural place of freedom, as represented by Barbin's intersexuality in Foucault's account, is drawing on the same repressive hypotheses that Foucault rejects in per genealogical work. Butler claims that Foucault's foreword to *Herculine Barbin* maintains 'an unacknowledged emancipatory ideal' (Butler 2007: 127). Ze is also accused of undermining the 'critical genealogy of the category of "sex" he offers toward the conclusion of the first volume of *The History of Sexuality Vol I*' (Butler 2007: 128), by romantically suggesting that Barbin exceeded the limits of sex and enjoyed desire and sexuality outside of the assumptions of sexual difference. Butler claims that Foucault's interpretation of Herculine Barbin refers back to a 'prediscursive libidinal multiplicity' (Butler 2007: 131), which, ze posits, would serve only to reify a new dominating essentialism. Butler also reminds readers that the pervasiveness and constitutive nature of sexual difference makes any kind of prediscursive selfhood impossible, and that Barbin's use of gendered language and description demonstrates that this idealisation is just that, idealisation. Foucault's *Herculine Barbin* has, then, been interpreted as drawing on the trope of some kind of foundational self beyond sexual difference and, while resting on a productive notion of power, of making a totalising gesture by appealing to a repressed essential aspect of the self, a pre-cultural desire. Butler concludes that:

> According to this Foucauldian model of emancipatory sexual politics, the overthrow of 'sex' results in the release of a primary sexual multiplicity, a notion not so far afield from the psychoanalytic postulation of primary polymorphousness or Marcuse's notion of an original and creative bisexual Eros subsequently repressed by an instrumentalist culture. (Butler 2007: 131)

Butler's analysis seems to be suggesting that behind many deconstructive approaches to sex and sexuality *really* lies a normative and foreclosed dedication to an alternative conception of a more free or multiplicitous sexuality. I opened this book with a quotation from *Herculine Barbin*, indicative of Foucault's value-based idealisation of 'the happy limbo of a non-identity' (Foucault 1980: xiii). I maintain that, so long as it is explicitly expressed or acknowledged as an 'emancipatory *ideal*' (Butler 2007: 127, my emphasis), rather than a foundational, closed identity, an ideal utopian telos of androgyny akin to this can constitute a more enabling, less restrictive way of constituting selves than that of compulsory sex/gender identity, so long as it is sufficiently open in character. My question is, given a non-foundational ontology of *potentiality*, might androgyny be able to exemplify a cultural resource for the constitution of selfhood instead of the prediscursive and constitutive sexual difference currently prevalent?

In the second half of this chapter, I will outline some specific modes of thinking and operating that an androgynous impulse or ethos such as Foucault's could inhere such that it does not reify into a fixed identity or foundational aspect of the self. Indeed Allen (1998) and Stoetzler (2005) posit that Butler's own work, in implicitly valuing deconstruction so much, itself holds such an unspoken 'emancipatory ideal', one that ze has been more explicit about in recent work, and one that may in fact be just the reconstructive, but non-foundational complement to per deconstructive impulse. This is an issue illustrated in parallel also by Butler and Benhabib's oppositional positioning of poststructuralism vs. critical theory in *Feminist Contentions*, which taps into the broader issue that is at stake in these issues of identity vs. non-identity, deconstruction vs. reconstruction, which I consider to be resolvable through a politics centred on an ethos rather than identity.

Illustrating this in an applied manner, before returning to mechanisms to aid a more transcendent use of androgyny in the second half of this chapter, I will consider briefly another, related problem of closure that exemplifies these oppositions: the potential for critical norms to collapse into negating norms exemplified by the trajectory of the notion of 'queer' since the 1990s. This will again clarify the dangers of which a truly reciprocal ethic must be mindful and must attempt to transcend and will help me to draw out the useful, ethical aspects of queer theory, whatever moniker they are under.

'Queer' and the reification of identity

As I outlined in the Introduction, the queer theory that has influenced this project represented a critique of the limiting and exclusionary impulses, or 'heteronormativity' (Warner 1991), of the assimilationist

political strategies and the identity categories of gay liberation or identity politics (Butler 1990; de Lauretis 1991; Halperin 1995; Phelan 2004;
Sedgwick 1990). While, as I outlined in Chapter 2, collective identities
have been critiqued for their homogenising impulse, collective identity
has also undeniably been an essential lifeline for many people margin-
alised by gender and sexuality norms (Butler 2004). However, in these
earlier chapters, I also emphasised the impulse of further marginalisation resulting from the construction of coherent community and identity. This is further illustrated through the ways in which the discourse
of 'queer' has been constructed and reconstructed, from the ideal of a
critical stance to, arguably, the reality of a homogenised identity. Queer
theory, as articulated in the early 1990s (de Lauretis 1991; Halperin
1995; Sedgwick 1990), seemed a promising basis for just what Butler
seemed to be idealising: a negative (as opposed to identity-based) ethics
without foreclosure (i.e. without a blueprint). It was, however, critiqued
for lacking any positive foundations, with critics claiming that its only
'appeal is one of rebellion, defiance, and transgression' (Dynes 1995:
37). However, many saw (Butler 1990; 1993a), and still do see (Giffney
2004), this lack of prescription to be queer theory's strength. I will
extend this strength below, articulating it as queer theory's normative
premise and telos, when formulating ideal modes of thought for cultivating a truly reciprocal, but still normatively informed, ethic.

Whether or not this definition of 'queer' in terms of the negative
'non-heteronormative' (first coined by Warner 1991) was desirable,
many commentators consider that this is anyway no longer the dominant understanding of queer (Butler 1993a; Giffney 2004). Queer has
struggled to resist congealment in to a positive identity, and many
thinkers now 'continually substitute ... queer for gay' (2004: 73):

> In the process they have reduced queer to an identity category alone,
> or the ontological and epistemological extensions of an identity
> category/umbrella descriptor. Those who employ queer theory for
> anything other than the location of non-heteronormative – yet non-
> gay or lesbian – identities risk charges of mis-appropriation, mis-use,
> mis-understanding. (Giffney 2004: 73)

Indeed, in an early discussion of the changing uses of queer, Butler
emphasised 'the constraints on and in resignification [and] ... its propen-
sity to return to the "ever old" in relations of social power' (Butler 1993a:
224). An example of this same problem in the queer activist community,
as opposed to the academic context, is the observation by some attendees

of a *Queeruption* radical queer gathering that there had been a shift in the shared understanding of queer. Attendees of *Queeruption* Berlin in 2003 commented that, even in these usually and ideally self-consciously critical and *de*constructive spaces and communities, there had developed 'dogmas' and 'the establishment of a queer "convention"' (Les Pantheres Roses 2003: n.p.) (in this case hypersexuality), such that there is an expectation of participation in norms and 'People who don't fit in are either excluded or, worse, forced to participate against their will' (Les Pantheres Roses 2003: n.p.). This points in the direction of an impulse, in situations where there are not mechanisms to prevent it, towards informally authoritarian congealment or solidification and homogeneity in alternative gender and sexuality practices, something Gamson considers to result from 'haphazardly attempting to build a politics from the rubble of deconstructed collective categories' (Gamson 1995: 390).

Some science fiction, playing with the utopian genre, has illustrated how this closure and slide into totalising norms might happen. The ways that separation and certain approaches to particularism (which are arguably allegorical characteristics of identity politics) can result in homogenisation is a theme of Ursula Le Guin's *The Dispossessed* (1974). Here a separate community based on anarchist ideals not only fails to catalyse change by example outside of its community, but also congeals into tradition, homogeny and power inside the community: 'Like all walls, it was ambiguous, two-faced. What was inside it and what was outside it depended upon which side of it you were on' (Le Guin 1974: 1). This mechanism of the congealment of power is a problem central to *The Dispossessed*, and a problem presented as one central to anarchism, wherein a major ambiguity of this 'ambiguous' anarchist 'utopia' is the seemingly inevitable slide into tyranny, the problem of the potential 'will to power that slumbers in everyone' (Beauvoir 2004: 251).

The planet of Annares in *The Dispossessed* ostensibly has *official* measures to protect against the reification of power, akin to those recommended in some theoretical anarchist texts (such as the rotation of work such that all members of society undertake all types of work). But in the period in which the book is set some members of the society have found ways to avoid this measure, such as the protagonist Shevek's university 'mentor' Sabul, who has managed to gain the privilege of working only on Physics. Ze communicates this privilege to Shevek when Shevek joins the institute: 'Listen. You're now a member of the Central Institute of Sciences, a Physics syndic, working with me, Sabul. You follow that? Privilege is responsibility. Correct?' (Le Guin 1974: 92). In addition to this institutional reification, the book serves to illustrate the power of more informal social reification of norms through the extent to which a 'communal' ethics or way of being is valued in Annares to the omission of alternatives, such that Shevek's preference for solitude is socially sanctioned. Additionally, despite the rejection of prisons in 'Odonianism' (the anarchistic doctrine followed), the asylums on Annares have come to do the work of prisons and serve as euphemistically named 'corrective centres' for dissident thinkers. Indeed, Andrew Reynolds (2005) suggests that Odonianism has much in common with Marcuse's utopian vision in *Eros and Civilization* (Reynolds 2005: 85). For example, an individualistic 'radical freedom', which, according to Reynolds, even if situated as part of an organism, could 'easily provide validation for authoritarianism' (Reynolds 2005: 86). In this vein, another novel by Le Guin, *The Lathe of Heaven* (1978), illustrates the ease with which power can congeal into tyranny. The actions of the character of Haber, a doctor with the pretensions of social engineer who discovers he can change the world by controlling another character's 'effective dreams', are analogous to the ideology of communism. Despite Haber's seemingly benevolent intentions, in attempting to *enforce* equality the result of his actions is homogenisation and social control. This, then, can be allegorised to this tendency even in self-consciously 'queer' communities for prescription and norms to take hold.

Such a tendency towards homogeny has long been identified in anarchist and feminist communities. The premise of 'Jo Freeman's' germinal anarcha-feminist article/pamphlet originally published in 1970, 'The Tyranny of Structurelessness', can be extended to most informal communities. This article identifies that 'there is no such thing as a "structureless" group ... [a group] will inevitably structure itself in some fashion' (Freeman 1996 [1970]: 1). Because of this inevitable informal structuring, which is usually not explicit, 'the idea [of structurelessness] becomes a smokescreen for the strong or the lucky to establish unquestioned hegemony over others' (Freeman 1996 [1970]: 1), and it goes on to argue that some 'principles of democratic structuring' (Freeman 1996 [1970]: 4) need to be applied to informal communities and collectives to ensure against such tendencies. I will discuss in the second half of this chapter what modes of thought would be useful in avoiding closure and maintaining reciprocity, and come back to the practical suggestions in Freeman's article in the next part of the book when considering practical strategies for putting a reciprocal ethics into practice.

Despite this potential and actual congealment of queer, Giffney maintains, diverging from the purview of lesbian and gay studies, that

ze understands 'queer theory to be, in Ruth Goldman's words, "a theoretical perspective from which to challenge the normative" ... even if
that normative is itself' (Giffney 2004: 74). Understood in this way, as a
critical perspective and not as an identity, queer theory could still be a
useful impulse in developing a truly reciprocal ethics that does not foreclose through assumption or congealment. Especially useful is the possibility, considered by Giffney above, that queer may have the capacity
to take up a critical stance towards itself, an *auto-critical* stance. Butler
also celebrates the aspect of queer theory that represents 'a self-critical
dimension within activism':

> ... if the genealogical critique of the subject is the interrogation
> of those constitutive and exclusionary relations of power through
> which contemporary discursive resources are formed, then it follows
> that the critique of the queer subject is crucial to the continuing
> *democratization* of queer politics. As much as identity terms must be
> used, as much as 'outness' is to be affirmed, these same notions must
> become subject to a critique of the exclusionary operations of their
> own production. (Butler 1993a: 227)

The important tenets to be derived here are that an ethics of reciprocity must be premised on a normatively argued-for principle, not
essential foundations, and must contain *a priori* a self-critical element
in order to remain reciprocal. In formulating an ethics of reciprocity
between self and others, and considering how it may be realised, the
more practical and procedural question of how exactly we would need
to perceive the other in order to maintain this ideal of reciprocity and
evade the problems of closure identified above and in previous chapters
needs to be considered. I will briefly return to the issues of recognition
in order to clarify how some models of recognition inhere closure, and
illustrate how reciprocity as a way of relating to the other, and consciously co-constituting oneself with them, can seek to recognise the
other instead 'in their otherness' (Beauvoir 1976: 67), according to a
principle of inexhaustible openness.

Who is the other? The limits to recognition and the closure of sameness

As I indicated in Chapter 3, many ethical visions for perceiving and
conducting oneself in relation to others posited as alternatives to liberalism (such as communitarianism) inhere the same problem of hidden,

and possibly homogenising and obliterating, assumptions regarding subjects. The seeming ease with which collective identity can slide into reification and exclusion demonstrates an important problem for an ethics of reciprocity concerned with relations between self and other, and binary-transcendent solutions are essential for overcoming the impasses inherent to the debates outlined: self/other, im/partiality, universal/particular. These are impasses to which I will deign to offer alternatives in the second half of this chapter, which will take me closer to the specific qualities of a practicable reconstructive, and truly post-gender reciprocal ethics. I will precede this discussion by outlining the problem of recognition in more detail.

Further to the ontological theorisations about recognition in Beauvoir's ethical existentialism, this problem of recognition of the other was also addressed in highly practicable and applied terms by Beauvoir long before the 'recognition debates' spurred by Taylor's essay 'Multiculturalism and the Politics of Recognition' (1992). Taylor's work spawned debate about recognition in different contexts, notably in the collected volumes *For Love of Country: Debating the Limits of Patriotism* (Nussbaum 1996) and *Is Multiculturalism Bad for Women?* (Okin 1999).

In *Pyrrhus and Cineas*, Beauvoir (1987) couches this problem in terms of the metaphor of ploughing one's garden, but not knowing its borders. Beauvoir asks, 'How do I know who more closely resembles me? ... Who is my neighbour?' (Beauvoir 1987: 136). This ethical and philosophical problem of exactly to whom we are responsible, whether this can be universalised, and how exactly (and procedurally or practicably) we *can* feel benevolence to others who are not directly connected to us, is also central to Beauvoir's novels *The Blood of Others* (1978) and *The Mandarins* (2005) as well as per play *The Useless Mouths* (2011) and per philosophical essays.

As I outlined in Chapter 3, like some critiques of Taylor's – and related – notions of group-defined rights (McNay 2008), some discussions of feminine ethics have been critiqued for their possible obliteration of intra-group difference. One of the central problems identified by Iris Marion Young's (1995) critique of feminine ethics, for example, is that often the ethic of care extends only so far, to women to the exclusion of men, but also only to those women who we most closely resemble and with whom we can empathise, effectively rehomogenising women on the terms of those dominant in the group as characterised in 'The Tyranny of Structurelessness' (Freeman 1996 [1970]). Indeed, in critiquing Nussbaum's argument for a universal ethic of pluralistic cosmopolitanism in *For Love of Country: Debating the Limits of Patriotism* (Nussbaum 1996), Elaine Scarry proposes that it is impossible for an ethic of care to be extended to those with whom we cannot identify, arguing that 'the human capacity to injure other people is very great precisely because our capacity to imagine other people is very small' (Scarry 1996: 103). The (presumed essential) difficulty of imagining *all* other people is a central critique of universalised ethics of benevolence, alongside a possible homogenising of one's own experience in empathising with those who are actually different. Thus Young (1995) concludes that instead of universally extending tolerance and freedom, these kinds of ethics assimilate the needs of the other into the assumption of a universal self through substitutionalism. This was a major criticism that many third wave feminists and feminists of colour made of earlier forms of feminism. Likewise, critics of dominant forms of international development studies and practice – especially as it pertains to gender and sexuality – have made similar charges (Bhabha 1999; Parpart 1993), warning that some development discourses risk 'women in the Third World (or the west) [being] lumped into one undifferentiated category' (Parpart 1993: 454). I will discuss some alternatives to substitutionalism in development studies and politics in the second half of the chapter.

Caroline Whitbeck's (1989) maternal ethics (discussed in Chapter 3) is exemplary of this, in that it works in practice on the basis of identifying with others through 'analogy' (Whitbeck 1989: 61) to the self. The idea of analogy here involves trying to understand others in terms of oneself, the corollary of which is that the self is held to be the norm and, as Young suggests, those who cannot be understood in this way cannot be related to or are else fitted to an understanding drawn from one's own point of view, that is, they are understood according to the 'cognitive instruments' of the dominant group, the very definition of 'symbolic violence' (Bourdieu 2004: 339). The notion of analogy has thus attracted criticism, in that 'those motivated by it will tend to suppress differences among themselves or implicitly to exclude from their political groups persons with whom they do not identify' (Young 1995: 300).

Indeed, Whitbeck's ideal of communities of analogy explicitly values a separatism that appears to imply intra-group homogeny as a strategy: 'This liberation is a social task, and for this reason communities committed to this transformation have often undertaken to separate from those unwilling to take part in it' (Whitbeck 1989: 68). This demonstrates a reluctance to deal with conflict, difference and divergence of opinion, and represents exactly the homogenisation that Young, Fraser

(2000) and Friedman (1993) fear that 'repressive forms of communitari-anism' (Fraser 2000: 3) foster. In terms of gender politics, this demon-strates the limits inherent in associating a feminist ethic with just the female. Indeed, such concerns led Young to return to some of the values of liberalism as potentially more progressive, developing the metaphor of the 'unoppressive city' (Young 1995: 317), the pluralism of which ze argues is preferable to the possible conservatism and homogeneity that results from communitarianism:

> For many people deemed deviant in the closeness of the face-to-face community in which they lived, whether 'independent' women or socialists or gay men or lesbians, the city has often offered a welcome anonymity and some measure of freedom. (Young 1995: 317)

However, in attempting to not capitulate to the binary logic of either liberal impartiality *or* communitarian partiality, below I will argue for another approach that deems to transcend the either/or logic of par-ticularism vs. universalism. Given the tendency to closure outlined in these three examples of androgyny as identity, queer as identity, and empathy as analogy, I propose that what is required for an eth-ics of reciprocity is a way to deal with and value conflict, difference and divergence of opinion positively without imposing closure and homogeny, but also without losing normative distinctions and the abil-ity to account for power. Additionally, it requires the elaboration of an ethical premise for caring for and being concerned with the other that is not dependent on sameness. A reciprocal ethic needs not to avoid conflict, difference or disagreement, but instead find a reciprocal way of channelling it.

Being reciprocal

In Chapter 4 I outlined that the ideal form for maximising freedom of being is through an ethic of reciprocity, in place of identity. In this chapter I have emphasised the ways that attempts at greater freedom of identity or being can collapse back into closure, and now want to out-line some specific characteristics of a reciprocal way of being that offers resources for maintaining reciprocity, and minimising closure.

While I concede that a relationship between two people can never achieve '*complete* mutual understanding and reciprocity' (Young 1995: 310, my emphasis), and recognise that complete understanding of the self is impossible, I also argue that it is normatively imperative to strive to make relations more reciprocal, or as reciprocal as possible ('with as little domination as possible' (Foucault 1997: 298)). This is the ontological ethical position elaborated through Beauvoir and Butler in Chapter 4 above of an opacity that forms the very (intersubjective) basis of agency. Along with the normative argument for a freedom of 'transcending immanence', how exactly can the other be most ideally perceived, knowing that we can never quite analogise to them, and how can we ensure that, as much as possible, we don't impose our own values and premises on them so that they can continue to 'transcend immanence'?

Young critiques many collective approaches to freedom as 'hopelessly utopian', arguing that they necessitate the fictional ability to get rid of the opacity of both self and others (Young 1995: 310). However, as I outlined in Chapter 4, both Beauvoir and Butler concede that the self is never known fully to the self *because* of a fundamental intersubjectivity, and formulate this as the very basis for an ethics of reciprocity. They thus conclude, as I outlined in Chapter 4, that this ontological premise means that my freedom is necessarily contingent on that of the other:

> It is only as ... something free, that the other is revealed as an other. And to love him [sic] genuinely is to love him in his otherness and in that freedom by which he escapes. (Beauvoir 1976: 67)

What I am interested in here is *how* to 'love him in his otherness and in that freedom' that is central to an ethic of reciprocity, and central to fostering an ethos of androgyny.

Following Benhabib, Fraser and others, here I will argue that the universalism/particularism debate constitutes a debilitating 'false antithesis' (Fraser 1995). Further, I will argue that the ideal *mechanism* through which the other can be related to in this truly reciprocal way that transcends this repetitive debate is that of universalised particularism (although with some differences from Benhabib and Fraser in terms of the *content* of this approach to ethical relations). I will illustrate how a post-gender ethos of universalised particularity can be conceptualised in relation to sexuality, and how it has been applied in the context of international development concerns about sexual freedom. Finally, I argue that this *ethic*, or way of conducting oneself, has the capacity to transcend the sameness/difference impasse, and should be seen as an androgynous utopian end-point in itself, as well as inhering mechanisms to prevent closure.

Universalised particularism

The particularism advocated by Friedman that I charted in Chapter 3 is a good starting point for thinking about the other without considering them in terms of sameness, but still departing from a *universal* principle of caring. Freidman's analogy draws on the ethic of care as applied to friends, because it acknowledges that partiality is inevitable but also that it can be chosen rather than being compelled by, for example, supposed biological or other intra-group imperatives. In this way it can be extended to social relations, demonstrating that there tends to be a universal code of ethics in friendships, and a generosity and concern that is applied to the other in their particularity. Recall that for Friedman, this:

> ... commitment to a person in her unique particularity, a friend, for example, takes as its primary focus the unique concatenation of wants, desires, identity, history, and so on of a particular person. It is specific to that person and not generalizable to others. It acknowledges the uniqueness of the friend and can be said to honor or celebrate that uniqueness. ... Just how we care for a particular friend depends on her specific needs, interests, and values. (Friedman 1993: 190–191)

While above I outlined Young's argument that 'the ideal of community... privileges ... immediacy over mediation' (Young 1995: 300), in *Woman on the Edge of Time*, Piercy (1979) also envisages a different ethic for community where the ethics of friendship is extended as a metaphor for social relations generally, and the relationship between people is not assumed to be one of antagonism, and also, crucially, not assumed to be inherently complementary either.

Nussbaum (1996), Benhabib (1985) and Fraser (1995) all aim to demonstrate that universalism and particularism are not mutually exclusive. The universalist/particularist debate omits the more complex nature of how ethics are put into practice and how these different approaches intertwine. For example, Nussbaum emphasises that the particularism of nationalism also relies on the universalism of the culture that the nationalist belongs to, so that nationalism is an 'ethnocentric particularism' (Nussbaum 1996: 5). Despite the critiques discussed above, Nussbaum's cosmopolitan ideal in *For Love of Country* seeks to evade the presupposition that 'the primary alternative to a politics based on patriotism and national identity is what [Rorty] ... calls a "politics of difference", one based on internal divisions' (Nussbaum 1996: 4). In this way, per cosmopolitanism relies on both the particularity of community and a universalised approach to pluralism, privileging moral principles over shared identity while respecting difference (Nussbaum 1996: 4). Nussbaum calls for identity and divisions to be outside of the purview of a cosmopolitan ethic, stating that 'Only the cosmopolitan stance ... has the promise of transcending these divisions, because only this stance asks us to give our first allegiance to what is morally good' (Nussbaum 1996: 5). This transcendence of the universal vs. particular through allegiance to a principle governing conduct with others rather than allegiance to identity groups to me represents what I have already outlined as a mechanism to avoid exclusion and reduction to identity, by making the unifying aspect an ethic or principle. This principle would, however, need to be sufficiently open and critical to remain truly reciprocal and 'democratic', and avoid the impulses to closure described above. I will consider in Chapter 6 some characteristics by which an ethos may attempt to remain open in this way. There are some limitations of liberal visions such as Nussbaum's cosmopolitanism that to a certain extent are rendered merely utopian because of their reliance on a first principle of pre-cultural and equal rationalism. Also, Fraser's positing of the possibility of 'universalist recognition, and deconstructive recognition' (Fraser 2000: 5), while a useful illustration of transcending the choice between these two approaches, holds the spectre of a notion of a more true self by using the terminology of 'misrecognition'. However, the procedural aspects of this binary-transcendent principle are of great use to the type of ethics I am proposing, and worth extending.

Seyla Benhabib's (1985) formulation of precisely how to relate to the other in a manner transcendent of the universalist/particularist binary is particularly developed, where the other is characterised as the 'concrete other'. Ze distinguishes the 'concrete other' from the generalised, universalised other of liberal theory, proposing that in acknowledging the concrete other:

> We seek to comprehend the needs of the other, his or her motivations, what s/he searches for, and what s/he desires. Our relation to the other is governed by norms of *equity* and *complementary reciprocity*: each is entitled to expect and to assume from the other forms of behaviour through which the other feels recognized and confirmed as a concrete, individual being with specific needs, talents and capacities. (Benhabib 1985: 411)

While drawing on a few particular universalised principles, then, in this case 'equity and complementary reciprocity', Benhabib's reciprocity calls for application of these universal principles alongside the acknowledgement of 'the other as *different* from the self' (Benhabib 1985: 412, my emphasis), avoiding the subsuming of the self to other/s that Butler, McNay, and Young, among others, warn against.

Further elaborating the problems with a purely substitutionalist way of cognising the other, but also considering what we would have to do to perceive the other in a way that honoured them in their otherness, Nel Noddings (2006) argues that:

> We could not formulate principles of justice for these people [people whom we would not want to live the same as] by imagining ourselves one of them. We would have to listen to those others and try to understand that they find their lives worth living. Then we would have to want to improve their condition, to make it bearable – or to recognize that it is already bearable. (Noddings 2006: 10)

One of the keys activities in such an ethos of approaching the other *in their otherness* is *listening*, which I will return to and elaborate in Chapter 8 in the practical and procedural consideration of fostering the ethic. As I have commented, Noddings (2003) considers choosing to care to be a more ethical form of caring than caring that is 'natural' and compelled. As such, in order to be an enabling as possible, there needs to be an element of both universalism in the ethic of openness and mutual respect, as well as particularism in considering the needs and wants of the concrete other, which would help us to care for and respect them in their otherness. I am not the first to propose an approach to recognition that can include both universalism and particularism. However, I am interested in considering how an ethics of reciprocity might enact and enable a universalised ideal of maximum 'freedom' in terms of selfhood and sexuality, co-constituted with others in their maximum freedom. That is, I want to consider its practicability as a cultural resource to *replace* sex/gender as a way of guiding our being/becoming and interacting in the social world, how it might work in practice, how it might prevent collapse or congealment in to only one side of this universal/particular binary, and what it might look like.

(Global) queer ethic: 'sex for pleasure'

How, then, can the other be perceived in an androgynous or queer way? Returning to sexuality, some early characterisations of queer theory and gender deconstructive theory seem to inhere precisely this universal/

particular ethics or mode of recognition, in combining a deconstructive, pluralist ideal in terms of behaviours and personal characteristics, and a universalist ideal in terms of an enabling value to realise this proliferation. This approach idealises a politics premised on a *positionality* rather than identity, which I will outline below. Additionally, some thinkers and activists have applied a similar impulse to more contemporary sexual ethical visions and practices.

Martha Nussbaum critiques Judith Butler's work (up to the late 1990s) for being unable to elaborate 'any positive normative notion', suggesting that 'for Butler, subversion is subversion, and it can in principle go in any direction. Indeed, Butler's naively empty politics is especially dangerous for the causes she holds dear' (Nussbaum 1999a: 8–9). That is, Nussbaum argues that Butler's deconstructive impulse has no 'universalist' element at all by which normative distinctions can be made, a relativist danger in work that attempts to evade the negations perceived in imposing a universalist morality (discussed in Chapter 3). It is true that in per deconstruction of the possibly foundational and foreclosing premises of the normative aspects of Foucault's and Wittig's work on sexuality, with which I began this chapter, Butler (1990) is very clear about modes of perception that are to be avoided in the quest for nontotalising modes of being and less explicit about characteristics of possible non-totalising, non-essentialist alternatives.

However, Stoetzler (2005) and Allen (1998) seek to emphasise the ethical imperative in Butler's work in *Gender Trouble* and beyond, an implicit ethical principle that can be interpreted as precisely a universalised particularism. Per project of deconstructing totalising modes of thought itself inheres a universalist valuing of critical modes of thought and non-closure, and of 'proliferation' (Butler 2007: 100). Moreover, in queer theory and gender deconstructive theory more broadly, as formulated in the early 1990s (and the impulse of which has been extended in various guises, for example Muñoz (2009)), a similar ethic or code of conduct can be identified, a positionality that constitutes a 'queer bond' (Weiner & Young 2011). The bonding, ethical element of queer could usefully be interpreted as a universal dedication to enabling the other according to their particularity (their otherness), 'a bond spanning differences that may remain irreducible' (Weiner & Young 2011: 227). I argue that such a deconstructive ethical imperative is just the robust normative principle *and practice* that could strengthen a reciprocal ethics beyond sexual difference and could exemplify a reconstructive ethos. I will attempt to distil, explicate and develop this normative baseline more fully in Chapter 6, where I will test reciprocity against real and imagined non-ideal situations and contexts.

To illustrate, Butler discourages the use of the plural term 'we' in an effort not to reduce the particularity of the individual and, similarly to existentialism, emphasises that while we are always self/other, we can never fully identify with an other or with a collective and remain singular and non-substitutable (Butler 2005: 34). Likewise, Muñoz (2009), in considering what a positive queer position that simultaneously heeds queer's critical relation to reducing others to homogeny might look like, invokes Nancy's notion of 'being singular plural' (in Muñoz 2009: 10). In remarkably similar terms to Butler, Muñoz reaches a parallel potentiality for reconstructive sociality: 'an entity registers as both particular in its difference but at the same time always relational to other singularities' (2009: 10–11), allowing for a 'belonging-in-difference' (Muñoz 2009: 20). A definite utopian, or ontological ethical, value can be identified as emanating from Butler's universal particular position. Ze argues that because 'the "I" that I am finds itself at once constituted by norms and dependent on them' all we can hope for, as actors, is to 'endeavour ... to live in ways that maintain a critical and transformative relation to them' (Butler 2004: 3). This represents a simultaneously deconstructive and reconstructive ethos.

Thus, despite the examples of 're-entrenchment' (Fuss 1989: 32) of some of its trajectories, outlined above, there are characteristics of queer theory that are worth hanging on to for their ethical, but not prescriptive, visions. These trajectories exemplify the characteristics of ontological ethics as developed from Beauvoir in Chapter 4: an ontology of potentiality, and a normative valuing of intentionality. These characteristics will be particularly useful in Chapter 6, where I will consider how this ethics can inform a useful politics in non-ideal contexts, without capitulating to norms, by constituting a positionality of simultaneous, and inexhaustible, de/reconstruction.

In terms of being reciprocal in one's sexuality, I conceive of Rubin's (1993 [1984]) germinal vision for 'a radical theory for the politics of sexuality' to foreshadow a similar position or ethos of universalised particularism applied to sexuality. This model is particularist (or deconstructive and non-universalising) in its premise of 'sexual variation' (Rubin 1993 [1984]: 14) that values the particularity of individual desire and sexual practices, and does not reduce this to identity categories, along with a reconstructive, universal ethic that denounces oppression. Rubin's is a 'sexual value system' (Rubin 1993 [1984]: 12) concerned with the reciprocal freedom in sexual relations (conduct) rather than the identities of those carrying them out or the acts undertaken (orientation). This is paradigmatic of a sexual ethics that is able to depart from a collective ontology of potentiality (i.e. is post-identity), but can also account for and denounce oppression.

The same can be said of early queer theory, the universal particularism of which can, in my view, best be summed up by the 'singular plural' (Nancy, in Muñoz 2009) ontological *and* ethical axiom, 'People are different from one another' (Sedgwick 1990: 22). This is a universalising claim, but one that calls for proliferation. This is echoed in de Lauretis's normatively informed vision for subjective 'multiplicity' and 'heterogeneity' (1987), and Butler's 'proliferation' or 'variable construction of identity' (Butler 1990: 5). This is perhaps the defining position of queer theory's thin, but useful, universal normative premise.

What kind of political subject can be posited around such non-reductionist, proliferated ontological and normative premises, that is, what constitutes the queer bond? Given the anti-essentialism of all of these approaches, then, they become politics of 'place or positionality' (Fuss 1989: 29). Likewise, in deconstructing identity politics as reifying the foundations that are the very cause of identity-based hierarchy, Butler's overall conclusion in *Gender Trouble* is that such a deconstructive *position* is a valid, and more effective premise for gender politics – 'there need not be a "doer behind the deed"' (2007: 195). For post-gender queer politics, then,

> If identities were not longer fixed as the premises of a political syllogism, and politics no longer understood as a set of practices derived from the alleged interests that belong to a set of ready-made subjects, a new configuration of politics would surely emerge from the ruins of the old. (Butler 2007: 203)

This future-oriented positionality is what Fuss (1989) argues is essential to anti-essentialist perspectives. The subject position that can be derived from these approaches, given the ontology of non-foundational becoming, is a subject whose 'conception is in progress' (de Lauretis 1987: 10). This ontology lends itself to a gender/queer politics premised on contingent foundations, a position rather than a fixed identity. Thus the 'subject of [this kind of] feminism [and, we might add, queer theory] is a theoretical construct' (de Lauretis 1987: 10). This approach is also compatible with the queer and postmodernist developments of politics based on *chosen* coalition or alliance (Gutterman 2001; Phelan 2004).

Complementary or inherent to this becoming subject-position, there was a clear ethic of open-endedness and non-closure in these queer and feminist deconstructivist anti-normalising projects, a perpetual and self-aware becoming as the basis for the queer ethico-political project. For example, Fuss sees value in positionality because it 'works against the tendency of concepts such as "subject" and "ego," or "I" and "you," to solidify' (1989: 30). Combined with positionality, the collective subject of queer can be understood as 'a "we" that is "not yet conscious"', a "we" that is 'a logic of futurity' (Muñoz 2009: 20). In more practicable terms, there are proposals that there should be 'constant revision, reevaluation, and reconceptualization of that condition' (de Lauretis 1987: 20). It seems a shame that the non-foundational positionality and 'analysis interminable' (Fuss 1991: 6) that was a key companion to the early formulations of queer theory must be lost because of the recapitulation of the moniker. Indeed, in 2004 Giffney made similar claims that these are the qualities from queer theory that should be maintained:

> We as queer theorists must continue to chip away at, what Michel Foucault refers to as, the 'net-like organization' of the norm, and expose *all* norms for the way they define, solidify and defend their shaky self-identities by excluding those (dissident others) who fail or refuse to conform. (Giffney 2004: 75)

This positionality alongside 'analysis interminable' (Fuss 1991: 6) has been extended more contemporaneously by queer theorist Muñoz, who characterises queer as futurity, potentiality or ideality rather than identity: 'the here and now is a prison house' (Muñoz 2009: 1). Like those positional characterisations above, Muñoz's queer utopian end is an undefined 'critical mode of hope' (Muñoz 2009: 4).

While Butler was already suggesting that 'queer' had lost its critical power in 1993(a) owing to the reification of it outlined above, self-identified 'queer' communities are still drawing upon it as a non-foundational and non-foreclosing, interminable *position* or ethos in ways not determined by its popular co-option. For example, this can be observed in radical queer communities and gatherings such as Queeruption and Queer Mutiny, the practices of which I will discuss in more empirical terms in Chapter 8. Brown's research led per to the conclusion that '"queer" within these networks functions more as a relational process, rather than as a simple identity category' (Brown 2007b: 2687). It is, indeed, still for many a term that exemplifies alternative ways of thinking about the self that do attempt to resist normalisation and maintain an auto-critical element, thereby limiting the extent to which it congeals into a fixed identity, instead supporting different definitions that respect multiplicitous ways of identifying. For example, the authors of the article about 'Dogmas in the Queer Scene' cited above argue that this congealment of norms is, actually, contrary to the principles of 'queer' as they understand or utilise it, positing an alternative understanding that stays true to its critical roots, so that for them 'Queer spaces are about *Freiraum* – spaces where we have the freedom to dismantle restricting, acquired codes of sexual and bodily behaviour' (Les Pantheres Roses 2003: n.p.). The article defines 'Freiraum' as 'Literally "free-room"; more like "freedom". Defined as "the opportunity to move freely and develop one's individual ideas"' (Les Pantheres Roses 2003: n.p.). This definition allies the principles discussed, and also members of the queer community, with the ontological understanding of situated autonomy outlined in Chapter 4, in that it is concerned at base with individual autonomy but acknowledges that this is situated, context-based and collective. As such 'Freiraum' is a way of thinking about the normative ethic that underpins such anarchist and radical queer practices and is both 'normative, [and] reconstructive' but *not* 'normalizing and oppressive' (Fraser, cited in Allen 1998: 465). It also means that the impulse of queer can be useful across cultural contexts without subordinating or excluding more localised expressions of gender and sexuality owing to a predetermining identity politics.

It is this future-oriented and undefined, critical positionality or impulse that is worth holding on to, the principles of universalised multiplicity, along with inexhaustibility as modes of being, modes of 'reading' one another and relating to replace foundational and immutable identity.

In seeking more freedom of sexual expression, identitarian rights-based approaches can perpetuate substitutionalism by not recognising the more localised, particular modes of recognition in a diversity of cultural contexts (Gosine 2005; Kollman & Waites 2009; Parpart 1993; Waites 2009). However, as Foucault (1983) has articulated, sexual identity approaches are about 'the orientation of my desire', that is, sexual orientation. Foucault questions the way that 'the problem of desire became much more important than the problem of pleasure. Why do we recognise ourselves as the subject of desire and not as an agent of pleasure?' (1983). This prefigures the possibility of a sexual politics of pleasure, not identity. It is freedom to do, rather than freedom contingent on being recognised as what we (supposedly) are. This is the kind of sexuality imagined in Piercy's androgynous (post-gender) utopian society in *Woman on the Edge of Time*, wherein people 'couple. Not for money, not for a living. For love, for pleasure, for relief, out of habit, out of curiosity and lust' (2001 [1979]: 64). Indeed, in an international or cross-cultural context, in a particular vision of sexual politics from the Institute of Development Studies (Gosine 2005; Jolly 2007), a universal particularism is apparent wherein the universal principle is one of pleasure, and sexual identity or the orientation of desire is bracketed off, particularised.

Some thinkers in development studies or global politics express concern that the imposition of identitarian approaches constitute Bourdieu's naturalised symbolic violence wherein the dominated are forced to understand themselves and others according to the 'cognitive instruments' of the dominant (2004: 339). Empowerment- or participatory-oriented approaches to international development in both sexuality and gender have considered how some of the homogenising tendencies of universalising and identity-based rights discourses in development can be avoided (Antrobus, Harcourt & Sen 2010; Kabeer 2005). These approaches tend instead to universalise only the *principle* of empowerment, defined as 'the ability to make definitions of your own life and the capacity to realise them' (Antrobus, Harcourt & Sen 2010), but leave the particularities of how one will define – the cognitive instruments – to individuals. The founders of DAWN (Development Alternatives for Women in a New Era, a feminist organisation from the 'economic south' concerned with development and gender) hold that the recognition of the other on their own terms (i.e. in their otherness) is the key to real empowerment: 'the deeper problem is the non-recognition of the person' (Antrobus, Harcourt & Sen 2010: 153). This is then exemplary of an enabling ethic or politics of positionality that does not require identity categories.

In seeking to transcend both the homogenising and exclusionary tendency of identity-based rights approaches to sexuality in development, as well as the negative framing of sexuality as only a health issue, Gosine (2004) and Jolly (2007), in the Institute of Development Studies, developed a visionary rallying principle of the right not to sexual identity or orientation, but rather the right to sexual pleasure: 'it can be argued that people have a right to seek ... pleasures, and that an enabling environment should be created for them to do so' (Jolly 2007: 3). This, Gosine suggests, is able to transcend both the globally universalising and essentialising tendencies of identity rights discourses, and the intra-group homogeny that can result from more localised participatory models, that is, the limitations of those approaches often presented as the mutually exclusive two poles of political ethics: liberalism (universal) vs. communitarianism (partial and relative) outlined in Chapter 3. The principles at the core of IDS's vision are like those of Foucault and of Rubin's sexual ethics, concerned with sexual practices rather than being contingent on orientation, and maintaining the ability to make moral distinctions about conduct with the universal principles of 'sexual pleasure and erotic justice' (Rubin 1993 [1984]: 28). This approach seems particularly progressive in the way that it might have the capacity to challenge conservative counter-moves to gay identity politics such as 'the move in both mainstream religious organizations and the military [in the US] to separate "orientation" and "conduct," permitting the former ... but not the latter' (Duggan 1994: 12). This approach unabashedly shifts the moral locus to the conduct itself.

Queering utopia, queering androgyny

The problems with the particular utopian visions of androgyny critiqued earlier in this chapter are, then, that firstly their basis for formulating utopian visions is the humyn subject, and secondly, that they perceive the utopian as a particular ideal state of being. That is, they are concerned with formulating teleological end-points in the form of universal visions or blueprints of what an ideal androgynous humyn would be like. Following my rejection of the universal/particular dichotomy above, I outlined how a particular queer ethic or position could replace identity as a way of understanding oneself and others, and sexuality. Thus I argue that androgyny and utopianism could be used as modes of thinking or positions to be applied in different ways to different concrete individuals and situations, as 'universal particulars'. While Johnson states that 'traditional utopian thinking projects a quest for totalization and presents itself as a privileged standpoint able to yield an unmediated vision' (Johnson 2002: 30), ze also offers an alternative way of thinking about the utopian that is much more like the 'inexhaustible critique' that queer theory was originally premised on and that the above approaches to sexual politics represent. Indeed, Johnson goes so far as to state that 'this [deconstructive] forward-looking capacity to disrupt, critique, and transform a given situation *is* the utopian' (Johnson 2002: 35).

I propose that the ethical components of queer theory and gender deconstruction outlined above represent an androgynous utopian way of thinking that can both prevent negation and avoid closure.

This utopian impulse is reflected in Muñoz's future orientation, which nonetheless rests on queer deconstructions: 'we must strive, in the face of the here and now's totalitzing rendering of reality, to think and feel a then and there' (2009: 1). This impulse to non-closure is also present in contemporary (and some older) anarchist thought and practice, and can help me to reconceptualise the meanings of utopia and androgyny, demonstrating how I am using them to underpin a reciprocal ethic (both mind-set and code of conduct) that seeks to transcend foundations and closed end-points.

Andrew Reynolds (2005) suggests that Le Guin's *The Dispossesed* offers exactly this type of inexhaustible, process-based utopianism. This is illustrated by Le Guin not through the anarchist planet Annares, which Reynolds reads as comparable with the totalising limits of classical anarchism as discussed above, but in the impulse of inexhaustible critique present in the character of Shevek, 'an anarchist among anarchists' (Reynolds 2005: 86). Reynolds thus reads *The Dispossesed* as transcending the dichotomies of abstract vs. concrete, or the universal vs. the particular, by combining the non-dominating principle that has been identified as the common feature of contemporary anarchism (Gordon 2009: 262), with the relativism of 'Nietzschean post-modernism' (Reynolds 2005: 88). Ze asserts that Le Guin's work responds to 'the impossibility of setting an objective standard to human "needs" – or "pleasure" for that matter – and attempts to transform that relativity of value into the precondition to a philosophy of liberation' (Reynolds 2005: 88).

Gordon argues that, given anarchism's contemporary extension to a generalised critique of domination in all its forms, it must remain open by positing that domination may take myriad forms in different social figurations. Ze argues that this makes contemporary anarchism's concept of 'utopia' much less an imagined state of being and place, and much more the application of an ethics of non-domination:

> While it is possible to at least imagine the abolition of concrete institutions [as did many 'classical anarchists'], the way in which anarchists have come to conceptualise domination presents us with a concept to which the idea of abolition is not so easily attached. This is for a simple reason: in order to speak of the abolition of domination as such, we need to possess the complete list of all its forms and systems, the entire range of possible patterns of social inequality and exclusion. However, we can never be sure that we have such a complete picture: how can we know that there are no forms of

domination that remain hidden from us today, just as some that we do recognise were hidden from our predecessors? (Gordon 2009: 263)

Gordon concludes that a truly anarchist utopian or revolutionary concept must 'allow for the possibility of forms of domination that are hidden from us today and that will only become apparent in the future' (Gordon 2009: 261). Thus, anarchist utopianism must be a principle, an impulse applied perpetually. Contemporary impulses of anarchism, understood as the principle of non-domination, are central to my project of developing a reciprocal ethics in contradistinction to the oppositional nature of sexual difference, including in considering how this could be realised. Indeed, I will discuss some contemporary anarchist social practices in Chapters 7 and 8 as exemplars of relating to oneself and others in a reciprocal and enabling manner that does not replicate the negations of sexual difference. Reynolds thus views the anarchist normative ethical principle embodied in *The Dispossessed* in the same way that I articulated the basic normative premise of the existentialist ontological ethics of Beauvoir: 'For Le Guin ... freedom itself ultimately comes to stand as the sole reference point for judging the value of human life' (Reynolds 2005: 85), rather than by an appeal to a natural or biological anarchist state of being.

Likewise, in the face of as yet unknown possibilities for closure, Muñoz (2009) presents a future-oriented, but non-teleological, utopian queer vision. This is a key mode of thinking 'queer' that is critical of the present and its totalising tendencies and thus utopian in outlook, but this utopianism is not a point of closure. This mode of thinking is able to transcend binaries oft cited as impasses such as positive politics that invoke closure, or negative politics that lack ethical content. This line will be traversed further in Chapter 7 where I consider how, in practice, there can be a relationality between people that evades the closure that is charged to all relationality by proponents of antirelationality (Muñoz 2009: 11).

Utopianism as I conceive it does not need to inhere a pre-cultural essentialist ideal or a blueprint or utopian ideal that must always lead to totalising unity and foreclosing difference. By considering an ethics of non-closure to be the utopian telos or end-point rather than a particular vision or blueprint, and by considering androgyny to be a way of thinking and relating rather than a fixed way of being, it is possible to remain dedicated to a utopian post-identity queer and androgynous ethic.

Conclusion

While representing an ideal process, positing an inexhaustibly critical and open relation to the other does not solve all problems. It produces, for example, the paradox that 'Fixed identity categories are both the basis for oppression and the basis for political power' (Gamson 1995: 391), because of the facticity of social context and the ontological situation. Impure starting points necessitate impure strategies to achieve reciprocity. Chapter 6 will consider the related problem of the reality of implementing such an ideal principle and mode of being in 'contaminated' non-ideal, already limiting circumstances, and foreground the most practical, final section of the book. In the next chapter I consider whether impure strategies can be justified, and how they can avoid congealment or solidification into totalising discourses, applying some of these strategies. This will allow me to return at the end of Chapter 6 to what exactly this inexhaustibility, and this ongoing concurrent de/reconstruction may 'look like' in terms of understanding oneself and sexuality. I will go on in the final part of the book to consider some practices that may be able to foster this androgynous ethic of reciprocity and challenge the pervasiveness and compulsarity of sexual difference.

6
The Politics of Implementing Post-Gender Ethics: Beyond Idealism/Realism

Here I mean to consider how the ethical ideal that I broadly outlined in the previous chapter may be applied. It is a central tenet of deconstruction that all 'saying' (the context) must be done within the language of the 'Said' (which must, to an extent, assume universal meaning and understanding). In this respect, Critchley suggests that for philosophers who critique the assumption of an autonomous self, a central problem is: 'How is the saying, my exposure to the Other, to be Said, or given a philosophical exposition that does not utterly betray this saying?' (Critchley 1999: 7). This is the theme of this chapter, that there often has to be an engagement with discourses or behaviours that are at odds with our ideal ethics because of the ontological necessity to act.

How can an ideal queer ethics centred on the principle of reciprocity inform an efficacious politics, and guarantee the outcome that it is intended to engender, that is, a more enabling way of being? Additionally, *can* such an ethics draw on means that are not continuous with its ends, and if so, how? Completely pure, ideal circumstances rarely, if ever, exist, and various aspects of situation mean that these ethics must be applied in non-ideal, non-equal circumstances. Beauvoir directly addressed this precise impasse in per 1945 essay 'Moral Idealism and Political Realism' (2004), encouraging submission to neither end of this seeming dualism:

> [An] Ethics [that] attempts to remove itself from time ... simply relegates itself to the past and appears as a useless relic of bygone ages. Wishing to be absolute, it severs its earthly roots, and the man of action who is rooted on earth no longer recognizes foundations there ... an ethics that does not bite into the world is nothing but an ensemble of dead structures. (Beauvoir 2004: 178)

... no end can be inscribed in reality. By definition an end is not; it has to be; it requires the spontaneity of a consciousness that, surpassing the given, throws itself toward the future ... and coherent and valid politics is idealist inasmuch as it is subordinate to an idea that it intends to carry out. (Beauvoir 2004: 179)

Applying this, in this chapter I will consider the inescapability of power, and the contextual, political need for identity claims. I will also 'test' the ideal ethic of reciprocity outlined in Chapter 5 in terms of real-life problems and through considering thought-experiments such as those of utopian and feminist science fiction. This will help me to refine these ideal elements of the ethic in order to further consider how, given the impurity of situation, such ethics can remain true to their basic principles of a developmental and non-violent relation to the other and also evade collapse and closure. I will attempt to transcend the binary impasse of means/ends (realism/idealism) and concede that there is some space for 'strategic violence' in an ethic of reciprocity in order to restore initial imbalances (Beauvoir 2004: 237–260; Fanon 1974; Sartre 1974), but also propose that there is a danger in 'strategic violence' of a slide into tyranny. Offering an overview of feminist and queer thinkers concerned with the same issue, I will then apply this model to the problem of gender, given that there is the danger of reification of identity in uses of 'strategic essentialism' (Fuss 1989; Spivak 1994). Further to this, I will propose some internal mechanisms that such a strategic politics (or means) would need to inhere to avoid this reification and ensure the desired ends. I will thus elaborate the characteristics proposed in Chapter 5 to emphasise how this ideal ethic of reciprocity may inform a practicable and positive politics, and not betray its own premises by remaining inexhaustibly open.

The inescapability of power and norms

I start with the same assumption as Foucault (1997) and Mouffe (1997), that power is inescapable (or in the Beauvoirian terms I have been using, that non-reciprocal relations are inescapable), that some level of hierarchy, power and development of norms is unavoidable, but that resignation to this can be made politically and ethically more useful by making value distinctions between different forms of non-reciprocal relations. Foucault's ontological ethical statement on this issue is as follows: 'I do not think that a society can exist without power relations. ... The problem, then, is ... to acquire the ... morality, the *ethos*, the practice of the self, that will allow us to play these games of power with as little domination as possible' (Foucault 1997: 298). Foucault, then, makes a normative distinction between power and hierarchy, which are often unavoidable and can be enabling, and domination, which is avoidable and undesirable. Likewise, Mouffe suggests that 'the main question of democratic politics is not how to eliminate power but how to constitute forms of power that are compatible with democratic values' (Mouffe 1997: 25). This echoes the distinctions made in Chapter 4 between 'extractive' and 'developmental' power (Patton 1994). This means that in the quest for a non-oppressive ethic, the aim shifts from eradicating norms to making value distinctions between desirable and non-desirable ones. The first half his chapter will be concerned with how to *choose*, with how such distinctions between the desirably developmental and the undesirably extractive can be made.

Beauvoir's position is that choices need to be made between different negations (or oppressions) that constitute symbolic violences, and sometimes a choice between means and ends has to be made. This relates to my central problematic of developing a reciprocal ethics because it suggests that, to some extent, some negation is unavoidable, and means need to be engaged with that are at odds with the desired ends. For example, negation may result from drawing on limiting discourses (the 'cognitive instruments' of the dominant (Bourdieu 2004: 339)) in the service of an 'identity' that is at odds with my ends, or in order to stop a greater negation, as considered in some science fiction where the treatment of those who commit murder or are perpetrators of sexual violence in utopian societies is explored. This central moral issue of how and what to choose and assign value to was explored by Beauvoir throughout per writing career. For example, in *The Blood of Others* (1978), written in 1945, Beauvoir considers the very real choices that those resisting the Nazi occupation of France had to make between undermining their own ethics by undertaking the ultimate negation of an other through murder, or allowing others to enact even greater negation through the murder of many more people. There are other examples of Beauvoir's engagement with this problem discussed below in considering how value distinctions can be made.

The second half of the chapter will analogise the antinomy of strategic violence with the problem of identity, and my critique goes hand in hand with acknowledging that, in given social situations, it must necessarily be engaged in. This discussion is premised on Butler's paradoxical picture of agency wherein one cannot be without doing and citing norms, and that 'a citation is only an *occasion* to subvert a norm; it is no *guarantee* that the norm will be subverted ... some citations will unwittingly reproduce the very norms that they seek to subvert' (Allen 1999: 72). This is the paradoxical problem of whether 'using gender to undo gender' (to borrow a phrase from Judith Lorber 2000) is efficacious. My question here is thus, having outlined the ideal reciprocal ethic, how can a deconstructive (or subversive) citation or reiteration, as far as possible, be *guaranteed*? I will argue below that, in engaging strategically with dominating cultural resources, mechanisms of inexhaustible dialectics and 'scrupulous visibility' (Spivak 1994: 153) may prevent the 'recuperative tendency' (Bordo 1993: 294).

Negation of negation: justifying strategic violence

As I emphasised in Chapter 4, Beauvoir's collective and purposive conceptualisations of freedom and negation mean that not taking a stance and attempting to evade responsibility (that is, knowingly *allowing* the negation of others) through inactivity is as much a violence as doing the violence oneself: 'for years now, the French people had been just as much accomplices to what was going on as the Germans under Nazi rule; the belated uneasiness some of them were feeling about this fact did nothing to reconcile them with me' (Beauvoir 1968: 615). As such, distinctions between desirable and undesirable negations or violences need to be made as there are occasions when some form of negation seems, in this model, ethically preferable, when 'one finds himself forced to treat certain men as things in order to win the freedom of all' (Beauvoir 1976: 97). This issue again taps into the central philosophical issues of the particular vs. the universal, and means vs. ends, binaries that I argue need not be capitulated to. Sartre was especially direct in per defence of strategic counterviolence by colonised people in per preface to Frantz Fanon's *The Wretched of the Earth* (1974), first published in 1961, an ethical sentiment that echoes Beauvoir's much earlier 1946 essay 'An Eye for an Eye' (in Beauvoir 2004). Here, Sartre made the bold claim that 'violence ... can heal the wounds that it has inflicted' (Sartre 1974: 25) by arguing that these are the 'inhuman means that these less-than-men [the colonised] make use of to win the concession of a charter of humanity' (Sartre 1974: 18). Sartre defends this strategy by recourse to the violent *context* (a parallel ontological concern to that of Beauvoir's emphasis on the irreducibility of situation) in which the colonised must attempt to find their humynity, which renders non-violent resistance impossible:

> ... if violence began this very evening and if exploitation and oppression had never existed on the earth, perhaps the slogans of

non-violence might end the quarrel. But if the whole regime, even your non-violent ideas, are conditioned by a thousand-year-old oppression, your passivity serves only to place you in the ranks of the oppressors. (Sartre 1974: 21)

Likewise, Hanssen (2000) suggests that Fanon's ethics of recognition is able to evade the either/or logic that leads to the impasses of a simple violence/nonviolence binary, something I will return to below. Hanssen comments that, while idealistic, owing to situation 'staged by white others' Fanon was willing to engage in means at odds with the ends as 'counterviolence':

> Thrown between a desire for activist force and a tranquil Kantian-inspired universalism, *Black Skin, White Masks*'s muted call for counterviolence still remained framed by a pacifistic poetry that yearned for the unmediated encounter with the other. In so positioning his work, Fanon resolutely rejected the choice offered between sameness and difference. ... For the two positions, that of 'colour-blindness' versus the 'colour-conscious' embrace of the racial mark, merely amounted to two alternatives in a drama staged by white others. (Hanssen 2000: 202)

This demonstrates a co-existence of idealistic ends and strategic means. Further to this, the central metaphor of Beauvoir's novel *The Blood of Others* is that a dedication to *means* in the service of an ideological moral or ethical purity, to the omission of considering the *ends* involved, is as flawed as the inverse of subordinating the means to the ends in 'political realism', an approach that values political ideals over humyn life and ethical values. The character of Blumenfeld in *The Blood of Others* serves as an allegory of the folly of means-centric pacifism more generally:

> He was so sure of his pacifism, so sure of himself. 'I am a pacifist.' He had given a definition of himself once and for all, he had only to act in accordance with his own idea of himself neither looking to left or right, as if the road had been already marked out, as if the future had not, at every instant, been that gaping void. (Beauvoir 1978: 119)

In the context of this dilemma in anarchist politics, Ward Churchill (2004), a revolutionary insurrectionary anarchist, proposes that continual negation is the inevitable corollary of a means-centric pacifist ethical prefigurative approach to politics, as opposed to a revolutionary politics that confronts 'oppressive' power. Similarly, ze emphasises the extent to which Western pacifists are exemplary of this 'moral purism' and, because the state that pacifists passively oppose remains undisturbed, this purism is counter-productive. Churchill suggests that this type of 'non-disruptive' (to the state) activism is 'a husk of opposition' (2004: 16):

> ... those who remain within the parameters of non-disruptive dissent allowed by the state ... can devote themselves to the prefiguration of the revolutionary future society with which they proclaim they will replace the present social order (having, no doubt, persuaded the state to overthrow itself through the moral force of their arguments). Here, concrete activities such as sexual experimentation, refinement of musical/artistic tastes, development of various meatfree diets, getting in touch with one's 'id' through meditation and ingestion of Hallucinogens, alteration of sex-based distribution of household chores, and waging campaigns against such 'bourgeois vices' as smoking tobacco become the signifiers of 'correct politics' or even 'revolutionary practice.' This is *as opposed to* the active and effective confrontation of state power. (Churchill 2004: 17)

Clearly this logic is derived from Churchill's adherence to a classical anarchist reduction of 'power' to a repressive power primarily from 'the state' and also per adherence to another simple idea, that of 'The Revolution' that overthrows this state. However, this analysis is still of interest, in that it points to the need for an effective politics to address and challenge oppressive power at the same time as attempting to foster enabling power, or empowerment. The aggregate of 'the state' can indeed represent one aspect of the negative type of power, defined as 'extractive' power in Chapter 4 (and not thereby precluding productive and developmental forms of power). In this context, Churchill's formulations for dealing with and attempting to prevent this 'extractive' power are potentially useful, and I will discuss the co-existence of different forms of ethico-political action that include oppositional and prefigurative 'politics' in Chapter 8. However, focusing on the principle for now, Churchill suggests that a reaction to dominating negation must be on its own terms, that is, must be a retaliation. Muñoz similarly cites Virno's support for the 'negation of negation', which 'resists an oppositional logic that clouds certain deployments of negativity' (2009: 12). This demonstrates another argument in favour of the strategic engagement with means that are at odds with the desired ends.

In considering how such strategic engagement can be distinguished and justified, like Fanon and Sartre, Beauvoir (while holding a different social ontology) concedes that some form of retaliation is justifiable, because there are some acts which, even taking into account the force of situation, *are* 'absolute evil' (Beauvoir 2004: 257) and for which responsibility must be taken or, if not freely taken, forced, in the name of an ethics of freedom. Indeed, Hutchings argues that Beauvoir's ethics 'illuminates the irremediable difficulty and inescapability of such judgments [regarding the legitimacy of violence] in a violent but also intransigent world' (Hutchings 2007: 111). The problem then becomes the ethical distinction between and judgement about justified negation, which is 'made to work in the service of enacting a mode of critical possibility' (Muñoz 2009: 12), and plain negation. This application of means discontinuous with ends necessitates strategies to ensure that these engagements with impure strategies remain strategic and do not congeal into equally oppressive practices, a dilemma central to the issue of 'using gender to undo gender'.

As previously stated, Beauvoir's novel *The Blood of Others* dramatised the dilemma of choosing whether or not to engage in violent resistance to the Nazi occupiers, a choice that would inevitably have 'unintended consequences for third parties' (Naji & Stanley 2011: 11) in the form of the deaths of individuals who were bystanders. In 'Moral Idealism and Political Realism', Beauvoir (2004 [1945]) directly considered the issue of choice around per critique of the philosophical privileging of either means (in the case of moral idealism), or ends (in the case of political realism). This ethical problematic is also the central metaphor of Beauvoir's play *The Useless Mouths*, written in 1945. Naji & Stanley translated this play and argue that 'The ethical import of *The Useless Mouths* is that no separation between ends and means is possible, let alone ethically desirable' (Naji & Stanley 2011: 22). Likewise, Beauvoir faced this dilemma of applying per ethics to the French war in Algeria, discussed in *The Force of Circumstance*, the third of per autobiographies, published in 1963. Beauvoir further rejects the opposition of means or ends in per previously discussed 1946 essay 'An Eye for An Eye' (Beauvoir 2004). This essay is particularly useful as it strongly underlines the normative bottom line in Beauvoir's reciprocal ethics, for within it ze advocates counterviolence in the form of punishment.

'An Eye for An Eye' (Beauvoir 2004), Beauvoir's explanation for per support for the execution of Nazi war criminals, rejects valorising means over ends, in that per support of the decision to execute Robert Brasillach supports an act that is the ultimate negation. However, Beauvoir's rationale is that punishment should not be defended using an ends-based rationale that presents punishment as prevention, expressing it instead as an act of intersubjective vengeance. This is vengeance as a 'metaphysical requirement' (Arp 2004: 241) because it re-establishes 'concretely and genuinely the reciprocity between human conscious-nesses the negation of which constitutes the most fundamental form of injustice' (Beauvoir 2004: 249). Beauvoir comments that punishment should be about 'reinstitut[ing] a lasting equilibrium' (Beauvoir 2004: 247) rather than satisfying a grudge. So Beauvoir's concept of venge-ance is not the separation of ethics and politics that ze criticises both moral idealism and political realism for (Beauvoir 2004: 175–193), but is rather premised in per ontology, in that its aim is that 'the totality of a situation must be revived' (Beauvoir 2004: 248). To illustrate this, Beauvoir elaborates:

> The torturer believes himself to be sovereign consciousness and pure freedom in the face of the miserable thing he tortures. When his turn comes to be made into a tortured thing himself, he feels the tragic ambiguity of his condition as man. (Beauvoir 2004: 248)

Beauvoir's ultimate principle, as elaborated in Chapter 4, is the abhor-rence of negation, the negation specifically of 'reciprocity between human consciousnesses' (Beauvoir 2004: 249). In 'An Eye for An Eye', per ontological premises provoke an argument for a *social* understand-ing of crime and a support of rehabilitation, but importantly, Beauvoir states that negation is a real abomination 'when a man *deliberately* tries to degrade man by reducing him to a thing' (Beauvoir 2004: 257, my emphasis). Beauvoir's contention is, then, that sometimes an impure situation necessitates means that do not match with ends.

There is a shared theme in the thought-experiments of some utopian science fiction of comparing different (groups of) people so as to prob-lematise the application of an idealist ethics and consider ethical bot-tom lines and value systems. For example, in Piercy's (1979) *Woman on the Edge of Time*, the final act of the protagonist, Connie, is to murder two doctors in order to escape the facility she is forcibly kept in. This is a choice between freedoms. The act of choosing also tests the ethics in Le Guin's (1974) *The Dispossessed*, where characters have to apply their ethics to, and make value decisions in, situations in which the collective good requires delimiting the individual good, or the good of other sub-groups within the collective. For example, the reader learns of a train driver who, during a famine, was forced to make a decision between knocking down starving individuals who were attempting to intercept the train for its supplies in one place, in order to take the supplies to another part of Annares, where people were also starving. On what value-basis can such a decision be made?

> They tried to take a grain truck off his train. He backed the train, killed a couple of them before they cleared the track, they were like worms in rotten fish, thick, he said. He said, there's eight hundred people waiting for that grain truck, and how many of them might die if they don't get it? More than a couple, a lot more. So it looks like he was right. But by damn! I can't add up figures like that. I don't know if its right to count people like you count numbers. But then, what do you do? Which ones do you kill? (Le Guin 1974: 270)

Reynolds considers the important issue is that Le Guin implies the moral superiority, and greater deserving, of the group who do not attack the train. In comparing one community that chooses to attack the train against another that debates such action but chooses not to, there is a greater value awarded to those who embrace the possibility that such an impulse *can* be overridden with ethical judgement. Ze suggests that this is Le Guin's demonstration that 'A psychology of freedom and solidarity ... can potentially be more powerful than "biological instincts"' (Reynolds 2005: 88).

Choosing between the value of different humyns may be ambiguous and the issues irresolvable, as suggested by Hutchings (2007); however, an attempt can at least be made to apply the broad normative principle that deliberate negation is undesirable and preventable.

Strategic essentialism and preventing closure

The unfortunate necessity of sometimes 'treating people as things' underpins strategic violence, and this is connected with the 'strategic essentialism' of using identity categories that reduce certain people to pre-constructed things, a 'symbolic violence' that I critiqued in the first two chapters. While in Chapter 5 I emphasised the tendency of the trope of queer to reify, I did also hold that, regardless of moniker, some of the impulses inherent to the original project of queer theory are worth retaining, re-exploring and extending to a practice concerned with replacing gender and sexuality identity with something more enabling. I identified a normative core principle in some queer theory or gender deconstructive theory of a universal enshrinement of the irreducibility of selfhood. Inherent and necessary to maintaining these visions, however, were the internal characteristics of a 'critical and transformative relation' (Butler 2004: 3), an 'analysis interminable' (Fuss 1991: 6) or 'a critical mode of hope' (Muñoz 2009: 4) that is always 'for and toward the future' (Muñoz 2009: 1).

Here I will elaborate the careful negotiation of the ideal/real often considered in the political strategy of strategic essentialism, and specifically the characteristics or tactics recommended for attempting to protect such a strategy from the 'recuperative tendencies' of 'current power-relations' (Bordo 1993: 294). I will consider the debates about the perceived idealism of some ideas from queer theory, and demonstrate how idealism and realism can co-exist in queer (understood as a verb) politics. Some of the tactics offered by early queer theorists and other proponents of strategic essentialism usefully examine how such strategies can be prevented from reifying with and consider some strategies for maintaining the ethical core of these ideas while attempting to make them efficacious for the 'real world'. This will then inform and foreshadow my discussion of the fostering of this ideal post-gender ethic in Chapters 7 and 8, by offering a set of considerations and precepts that need to be borne in mind.

That 'the logic and political utility of deconstructing collective categories vie with that of shoring them up' (Gamson 1995: 391) was a key issue for early queer theorists, the titles of many of their works reflecting this inside/outside dialectic (cf. Fuss 1989; 1991; Sedgwick 1990). The attempt to transcend such dualisms and refusal to settle this once and for all was taken by some as evidence of queer theory's undertheorisation or at least deconstructive limits. For example, Seidman argues that, in articulating the need for strategic essentialism, 'Sedgwick seems to be acknowledging that the social force of the deconstructive critique is contingent upon its being connected to a politics of interest' (Seidman 1995: 133–134). In more sympathetic critique, Duggan worries about the political efficacy of the denaturalising project and language of queer studies, framing this limit as 'the difficulty of communication across the gap between the predominantly constructionist language of queer studies and the essentialist presumptions of public discourse' (Duggan 1994: 4).

This is directly allegorical to the polarisations between idealism/realism elaborated above, and those sometimes perpetuated in anarchist politics between 'pure' prefigurative politics and more strategic approaches that engage power on its own terms. Some have used this pervasive reality of essentialism in public discourse to propose identity as a 'necessary fiction' (Weeks 2003). Likewise, the reality that 'norms ... precede, constrain, and exceed the performer' (Butler 1993a: 234) could be extended to argue that queer theory is politically redundant. The debates over identity and its necessity and usefulness, or not, have been played out at length in feminism, queer theory, postcolonial studies and gender theory in various guises, and are covered elsewhere in this book. Various solutions, compromises and ways of approaching identity have been developed that are of interest to my project of developing a non-foreclosing, deconstructive and inexhaustible ethics of reciprocity, but the most useful are the various approaches advocating strategic essentialism (Spivak 1994).

What is most important here, as with the broader debate above around applying an ethos, is that a guarantee of the normative baseline is aimed for. First I will outline some illustrations of a co-existence of deconstructive ends with this 'necessary fiction' of identity-based means in the 'real world' of queer activism and communities, after which I will elaborate on the risks of this, and consider various strategies that have been developed to maintain an 'analysis interminable' (Fuss 1991: 6).

Beyond means/ends in gender and sexuality politics

One particular ethico-political campaign concerned with maximising gender choice in a gendered world provides a case study in miniature for teasing out the idealism/realism dualism. The PAN toilet campaign, and similar campaigns, sometimes called gender-neutral bathroom (US)/toilet (UK) campaigns, are activist campaigns for gender-neutral toilets that have taken place mostly on university campuses, but also in some workplaces and public spaces. In my reading, this exemplifies a politics that holds the aim of transcending gender, without this neglecting the specific strategic needs of those considered trans or women. These campaigns take place as both identity-based advocacy for the trans community, so that those who are either transitioning or have an identity permanently neither male or female can feel more comfortable and safe, hopefully reducing the violence sometimes experienced by trans/gender variant folk as a result of being 'mis'-read (the 'toilet problem' outlined in Chapter 1), and as awareness campaigns to highlight and deconstruct the restrictive binary nature of sex/gender.

These campaigns have sometimes received objections from feminist perspectives for undermining awareness of the extent to which this would impact negatively on women, echoing the warnings that in a patriarchal society, so-called 'androgyny' can mask androcentrism (Rosinsky 1984: x; cf. Pacteau 1986: 70). Greed emphasises the extent to which public toilet design impacts negatively on women and argues that such design takes place from the universalised subject position of the male architect and represents 'deep cultural taboos about the place of woman in the city of man' (Greed 2003: 71). Prioritising concern for women leads per to conclude that 'mixing boundaries does not work unless women's needs are prioritised' (Greed 2003: 76). However, the PAN campaign has called for gender-neutral toilets *in addition to* the current sexed toilets, not the dissolution of those.

Additionally, PAN campaigners view the function of their campaign – like the broader aim of getting rid of gender identity outlined in this book – as 'liberating' for people of all genders, including women. Australian activist Larx mentioned resistance from the women's collective at Melbourne University to the PAN campaign on similar terms to those articulated by Greed above. Larx rejected these 'identity-politics based' objections, emphasising that ze considered the aim to be liberating not only for transgender people, but also as ultimately helping to deconstruct sex/gender towards 'liberating' all humyns:

> ... the campaign was to advance the struggle of trans/intersex people in society, but also to break down constricting social norms about gender so that all people can feel more comfortable/liberated/etc. so [it was on behalf of] the whole of humanity, basically. (Larx personal correspondence)

For many people, then, the aims of transcending gender are ultimately the best solution to *all* aspects of the gender hierarchy, *including* the oppression of women:

> For me, the success of the degendering movement will be marked by unisex bathrooms. This is not a trivial goal – gender divided bathrooms replicate the supposed biological base of the gendered social order and the symbolic separation of men's and women's social worlds. They are also constant evidence of gender inequity, since there are never enough ladies' rooms in public spaces. (Lorber 2000: 91)

Lorber's 'degendering' aim implicitly departs from a feminist position that critiques the negation of women's needs, but views the valorisation of the different needs of women as a strategy contingent on an unequal context, not an end in itself. The PAN campaigners were not attempting to take away choice and undermine the 'safe space' of women's toilets, but rather campaigning for gender-neutral toilets *in addition to* current toilets such that more choices could exist. Likewise, PISSR (People In Search of Safe Restrooms) researcher Stavis:

> ... believes that gender-neutral bathrooms will not only help to reduce harm to transgender and gender variant people, but will help parents escort their small children of different genders to the restroom and will create more restrooms for women. (Linden 2003: n.p.)

In this way, the campaigns seem multi-layered as identity-deconstructive campaigns, *and* identity-based campaigns. This seems to depart from a queer analysis of sex/gender as oppressive for all humyns, while also working strategically to advocate on behalf of those currently considered subordinate 'other'.

In a similarly strategic way, many activists in 'real-world' contexts do not find an impasse working strategically with identities while also taking a deconstructive approach to them. Despite some postulations around some trans practices as inherently reifying heterosexuality, and some evidence that there are 'conformity pressures' (Gagne & Tewkesbury 1998), Dean Spade's discussion of per encounter with trans community demonstrates a different experience, wherein ze found a capacity for a more pluralistic co-existence of narratives of the self. Spade links this to an overarching shared (universalist) ethic of autonomy and respect that transcends particular differences of identity, an approach I consider to be useful for the ethics I am arguing for. Contrasting it to the medical framing of trans, Spade explains:

> I've found that in trans contexts, a much broader conception of trans experience exists. The trans people I've met have, shockingly, believed what I say about my gender. Some have a self-narrative resembling the medical model of transsexuality, some do not. However the people I've met share with me what my counsellors do not: a commitment to gender self-determination and respect for all expressions of gender. (2003: 22–23)

Likewise, Hennen suggests that within the radical faerie community, although many members share a fairly essentialistic notion of their identity, a real-world pluralism of narratives of selfhoods is sometimes possible and effective. A statement on the faerie culture describes an underpinning assumption of 'gays and lesbians as a distinct and separate people, with our own culture, ways of being/becoming, and spirituality' (Cain 2013). However, in Hennen's account, in reality 'a postmodern emphasis on fluidity and incoherence ... paradoxically exists quite comfortably alongside some strongly essentialist notions emphasizing the fixity of faerie identity' (Hennen 2004: 508). My own research in one particular part of community led me to similar observations through facilitating a discussion group around the (continuing) usefulness of the discourse of 'queer' (April 2009) and its compatibility with the faerie ethos. A gathering combined of older, more traditional members of the faerie community, who tend to be men who identify in the above way, with younger, mixed-gender, queer community members, proved surprisingly harmonious on the whole. The general consensus seemed to be that, although participants had greatly divergent ontological perspectives, from radical social constructionism to essentialist notions of a 'queer spirit', they shared an ethic of openness to, respect for, and non-oppression of, the other, whether or not they identified in the same way. What both of the loose groupings combined there shared, however, was some kind of dedication to anarchist politics or ethics. The faerie statement quoted above describes the movement as 'radically (at the root) decentralist and anti-authoritarian' with values of 'self-discovery and nurturing ... [and] self-definition' (Cain 2013). As I suggested in Chapter 5, it seems possible that, by focusing a desire for uniting on an ethics or principle rather than an ontology or identity, it is possible to by-pass much antagonism, closure and exclusion, although I do not wish to paint the picture that either of these social movements or communities is immune to the congealment of norms or authority.

Foreclosing foreclosure: doubled vision

What strategies, then, can guarantee reciprocity and perpetuate 'analysis interminable' (Fuss 1991: 6) such that (positivistic) means do not undermine (deconstructive) ends? Articulated differently, how can the dual impulse of de/reconstruction be *maintained* and *guaranteed*?

Butler is sometimes cynical about the outcomes resultant from the use of identity because of per poststructuralist position that 'it is ... impossible to sustain ... mastery over the trajectory of those categories within discourse' (Butler 1993a: 227). However, per practical conclusion from this, in particular responding to considerable criticism from those who perceived *Gender Trouble* to be an attack on identity politics, is that per work is 'not an argument *against* using identity categories, but it is a reminder of the risk that attends every such use' (Butler 1993a: 227–228). Like Butler's premise, Critchley argues that the ontological delimitation that deconstruction departs from is that 'the resources of metaphysical discourse are the only ones that are available, [thus] one must continue to use them even when trying to promote their displacement' (Critchley 1999: 15). Likewise, having advocated 'negation of negation' as a possibly transformative and enabling strategy, ever hopeful, Muñoz proposes that 'disappointment needs to be risked if certain impasses are to be resisted' (2009: 9).

A great number of thinkers have proposed political deployment of essential categories or identities as a strategy (Alcoff, in de Lauretis 1994: 10; Braidotti 1994; de Lauretis 1987; 1994). However, the 'risk' often referred to by many of these queer thinkers discussing the use of essentialism (Butler 1993a: 228; de Lauretis 1994: 33; Fuss 1989: 32) is a similar warning to that made in early deconstructive thought, where the premise of engaging with and departing from the discourses within which we are situated is accepted, but there is a warning to remain critical of them (Spivak 1976: xiv). Addressing this explicitly, Spivak wishes to 'remind the feminists who want so badly to be anti-essentialists that the critique of essence *à la* deconstruction proceeds in terms of the unavoidable usefulness of something that is very dangerous' (Spivak 1994: 156), hence per assertion of a tactic of *strategic* essentialism. Put otherwise, 'the "risk" is worth taking' (Fuss 1989: 32).

Given the ontological paradox, then, the refined distinction becomes that 'an *uncritical* appeal to such a system [of gender] for the emancipation of "women" is clearly self-defeating' (Butler 1990: 2), underscoring again the need for an inexhaustible auto-critique. The priority becomes identifying 'at what point … this move cease[s] to be provisional and become[s] permanent' (Fuss 1989: 32). This is what de Lauretis calls 'the practice of self-consciousness' or 'the consciousness of gender' (1987: 20), and is what distinguishes complicit and resistive engagements with identity. Likewise, Derrida has been read as suggesting that deconstruction is the limit of our escape from 'basic categories of Western intellectual life' (Baynes 1987: 121), but that deconstruction can be thought of as an alternative way of being and relating, that is, an end, *in itself*. This interminability was a key characteristic that I outlined as an internal mechanism in an ideal reciprocal mode of being in Chapter 5, where, drawing on queer and gender-deconstructive theory, as well as contemporary anarchism, I identified this openness as an androgynous impulse and as a utopian end in itself.

In this way, Butler's work has usefully been read as proposing a kind of inexhaustible dialectic. Following Stoetzler, I argue that dialectical thinking, if not understood as leading to closed resolution, does not inherently reduce 'the full diversity of the different to the straightforwardly contradictory' (Stoetzler 2005: 358). Stoetzler suggests that Butler would do better to explicate the normative premise to per work, a premise I have identified in Chapters 4 and 5 as valuing multiplicity and inexhaustible critique: 'the variable construction of identity as ... a political goal' (Butler 1990: 5). Stoetzler returns to Butler's early use of dialectics – which Butler developed from per reading of Beauvoir – and sees this as an alternative way of thinking that is required for 'inexhaustible critique', in that it is an 'open, dynamic form of thinking' (Stoetzler 2005: 354), which does not 'try too hard to settle the account once and for all' (Stoetzler 2005: 348). Thus a key precept for the next, and most practicable, part of this book, is that a post-gender mode of thought must be perpetually critical:

> If ideas and accepted practices have a way of hardening, of rigidifying over time, then criticism must not be an isolated event but an ongoing practice. If thinking differently, seeking freedom by creative engagement with new possibilities, is the objective, then there is no end to ethical criticism. (Cooper & Blair 2002: 529)

Another key aspect is that, in engaging strategically with norms or dominating discourses, there needs to be inherent resources to simultaneously 'promote their displacement' (Critchley 1999: 15). Examples of this might be the deconstructive strategies of doubled-reading or doubled vision, which can be promoted through an explication of the strategic nature of these engagements, what Spivak would call (to paraphrase) a scrupulous visibility (Spivak 1994: 153).

The ability to be critical, then, can be understood as a textual reading capacity contingent on training or discursive or cultural context, and many thinkers are keen to emphasise that these capacities themselves are contingent and it is on these that the subversive effectiveness hinges (Bordo 1993; Hutcheon 1994): 'different readings of texts indicate different trainings, not simply differences in subjective (private) point of view of a given text' (Hunter, in Hurley 1990: 157). Bordo is correct to emphasise that the fundamental intersubjectivity, and compulsarity, of binary sex/gender discussed in Chapter 2 means that most acts are 'readily interpreted as proof of the foundational nature of gender, the essential reality of the binary frame' (1993: 294). The capacities to read otherwise cannot be assumed, making tactical engagement like this particularly risky. I will briefly outline here the subject-positions required to be critical in an appeal to essences (i.e. to *read* critically), and whether there are 'possible distributions of subject-positions located in the text itself' (Fuss 1989: 32). Critchley proposes that deconstruction contains within it an auto-critical mode of double reading, quoting Derrida to the effect that deconstruction consists of 'Two texts, two hands, two visions, two ways of listening. Together at once and separately' (Derrida, cited in Critchley 1999: 18). As such 'deconstruction may therefore be "understood" as the desire to keep open a dimension of alterity' (Critchley 1999: 29), so avoiding the violence of reducing the other to the same. This concept of 'double reading' thus seems a useful way of approaching the other, a useful subject-position, by remaining open and also critiquing the initial understanding of the other. Applied directly to gender, de Lauretis (1987) proposed a similar mode of seeing or reading as the most strategically useful for challenging the reality of sexual difference. With a longer-term gender-deconstructive aim of fostering more 'multiple' or 'heterogenous' subjects, de Lauretis nonetheless also acknowledges that we are positioned in sexual difference, and thus suggests that the ideal being is 'one that is at the same time inside and outside the ideology of gender, and conscious of being so, conscious of that twofold pull, of that division, that doubled vision' (1987: 10). It is worth noting that such textual reading capacities have been identified and extended as practical strategies for many groups who are compelled to work within and from discourses that seem to negate them. For example, Nakata proposes that, in order to avoid assimilation into a knowledge system that negates their specificity, but in order also to be heard, indigenous Australians must 'work two knowledge systems together' (2012: 5).

An example of a practice that provokes, and attempts to guarantee, a deconstructive or double reading (i.e. attempts to construct a subject-position in the text itself, to paraphrase Fuss (1989)) in practice is the deconstructive strategy of placing problematised terms 'sous rature' ('under erasure') (Derrida 1976: xiv), such as writing a word with a score through it. Placing something under erasure is to acknowledge that simply behaving 'as if' it does not exist does not serve to diminish its material significance, accepting it as an 'inaccurate yet necessary ... philosophical exigency' (Spivak 1976: xiv). Butler accepted this just deconstructive premise in per characterisation of identity as 'necessary error' (Butler 1993a: 230). Just as Heidegger used the word 'being' under erasure to demonstrate and problematise that this is a concept that has reified into a taken-for-granted 'thing' (Spivak 1976: xv), using the term 'gender' or gendered terms, for example, under erasure could do the same: 'In examining familiar things we come to such unfamiliar conclusions that our very language is twisted and bent even as it guides us. Writing "under erasure" is the mark of this contortion' (Spivak 1976: xiv).

This exemplifies Spivak's careful refinement of how discourses may be engaged in strategically so that they do not collapse, best summarised as a *'strategic* use of a positivist essentialism in a scrupulously *visible political* interest' (Spivak 1994: 153, my emphasis). What distinguishes positive, non-subordinating and 'developmental' relations from normative engagements that uncritically replicate dominating relations here is that they are engaged in this *'scrupulously visible political interest'* (Spivak 1994: 153, my emphasis), or as de Lauretis puts it, *'conscious* of ... that doubled vision' (1987: 10, my emphasis). This transparency and self-critical element, co-existent with the provision of cultural resources to read in this doubled manner, is what makes repetitions of norms subversive rather than reifying. This means that, despite the inescapability of power and norms, in order to be 'developmental' rather than 'extractive' (Patton 1994), reconstructive norms need to explicate their own ethical premises in this scrupulously visible way, argue for them non-foundationally and foster deconstructive capacities within them. This scrupulous visibility is compatible with concurrent short- and long-term strategies such that the ultimate aim is not lost. Duggan is deeply suspicious of less visible strategic essentialism and, echoing the need for interminability and returning us to the necessity of not losing sight of the deconstructive, reminds those engaged in queer politics 'not to let everyone else [wider society] off the hook' (1994: 6). It is important for this strategic essentialism not to slide into exclusive minority politics and to continue the deconstruction of the norms in which it engages. However, the internal mechanisms suggested by various proponents on strategic essentialism seem to heed this danger and, owing to their concurrent and interminable de/reconstructive modes, seem prepared to challenge closure should it seem a risk. How, then, can this ideal subject that is conscious of this doubled positionality be fostered? That is the subject of Chapters 7 and 8.

Conclusion

The aim of the final part of this book is to consider, given the ontological and political risks, realities and precepts outlined here, some sites for intervention, where sexual difference might be challenged and ethics of androgynous reciprocity could be implemented, fostered and maintained. I will attempt to offer an account that is as comprehensive as possible, by focusing on the subject and their capacities, as well as enabling and reciprocal relations, and enabling and transparent social context. Chapters 7 and 8 will then complete my practicable and thorough vision of how subjects may be able to work towards understanding themselves and others with an outlook that is more enabling than the assumption of oppositional sexual difference. What I hope that this chapter has offered to this formulation of strategies is a commitment to inexhaustibility, what Noddings calls a 'conditional approach':

> A conditional approach moves carefully back and forth between ideal and actual worlds. It is liberally sprinkled with turning points: points at which we turn from thinking to feeling, from acting to listening, from moving ahead to pausing for reflection. In dealing with those whose interests we have embraced, we have to remember to respond to persons, not only problems and principles. (Noddings 2006: 13)

7
The Fully Armed Self: Cultivating Post-Gender Subjects

Multi-layered sites for post-gender ethics

The final part of this book aims to take on board and operationalise all of the precepts of the book thus far: that the attribution of sex/gender is restricting of freedom; that the self comes to be in relations with others and in social context; that there is the potential that this becoming could be more enabling; and that a collective enabling mode of being could be characterised by a queer ethic of androgynous reciprocity. I will identify some key sites where there are opportunities to 'intervene' in the symbolic violence of sex/gender difference and foster a more androgynous ethos, and a more reciprocal ethic, or way of being and relating. By applying these insights to practice, I am recognising, and attempting to contribute to, an alleviation of the problem that:

> A lot of voices tell us to think nondualistically, and even what to think in that fashion. Fewer are able to transmit how to go about it, the cognitive and even affective habits and practices involved, which are less than amenable to being couched in prescriptive forms. (Sedgwick 2003: 1)

In practical terms, given that I have identified the perpetuation of sexual difference taking place in the subjectivity of individuals, in their interactions with others, and through the limits dictated by their situation or cultural resources, effective intervention would require an 'integrative' multi-layered (Lorber 1986; 2000; cf. Risman 2004; Risman, Lorber & Sherwood 2012) or 'multidimensional' (Risman 2004: 434) approach. Chapters 7 and 8 will then be concerned with how sexual difference may be challenged across these dimensions, and what androgynous, reciprocal subjectivity, relations and social contexts might look like.

Thus I will focus on some strategies for fostering (i) subjects sufficiently critical to recognise external coercion (in this case that of the imposition of a framework of sexual difference) and reject it; (ii) subjects that would not perpetuate such coercion or negation upon others (in this case by reading or attributing others in terms of the limiting framework of sexual difference); (iii) situations or pre-existing norms that are not coercive by imposing compulsory sexual difference; and (iv) situations or social contexts that are enabling, making it practically possible for subjects to recognise and reject coercion and not perpetuate it (in this case by providing alternative discourses and modes of thought to attach to, and 'read' within, that are not premised on sexual difference).

Here in Chapter 7 I want to consider some sites for intervention in sexed/gendered subjectivation, that is, coming to subjecthood. I will outline what kind of subject might be most equipped to be as purposive as possible in subjectivation and be 'in the presence of their freedom' (Beauvoir 1976a: 98). In turn, I argue that this type of subject would be most equipped to engage in truly inexhaustible reciprocal sociality, that is, to engage with the other 'in their otherness' (Beauvoir 1976: 67) and avoid attributing them with preconceived sexed/gendered norms, in order not to negate them. Beauvoir, as previously outlined, refers to this as being 'fully armed'. I will suggest that to be the most armed to be purposive in their constitution of self and engage in reciprocity, and thus to resist 'gendering', subjects would need to be equipped to take up critical and reflexive subject-positions or reading capacities. This chapter will use the notion of pedagogy to explore subjectivation, how subjects learn 'to be' or become and teach each other 'to be', and outline some practices that seem fruitful for fostering these capacities and have potential for arming subjects in a manner consistent with the ends of androgynous reciprocity. I will draw on anarchist and queer pedagogical practices here as they share expanded definitions of pedagogy and because their normative premises and goals are that of fostering 'freedom'. I will then go on to consider gender-neutral childrearing as an obvious and possibly effective site for intervening in the process of sexed/gendered subjectivation, and for nurturing subjects with the capacity for more androgynous, reciprocal ways of being in the World.

In Chapter 8 I will consider some sights for intervention that might foster more reciprocal intersubjectivity, and consider social

communication practices that foster and maintain this critical relation and attempt prevent it from solidifying or congealing. Finally,
Chapter 8 will be concerned with how a social/cultural context can
try to support autonomous and reciprocal social relations by attempting to foster cultural categories and modes of intelligibility conducive
to this.

Fully armed: the ideal subject for androgynous reciprocity

The problem is, then, one of fostering individuals capable of engaging
with others and with social norms or cultural resources in a purposive,
reflexive manner. This can usefully be framed as an issue of learning
how to read in a critical, reciprocal manner if we understand reading
as 'a moral technology, a series of social techniques, skills and trainings
which produce and value a particular mode of subjectivity' (Hurley
1990: 156).

In Chapter 6 I indicated the importance of reading capacities as
subject-positions that make the difference between critical and non-
critical ways of 'reading' one's own subjectivity, and that of others. In
the context of challenging gender, Hausman articulates this necessity of
capable or enabled participants in interaction:

> The potential subversiveness of the performance is always deter-
> mined by its context as well as, Linda Hart might add, whether or
> not the audience is capable of *seeing* that context and *reading* it in
> relation to the performance. (Hausman 1999: 202)

Indeed, in considering the situated nature of freedom, Beauvoir
states that, ideally, to avoid actions being undertaken 'out of ignorance or out of constraint', a course of action is needed 'to expose the
mystification' and, through 're-education', to 'put the men who are its
[ignorance's] victims in the presence of their freedom' (Beauvoir 1976:
98). Likewise, Butler frames critical 'reading capacities' as a central site
of subversion of subjectivation, which allows for reconstructive reading
capacities, stating that 'Subversive practices ... challenge conventions
of reading, and demand new possibilities of reading' (Butler 1993b:
n.p.). In Chapter 6 I emphasised the importance, if reciprocity is to
avoid closure and collapse into hierarchy, of the capacity to read both
deconstructively and reconstructively, drawing on de Lauretis (1987),
Fuss (1991) and Hutcheon (1994), and suggested that a capacity for
perpetual openness would minimise collapse into closure. What, then,

would such a capacity for inexhaustible critique or 'analysis interminable' (Fuss 1991: 6) look like, and how could it be applied to 'identity' and sexuality?

I characterise Foucault's ideal of the critical attitude (2007) to be a useful way of characterising the internal qualities needed for 'queer cultural workers' (Muñoz 2009: 9) capable of 'the critical imagination' (Muñoz 2009: 10). This ideal was most clearly articulated in Foucault's essay 'What is Critique?' (2007). In this project, Foucault is concerned with how subjects might have the most self-willed 'techne of the self', so that the way that one comes to recognise oneself as an ethical subject, the *mode d'assujettissement* (which Foucault defines as 'the way in which people are invited or incited to recognize their moral obligations' (1984: 353)), is as much as possible a 'personal choice' (Foucault 1984: 356). This subjective capacity is also a capacity idealised in and sought through much queer pedagogy, which I will elaborate later in this chapter.

Friedrich Nietzsche's juxtaposition of the hierarchical, rigid (and human) construction and reification of metaphors into *schema* with what ze frames as the more ideal 'perceptual world of first impressions' (Nietzsche 1998: 360) is likewise a good illustration of what a less obliterating, negating, exclusionary capacity of intelligibility or mode of 'reading' might look like. Compatible with the ideal values of self-willed or purposive creation outlined and justified in the previous chapters, Nietzsche's ideal is a person who does not forget that they are 'self as a subject, and what is more as an artistically creating subject' (Nietzsche 1998: 361), who does not take pre-existing concepts or metaphors as fixed, but who is 'freely composing and freely inventing' (Nietzsche 1998: 361). This critical relationship to pre-existing norms or discourses would also aid in overcoming the attribution of others to pre-existing norms, and thus the negation of their freedom. This has clear normative and practice-based parallels with Foucault's ideal ethical practice of critique.

Both of these thinkers are, then, proposing that maximum autonomy can be obtained by the capacity to have an awareness of one's own genealogy. The capacity for genealogy is analogous to that of deconstruction as a transformative process in which understanding the historical constitution of discourses and practices and ways of being allows us to understand how this could be otherwise. Foucault implies that deconstructive or genealogical thinking is a strategy of freedom: 'Since these things ... have been made, they can be unmade, as long as we know how it was they were made' (Foucault 1988, in Cooper &

Blair 2002: 517). Cooper & Blair (2002) argue that Foucault's ideal of problematisation as an intellectual imperative opposed to polemics holds the promise of 'opening possibilities for transformation' (521). The subject of this 'genealogy provides us with the tools for a project of freedom, of going beyond our "limits"' (Wain 1996: 355). The implication of Wain's and Cooper & Blair's readings of Foucault are that education should be reunderstood as a process of deconstructive analysis that helps us to understand why things are as they are and to make it possible to render them otherwise. Foucault outlines how the critical attitude, which ze defines as exploring how to not to be 'governed quite so much', lays the foundations for alternative ways of being governed. Ze defines this critical attitude as follows:

> Facing them [practices of governing] head on and as compensation, or rather, as both partner and adversary to the art of governing, as an act of defiance, as a challenge, as a way of limiting these arts of governing and sizing them up, transforming them, of finding a way to escape from them or, in any case, a way to displace them, with a basic distrust, but also and by the same token, as a line of development of the arts of governing ... [the critical attitude is] a kind of general cultural form, both a political and moral attitude, a way of thinking, etc. and which I would very simply call the art of not being governed like that and at that cost. I would therefore propose, as a very first definition of critique, this general characterization: the art of not being governed quite so much. (Foucault 2007: 44–45)

This critical attitude represents perfectly a means of conceptualising the subject, of being, that could resist identity. The dynamic of deconstruction as co-constitutive with, and perhaps even synonymous with, reconstruction, and this as an ethical end in itself, allows for subjects that are not predetermined, in that it is 'a means for a future or a truth that it will not know' (Foucault 2007: 42). This leads Foucault to claim the 'critical attitude as virtue in general' (Foucault 2007: 43). If we understand critique as a process (i.e. a means) and as a virtue (i.e. an end) then it is possible to understand how 'Critique would essentially insure the desubjugation of the subject' (Foucault 2007: 47). Foucault explicitly advocates this subjective, genealogical approach to knowledge as a method for rejecting coercive authority: 'Instead of letting someone else say "obey," it is at this point, once one has gotten an adequate idea of one's own knowledge and its limits, that the principle of autonomy can be discovered' (Foucault 2007: 49). Beauvoir articulates a similar dedication to empowering pedagogy when ze claims that:

> One cannot hate [a person who blithely negates others because they] ... never had the possibility of criticizing it. One reeducates children, the ignorant, those populations that are ill-informed; one does not punish them. (Beauvoir 2004: 256)

Such a critical attitude would enable people to 'expose the mystification ... to put the men who are its victims in the presence of their freedom' (Beauvoir 1976: 98). Following my discussion of the threat of closure and the need for perpetual critique in Chapter 6, the internal processes of this attitude are exemplary of the attitude one would need in order to be 'fully armed' in the face of subjugating norms such as gendered identity and to prevent congealment in to norms and their imposition. This impulse is inexhaustible as it is both the means and the end.

Why pedagogy?

This chapter is concerned with how to foster subjects with the capacity for an androgynous mindset or ethos, for this enabling de/reconstructive process outlined above, and capable of ethical, reciprocal relations. Pedagogy has always been concerned with the cultivation of ideal subjects, however defined, and to more or less coercive and enabling extents. Like other critical theorists, Foucault identifies 'the art of pedagogy' (Foucault 2007: 44), that is, how we teach and learn, to be a central aspect of how we are governed, and therefore how we may be governed differently. This is because pedagogical contexts provide us with the 'cognitive instruments' (Bourdieu 2004: 339) with which, and within which, we can *be*. Hunter describes popular education as exemplary of just this '"moral machinery" ... [and sees it as] aimed, as Foucault puts it, at the "normalisation of the population"' (Hunter 1988: 75). In the contemporary British context, for example, 'Citizenship' education, which ostensibly intends to foster active citizens, has been critiqued as actually implicitly assisting liberal democracy to 'perpetuate itself' (Pike 2007: 472; cf. Kisby 2007).

For the purpose of this project, the issue is how more explicitly purposive capacities can be learned in a way that is enabling but cognisant of the productive, constitutive nature of power and subjectivity. Such reading practices are central to the project(s) of queer pedagogy (Britzman 1998; Sumara & Davis 1999). Queer pedagogy is a praxis that may be capable of 'exposing mystification', ensuring subjects are not prevented from having a critical relationship to the categories by which themselves and others are constituted.

Given the ontological picture I have presented thus far, there is the possibility of enabling, non-dominating modes of learning that directly inform more enabling, non-dominating modes of becoming and relating more broadly. Anarchists, in being concerned with maximising autonomy, have long defined education, not as instruction of particular information but, rather, as nurturing capacities (cf. Bakunin 1970; Chomsky 2003; Heckert 2009; 2011; Hern 2008; Suissa 2010). Thus, anarchist approaches to pedagogy are useful for an ethically oriented, non-foundational project such as mine. Although Geoffrey Fidler (1989) rightly notes that much early anarchist pedagogy departs from the classical anarchist assumption of the essential co-operative nature of humyns, there has always been an element of anarchism that has put aside the potentially never-ending debates about essential humyn nature and instead concerned itself with the *cultivation* or *fostering* of subjects who would be capable of self-willed action, and capable of living in a society of like-minded individuals. Anarchist pedagogy can alternatively be characterised as a practice of nurturing capacities (Heckert 2009) based on a thin ontology only of potentiality. Tolstoy, for example, suggests that instruction can either become oppressive and a prescriptive form of education ('Education is the action of one man [sic] upon another' (Tolstoy 2008: 5)) or can operate on a less oppressive dynamic: 'Instruction and teaching are the means of culture, when they are free' (Tolstoy 2008: 5). Tolstoy regards it as a socially organic, necessary and not inherently dominating process, to share information with others, and thus 'The difference between education and culture lies only in the compulsion' (Tolstoy 2008: 5).

This subjectifying mechanism in instructional education is a central concern and point of criticism by anarchist and queer pedagogues, and parallels my concern with critiquing the *objectifying* outcomes of identity. In this way, Robinson worries that the hierarchical adult/ child binary, which reflects the teacher/pupil binary, causes children to 'become the powerless and voiceless "other" within this relationship' (Robinson 2005: 22). That is, the pedagogical model of instruction reflects just those self/other hierarchical impulses that I have identified in sexual difference. Foucault's distinction between dominating and developmental power allows for a similar idealisation of pedagogy instead as 'cultivation' (Fidler 1989: 23):

> I see nothing wrong in the practice of a person who, knowing more than others in a specific game of truth, tells those others what to

do, teaches them, and transmits knowledge and techniques to them. The problem in such practices where power – which is not in itself a bad thing – must inevitably come into play is knowing how to avoid the kind of domination effects where a kid is subjected to the arbitrary and unnecessary authority of a teacher, or a student put under the thumb of a professor who abuses his authority. (Foucault 1997: 298–299)

The ontological assumption of this part of the book is, then, that 'there are ... structural alternatives to the carceral school, classroom, and society, because there are power relationships and technologies that are not dominating' (Wain 1996: 358).

Queer pedagogy

Queer pedagogy (and some anarchist and anarcho-queer pedagogy) is able to bring this ideal of a critical subject and the possibility of enabling pedagogy to bear explicitly on the construction of identity, aiming to foster in subjects an awareness of the genealogy of their selfhood (especially their sexual and gendered selfhood) and remaining inexhaustibly critical about this. Ideally, queer pedagogy can 'provoke ethical responses that can bear to refuse the normalising terms of origin and of fundamentalism, those that refuse subjection' (Britzman 1998: 79). This, in turn, is necessary for moving towards a more self-willed and recip-rocal social and discursive context.

Anarchist approaches to pedagogy, like the poststructuralist notion of textual reading practices that expands to 'reading' all aspects of culture, can usefully and realistically expand our understandings of the terrain upon which learning takes place. Acknowledging the fun-damentally social ontology of selfhood means that contemporary anar-chists usefully take off from the assumption that '"education" is not synonymous with "schooling"' (Suissa 2010: 4). However, this radical claim has been little acknowledged in pedagogical theory. As Judith Suissa remarks, 'even those who do explicitly acknowledge this fact ... tend to treat this issue simply as a factor to be dealt with in the debate conducted within the framework of the existing democratic ... state' (Suissa 2010: 4). Additionally, queer pedagogue Luhmann comments that 'even teachers dedicated to critical pedagogy when speaking about their pedagogy might refer to little else than their teaching style, their classroom conduct, or their preferred teaching methods' (Luhmann 1998: 120). Instead, as I have emphasised before (Nicholas 2012), it is possible to consider all aspects of cultures and subcultures that play a part in 'teaching' ways of being as pedagogical. I will return to some of these in Chapter 8.

Like anarchist pedagogy, the ends of queer pedagogy are also its means, and it is concerned not with what the subject should learn, but how, what Kopelson calls an 'epistemological position – a way of knowing, rather than something to be known' (2002: 25). A primary concern for both anarchist and queer pedagogues is procedural, then. Like Foucault's notion of an enabling transmission of knowledge or ways of knowing, queer pedagogy seeks to foster a particular relationship of subjects to texts, that is, a queer reading capacity.

Luhmann states that owing to queer pedagogy's primary epistemological concern with 'the question of how we come to know and how knowledge is produced', it must focus on and deconstruct the process by which this happens 'in the interaction between teacher/text and student. This orientation to pedagogy exceeds education's traditional fixation on knowledge transmission, and its wish for the teacher as the master of knowledge' (Luhmann 1998: 126).

In specific reference to essentialising and compulsory sexual and gender identity, in the service of this telos of deconstructing implicitly dominating discourses, queer pedagogy is primarily concerned with uncovering, or deconstructing, the tacit, implicit heteronormatising that occurs in dominant discourses and through which subjects learn to be, and learn to be sexual and gendered. Queer pedagogues have suggested that this critical mode of thought provides the way that subjects can resist the normatising discourses that queer theory deconstructs. Queer pedagogy seems ideal, then, for providing a mode of learning how to be (i.e. subjectivation) and how to read others (and therefore allow them to be) that is not premised on *difference*, specifically on the difference of gender and sexuality. In this way, Sumara & Davis (1999) assert that queer pedagogy is all about (re)cognition: 'Living within heteronormative culture means learning to "see" straight, to "read" straight, to "think" straight' (Sumara & Davis 1999: 202). In terms of the implications of this for intervening in and resisting sexing/gendering, the aim of queer pedagogy is fostering the capacity to 'see', 'read' and 'think' (i.e. to (re)cognise) in non-heteronormative ways, that is, resisting normative attribution. It has been suggested that this fostering of a deconstructive ethic is precisely the strategy needed to undermine the negation that heteronormativity performs upon those who exceed it:

> ... the way stable notions of gender, sex and desire are constituted, expressed and normalised through compulsory heterosexuality (that is, how gender is heterosexualised and sexuality is simultaneously

normalised as heterosexual) needs greater recognition in the field of early childhood education. This is particularly so if gender equity strategies employed in early childhood education are to be fully effective. (Robinson 2005: 21)

In terms of reconstructive potential for 'queer sociality', that is, a more positive, queer code of conduct, further to the notion of queer pedagogy as an 'epistemological position – a way of knowing, rather than something to be known' (Kopelson 2002: 25), queer pedagogy can be understood as a reading capacity or learning disposition premised on and oriented towards an ethic of universalised particularism (cf. Chapter 5). The key here is that 'if we read from multiple subject-positions, the very act of reading becomes a force for dislocating our belief in stable subjects and essential meanings' (Fuss 1989: 35). This open or dislocated disposition to what we 'know' would mean approaching and reading others, with the only universalised principle being that 'People are different from one another' (Sedgwick 1990: 22). Sumara & Davis extend this by proposing that the aim of queer pedagogy must be fostering the capacity to (re)cognise the *particular* differences among individuals, not *groups* of individuals (Sumara & Davis 1999: 194), that is, a universalised particularism. This, then, is compatible with a queer telos of allowing for non-defined 'variable construction[s] of identity' (Butler 2007: 7–8). Spurlin clarifies this normative position:

In one sense, a 'queer' pedagogy would imply not only an analysis of (sexual) difference(s) in the classroom but of interrelated, broad-based pedagogical commitments to free inquiry and expression, social equity, the development of more democratic institutional and pedagogical practices, and the broadening of dialogical spheres of public exchange within and beyond the classroom as sites for engaged analyses of social issues and collective struggles. (Spurlin 2002: 10)

Sumara & Davis conceive of this as having broader benefits for individuals and sociality, stating that 'Interrupting heteronormativity, then, becomes an important way to broaden perception, to complexify cognition, and to amplify the imagination of learners' (Sumara & Davis 1999: 201), that is, it is an *enabling* strategy. Below I will suggest that collective critical reading of discourses (widely understood) for both children and adults is an important strategy of queer and anarchist pedagogy that makes the underlying master discourses and ideological 'moral machin-ery' explicit, and can underpin the reconstruction of preferable modes of sociality. It therefore has the desired outcome of undermining its own subjectifying authority, as well as concurrently nurturing and imbuing the capacities of subjects to undertake other critical engagements in future.

In summary, I argue that anarchist and queer pedagogies feature the following principles that make them ideal pedagogical approaches for fostering reciprocal subjects and relations:

- the ideal of a nurturing, not compelled or coercing, relation between learning partners;
- a non-defined outcome in terms of learning *content* or identities of participants;
- a deconstructive motivation informed by an enabling ethic;
- a 'scrupulous visibility' (to paraphrase Spivak 1994: 153) in terms of these underlying ethics/discourses that the learning takes off from.

Teaching androgyny

First it is important to note the irreducibility of self, relationships with others and social contexts, and that in discussing enabling relationships and cultural resources in Chapter 8, I will be talking about 'learning' also. Hence this is to an extent a false separation for ease of communi-cation. This quotation from 'anarchist sex educator' Heckert challenges the terrain of 'sex education' and taps into just this co-constitution, and the tacit nature by which we learn how 'to be' from the fund of ideas available:

> If anarchism is about changing relationships throughout life, then sex education could be just as much a focus of anarchist practice as G8 summits, poverty or climate change (inasmuch as any of these are really separate). Anarchist ethics of prefiguration and mutual aid, of listening and appreciating difference, seem to me to speak clearly to the challenges of sex education (broadly defined). (Heckert 2011: 161)

The tacit means by which dominant identity norms are learned (cf. subject, Hunter 1988; Hurley 1990) is especially apparent in the ways that sexuality and gender are closed off as topics for consideration by children (let alone critical consideration) by denying that children have a sexuality (Robinson 2005). Robinson argues that this thereby enforces dominant discourses that create the restrictive culture of self and other, and also police heteronormativity (Robinson 2005: 22). This justifies even more the strategy of explication, of 'scrupulous visibility' proposed by Spivak as a means to minimise coercion (Spivak 1994: 153). By 'textualising' culture as I have in this chapter, a more thorough understanding of the nature of learning becomes clear, highlighting that most sexuality and gender learning is located in non-institutionalised settings and aspects of culture.

A first aspect of anarchist and queer approaches to teaching and learning, informed by this understanding of the tacit pedagogical nature of culture broadly and the more informal idealisation of knowledge sharing, is a purposive creation of culture that attempts to foster critical engagement with dominant norms. I have charted elsewhere (Nicholas 2007; 2012) the pedagogical function of many aspects of these cultures, such as music and zines, and gatherings or groups. Some other brief examples: contemporary anarchist collective CrimethInc. have been making and distributing their 'Gender Subversion Kit' (CrimethInc. n.d.[b]) for some years. This is a large poster based on a poem a poem by Nancy Smith about the restrictions that gender imposes on the freedom of both boys and girls (cited in full in Chapter 2). Complementing this call to deconstruction is a reconstructive counterpart on the reverse in the form of extracts from a gender-subversive colouring book for children, which depicts boys and girls undertaking a truly androgynous combination of tasks.

In a semi-formal context, as I have written elsewhere (Nicholas 2012), the 'developmental' (Patton 1994) ideal of 'work-partners' (Bhave 2008: 10) is carried out in anarchist communities in less formal, less institutional, but explicitly pedagogical settings such as 'skill sharing' and 'knowledge sharing' events instead of classes or other traditional fora. Free Skools represent this non-compelled, sporadically organised means of sharing and communicating information, practices and ideas, and are usually run by volunteers. 'Free Skool' appears in different spaces with different levels of organisation and regularity. In Brighton, UK, for example, there is a monthly Free Skool day on a Saturday at an autonomous social centre, which features one-off discussion groups, skill shares and workshops.[1] Other Free Skools may be established spaces and feature longer courses.

These 'pedagogical' aspects of culture offer new subject-positions or capacities to individuals, through non-coercive and dialectic means, as part of ongoing cultural conversations. In Chapter 8 I will relatedly discuss some community practices that are concerned with fostering 'safe spaces' in terms of sexual consent, practices that I argue are also anarchically ethical and fundamentally pedagogical in that they seek to transform the consciousness of those involved, as well as intersubjective and reconstructive because they are concerned with transforming the way that people relate to one another.

Given the open-endedness that I outlined above as characteristic of these pedagogical approaches, another important strategy of queer and anarchist approaches to pedagogy is the rejection of arbitrary restrictions and an openness to play. Robinson (2005), in per work with teachers preventing tacit homophobia or heteronormativity, suggests that an important strategy is the self-awareness of the 'educator' in not policing gendered behaviour in play, that is, the *freedom* in the narrative content of play. A practical recommendation from Robinson for this is resisting impulses to communicate that a child has transgressed rules when playing dress-ups in clothes commonly associated with the opposite sex/ gender, or when a child expresses a wish to 'marry' their friend of the same sex/gender.

As well as an enabling pedagogical environment, the ideal mindset outlined in this chapter – capable of 'reading' oneself and other in nongendered ways – can be a more explicitly fostered goal. Anarchist Free Skools, for example, seem particularly preoccupied with deconstructive ways of thinking, through the critique of modes of thought. The by-line on the Toronto Anarchist Free University website, for example, is 'a riot for the mind' (Anarchist Free University Toronto), neatly summarising their de(con)structive impulses towards the aim of 'not be[ing] ... governed quite so much' (Foucault 2007: 44–45).

Sumara & Davis undertook empirical research on school pupils' understandings of sex and experiences of mainstream sex education through a queer lens. This catalysed a critique of the didactic *means* through which sex education is delivered, and the naturalised relationship to dominant sex norms that this tacit inculcation into norms engenders in students:

> Because these curriculum artefacts were presented as information rather than as beginning places for critical inquiry into what might constitute experiences of sexuality and sex, Gina (and a number of her classmates) seemed unable to represent anything other than the usual cultural myths about sex and sexuality – particularly myths about what counts as sex (only intercourse, it seems) and as sexual partners (opposite sex only). (Sumara & Davis 1999: 199)

Carrying this forward to a practical implications for what a more enabled 'places for critical inquiry' may entail, Sumara & Davis idealise a deconstructive disposition:

> If sexuality is understood as a category of experience that emerges from various and overlapping technologies of self-formation and reformation, then the cultural mythologies around what constitutes the category of 'heterosexual' must be called into question. (Sumara & Davis 1999: 195)

Queer approaches specifically to sex education are, therefore, unsurprisingly concerned with having a critical, deconstructive attitude towards discourses around sexuality, with the activity of queering. Strategies proposed as queer pedagogy for 'interrupting heteronormativity' include genealogy, fostering reflection and deconstruction of existing discourses and modes of intelligibility. Robinson (2005) has focused on the ways that the learning materials in the discursive cultural context in which children learn, such as story books and animated films, are heteronormatised and must be engaged with from critical perspectives. Like Heckert's strategy of 'deconstructing stories' (cultural narratives) (Heckert 2011: 167) about sex in anarchist sex education, a suggested strategy for challenging this broader and more implicit cultural heteronormativity is that of critical co-reading/viewing, which makes explicit and critically considers the underlying narratives (Robinson 2005: 26). It also takes into account the co-constitutive ambiguity of agency, and is useful to both institutionalised schooling, home schooling and more informal sites of learning that do not even identify as schooling. Relatedly, this has become a fairly established recommended strategy for challenging the power that violent discourses in media may have on developing children (Jones 2003), instead of reducing the analysis to a simplistic idea that media passively shapes children. Robinson states:

> ... far from a call to dismiss the books identified in this discussion outright for their largely inherent heterosexism and sexism (or classism or racism), many such children's texts currently used by educators are critical resources that can provide opportunities to re-examine with children the cultural scripts implicit and explicit in the texts and how they operate to position the readers/viewers. (Robinson 2005: 27)

In this way, Heckert suggests that a specifically anarchist approach to sex education is simultaneously deconstructive ('Anarchist sex education might ... involve sharing skills of deconstructing stories' (Heckert 2011: 167)) and *re*constructive, in that it is 'a practice that changes the present and opens different possibilities for the future' (Heckert 2011: 162). Ze likens per ideal for sex education to amoeba sex (an analogy borrowed from Ursula Le Guin), which is mutual and non-hierarchical, given that amoebas have no sex/gender:

> Anarchic sex education might invite the possibility that human sex could be more like amoeba sex – with (many) genders and with nerve endings! Anarchic sex education might be like amoeba sex, an amoeba orgy in the classroom (or in a social centre or gathering, in the pub or around the kitchen table). Not a worker delivering a pizza: a group of people making a pizza together, or even a group planning to make a pizza, while open to the possibility that it may turn into something else entirely. (Heckert 2011: 163)

Such critical strategies make sense in the ambiguous ontological context outlined in Chapter 5, that currently sexual difference is a compelled norm that is attributed to a person with or without their consent, and the necessity of this critical attitude is exacerbated by the threat of closure. An explicit emphasis on discussing, and deconstructing, aspects of identity and selfhood, especially gender and sexuality norms, is common in Free Skools and similar learning events or spaces (Nicholas, 2009; 2012). Specifically, there is often a specifically queer deconstruction of the mythology of compulsory heterosexuality or heteronormativity. For example, the Between the Lines DIY fest held at the Cowley Club Social Centre in Brighton in 2008 and 2009 involved workshops and discussion groups that were pedagogical in the senses outlined above, with one specifically on the topic of 'different kinds of relationships' (Nicholas 2012). This had deconstructive and concurrent reconstructive aspects, denaturalising dominant relationships and their cultural compulsarity, alongside discussion of alternative means for conducting sexual relationships in a manner that would not oppress, restrict nor exploit others. These kinds of events, such as Between the Lines or Belladonna DIY fest (Wollongong, Australia) commonly have a scheduled discussion or workshop around anarchist or queer deconstructions of gender identity. Combined with collectively developed norms for interaction that are intended to enable all members of a group and resist 'the tyranny of structurelessness' (Freeman 1996 [1070]), which are (ideally) open to critique and improvement, the idea is that these are spaces of deconstructive and reconstructive free play. This is reminiscent of the previously cited 'queeruption' ideal of 'Freiraum', defined if we recall as 'Literally "free-room"; more like "free-dom" ... "the opportunity to move freely and develop one's individual ideas"' (Les Pantheres Roses 2003: n.p.).

Freeschool Vancouver holds explicitly deconstructive 'Sexuality Learning Groups' the genealogical approach of which can be sensed by their central use of Foucault's *The History of Sexuality*, which is a text dedicated to uncovering the origin of contemporary formations of sexuality identity. In a similar deconstructive manner, I have previously charted (Nicholas 2012) Free Skool Santa Cruz's workshop series 'Unpacking Gender Norms', which seeks to 'examine where the gender-binary system and heterosexism come from, how they are carried out, and how we reproduce them within our own communities' (Free Skool Santa Cruz 2008). Such genealogical strategies serve the function of exposing what Beauvoir calls the 'mystification' enacted by such norms, and allows for reinvention on more ethical and purposive terms.

Such practices and the capacity to undertake them are necessarily intersubjectively fostered. As such, Chapter 8 will go on to consider how the relationships between people, and the social/cultural contexts within which people are situated, which are necessarily co-constitutive with the self, can be as enabling as possible, developing these capacities for purposiveness rather than undermining them.

Gender-neutral childrearing

In discussing queer pedagogy, I have outlined that one of the key concerns is that the adult–child relationship is enabling rather than dominating and prescriptive (Robinson 2005), and parenting or childrearing is one of the key sites through which people learn how to be and interact. In an historical context, the 1970s saw some feminist calls for and visions of gender-neutral childrearing (Anderson & McIntyre 1976; Firestone 1972; Piercy 2001 [1979]), the most famous of which is perhaps Firestone's. Per call for the use of reproductive technologies in order that women may be freed from pregnancy and birth was premised on critique of the gendered maternal role and that

> children are defined in relation to this role and are psychologically informed by it; what they become as adults and the sorts of

relationships they are able to form determine the society they will ultimately build. (Firestone 1972: 72)

Contemporaneously gender-neutral childrearing has again become a common topic of controversy in mainstream media, which I will discuss below. What the accounts over both of these eras tend to share is an explicitly ethical basis for this practice, informed by a desire to develop more enabling forms of parenting, and more enabled, less restricted, children.

In Piercy's (2001 [1979]) *Woman on the Edge of Time*, for example, the authority and biological 'enchainment' of parenthood is broken in per imagined future because children are bred outside of bodies: every child has three non-biological mothers, and 'mother' is a non-gendered moniker synonymous with 'parent'. The goal is 'to break the nuclear bonding' (Piercy 1979: 105). Child-rearing is a fundamentally community-based practice, and is not restricted to just the three 'mothers' – a child can choose to live where they please. Challenging the traditional authority of parents, the role of the mothers is not ownership but rather guidance and coexistence. At around the age of 13, all children in Piercy's novel go through a naming ceremony, wherein their autonomy is fostered by being taken to the wilderness and left to choose their name and make their own way home. After this, they and their co-mothers cannot speak or live together for a year. This arrangement demonstrates a valorisation of non-hierarchical nurturing relations conducive to maximum autonomy in individuals. Similarly, Pearson (1977) cites Mary Staton's 1976 sci-fi novel *From the Legend of Biel* as illustrating and envisioning parenting relationships that are emblematic of a reciprocal self/other relation of mentoring: 'The mentor/charge relationship is based on mutual sovereignty [...] two people of relaxed and curious mind, who learn and share together, who confront the unknown, also create joy' (Pearson 1977: 56). Martin (2005) argues that 1970s accounts tended to have crude accounts of socialisation, which tended towards social determinism or structural reduction, and which have been superseded in gender studies. More recently, however, Lorber has argued that 'the separation of sexuality and reproduction, and biological and social parenting, if carried through into new family and kinship structures, might help to dislodge gender' (Lorber 1986: 573). Additionally, following a lull after the 1970s in feminist arguments for gender-neutrality in terms of the attribution of a child's sex/gender (Martin goes so far as to argue that this constituted 'a stalled revolution' (2005: 456)), there have recently been a small number of high-publicity, isolated accounts of attempts to carry out this practice (Green & Friedman 2013), as well as some media attention about gender-neutral toys and gender-neutral pre-schooling. In undertaking media analysis of the discourses around these parenting cases, I determined that the most heavily covered cases were those of Pop and per parents in Sweden, and Storm and per parents in Canada. Also of note was a child called Sasha in the UK.

In more recent cases, the motivations seem consistent with those of the 1970s thinkers. Most of the parents articulate positions that gendered behaviours are to some extent socially produced, paired with an explicit non-coercive principle. Storm's father stated the belief that to make decisions on behalf of your children is 'obnoxious' (Stocker, in Roth 2011: n.p.), Pop's mother hoped it will 'avoid preconceived notions of how people should be treated' (Parafinowicz 2009: n.p.), and Sasha's mother 'wanted to avoid all that stereotyping' (Higginbotham 2012). Storm's parents in particular explicate an enabling ethos and practices that characterise a relational, listening ethic:

> ... the idea to keep the baby's sex private was a tribute to authentically trying to get to know a person, listening carefully and responding to meaningful cues given by the person themselves. (Witterick 2011: n.p.)

As well as deconstructing sex/gender attribution, then, these practices inhere reconstructive, moral principles that transcend sex/gender identity, with an emphasis on the moral conduct of acts, rather than their gender appropriateness. Indeed, Witterick saves per 'energy for non negotiable limit setting related to safety, kindness, self respect, health, fulfilment and fairness' (Witterick 2011: n.p.), and Pop's mother focuses instead on 'self-confidence and personality' (Parafinowicz 2009: n.p.). In the following quotation, Witterick most clearly articulates this desire to foster an alternative value system and developmental context that bypasses gender identity but still offers some functional, positive social guidance about how to conduct oneself in the world:

> When faced with inevitable judgment by others, which child stands tall (and sticks up for others) – the one facing teasing despite desperately trying to fit in, or the one with a strong sense of self and at least two 'go-to' adults who love them unconditionally? Well, I guess you know which one we choose. (Witterick 2011, in Poisson 2011: n.p.)

This is all good and well in a society that has entirely transformed notions of gender, sex and parenting. But, again, this hinges on the issue of cultural resources, intersubjectivity and reading capacities. Often, in isolation, such practices are recuperated by the binary norm or serve only to draw attention to and underscore issues of sex/gender, as demonstrated by the excitement around Sasha's mother revealing that he was 'really' a boy in a dress all along (Higginbotham 2012; McDermott 2011). This can be understood in terms of constituting a

> boundary event (cf. Barthes) in which the collective norms for differentiating self and others are made visibly, viscerally apparent. Rather than being nullified or erased, boundary transgressions etch the boundaries deeper into the collective conscience. (O'Brien 1999: 84)

The power of social context or cultural resources and pragmatic issues of liveability are used as arguments against these longer-term strategies. The debate becomes one of morality and determining 'harm' to the child, commentators asking 'Is Gender-Neutral Parenting Right?' (de Miguel 2012).

Storm's parents' decision met with huge criticism for its potential to 'alienate' (Poisson 2011: n.p.) per from wider society, as evidenced by reader comments on many online news articles charting the story (see for example comments referenced in Roth 2011). Some commentators shared some or all of the analyses regarding the social nature of gender, but the pragmatic, realist concerns over rode this. Storm's mother commented: 'Storm will certainly need to understand his/her own sex and gender to navigate this world (the outcry has confirmed this clearly!)' (Witterick 2011: n.p.). Functionalism trumped utopianism in many critiques: 'kids need to know what their gender identity is as they need to put themselves into a certain position to fully understand social roles and fit in' (Miguel 2012). The reports often quote child psychologists to testify to the necessity of clear gender roles for mental wellbeing (James 2011). These accounts quoted child psychologists to confirm naturalistic ideas of sex/gender ('we all have sexual identity' (James 2011)) or simply asserted the commensense position that 'biological facts are difficult to supress' (Leonard 2011: n.p.), and so declared such practices to be merely 'crude social engineering' (Leonard 2011) and doomed to failure. This account departs from dominant ideas about the naturalness of gender coupled with a liberal voluntarism that does not attribute any effective power to the social, which means a characterisation of the parents as coercively 'imposing their ideology on the child' (Leonard 2011; cf. de Miguel 2012). At the extreme end, attempts to eliminate gendered language and stereotyping in a Swedish pre-school have been described as 'mind control' (Soffel 2011).

It seems, then, that to be effective more widely, such practices would need to inhere cultural resources for reflection by those 'reading' the practices. This requires nuanced reflection on the nature of choice and the constitutive – not just repressive – nature of power and the nature of sex/gender, its origins and its perpetuations, as well as its inherent 'violences'. There is evidence of more nuanced accounts, informed by academic research, creeping into the media, such as Orenstein's (2011; cf. Belkin 2011) piece, which reflects on the desirability of gender-neutral toys, drawing on biological research about the ways that 'gendered play patterns may have a more long-term impact on kids' potential than parents imagine'. An effective undertaking of this kind may seem deeply challenging, but in per visionary call for a politics not resembling 'the anemic, short-sighted, and retrograde politics of the present' (2007: 20) Muñoz argues that 'we must dream and enact ... other ways of being in the world, and ultimately new worlds' (2007: 1). Having outlined some 'other ways of being in the world' and ways of fostering this on an individual level in this chapter, the next chapter will be concerned with how intersubjectivity (i.e. relationships) and social contexts might be otherwise so as to enable, rather than restrict, these other ways.

8
Ethical Post-Gender Sexual Relationships and Communities

The previous chapter discussed some key sites for intervention that might foster individual subjects capable of perceiving themselves, and approaching the world with an androgynous ethos, and with a reciprocal code of conduct (ethics) – that is, subjects capable of resisting gendered subjectivation. In previous chapters I have outlined how greatly the capacities for purposive existence, and the ability to resist sexual difference and essentialising identity, are contingent on an 'equally free other' who is able to resist attributing identity with preconceptions – that is, enabling, reciprocal intersubjectivity between two purposive individuals. I have also, following many social theorists, emphasised throughout how these capacities are deeply contingent on the cultural resources or 'fund of ideas' from which individuals may act.

The example of gender-neutral childrearing with which I ended the previous chapter illustrated that many parents dedicated to an ethos and ethic of self-determination as the ideal mode of being for their children have sought to intervene in the cultural resources from which their children can choose, and through which others relate to them. This example is another illustration of how such practices are ineffective in isolation, and require intervention on a more social scale, as interventions like this can be meaningless or recuperated in a wider social context without the 'cultural resources' for other participants to also 'read' the practices in non-sexed/gendered ways and to not attempt attribution according to existing cultural categories. As Risman emphasises, 'Gender is deeply embedded as a basis for stratification not just in our personalities, our cultural rules, or institutions but in all these, and in complicated ways' (2004: 433).

This chapter is dedicated to considering how relationships between people, and how collective social norms or resources, may be as enabling as possible to maximise the self-determination of individuals in their selfhood and sexuality, and may even imbue these capacities. I will discuss how Foucault and others consider that complete equality in interaction is impossible, but are still dedicated to striving for the most enabling relations possible, and then go on to outline some practical strategies that have been attempted or recommended such that the individuals participating in relations with others can be empowered or imbued with the capacities to (inter)act with as much purposiveness and 'culpability' as possible.

Relatedly, the chapter will then consider how the social environments and cultural resources within which our relations are situated and within which we come to 'be' can be as enabling as possible. Crucially, however, as well as minimising negative coercion, I also consider how cultural contexts or discourses can explicitly foster *positive*, purposive and more 'autonomous' ways of being that I have already argued are ethically desirable. Here, then, I discuss the 'official' legal and medical sexed/gendered cultural categories that pre-exist and shape individuals and their sense of self and the ways that they are treated by others. I chart resistance to these from intersex and trans activists, as well as the development of alternatives and consider the effectiveness of this. I also outline some grassroots queer prefigurative subcultural communities that attempt to foster more androgynous cultural contexts, and imbue social participants with the capacities to be purposive and attempt to minimise the imposition of attribution. In discussing broader interventions, gender-neutral language practices provide the opportunity to discuss how fostering cultural resources might be made more effective. Finally, I will consider how sexuality might be understood and practised without sex/gender, understood instead around ethics of pleasure and consent.

Doing reciprocity together: enabling relations for post-gender ethics

How can intersubjective relations and communication constitute and perpetuate the principles of reciprocity that I have argued would allow purposiveness to flourish? How can the other be related to in their otherness and 'called to account' as a purposive subject without preconceptions? That is, related to without being othered and treated as 'an adversary, an enemy who is wrong, who is harmful and whose very existence constitutes a threat' (Foucault 1984: 382)? Related directly to sexual difference, how can relations be sufficiently open so as not to 'enforce interactional expectations of one another' (Risman, Lorber & Sherwood 2012: 9)? Lorber argues that feminists have to the date of writing 'tended to pay less attention to restructuring sexuality, friendship, and parenting so as to eliminate gender as an organizing principle of intimate relationships' (Lorber 1986: 572). This interactional maintenance of sex/gender is so central that Risman argues 'that the stalled gender revolution ... [can] be traced to the interactional/cultural dimension of the social structure' (2004: 436), that is, a failure to account enough for, and tackle, the weight of the intersubjective. As I emphasised in Chapter 3, there are now various feminist approaches that are concerned with just this, an alternative ethic or way of being within all relationships, such as Noddings' (2003) idea of a friendship ethic or 'ethical caring' that would radically rearrange *all* social relationships. Additionally, there are practices in anarchist, feminist, queer and activist communities that are concerned with transforming and restructuring relationships. These place great ontological emphasis on subjects, in order to minimise the extent to which they take off from hierarchy and dualism, including the negating assumptions of sexual difference. The interactional domain is, then, is a key site for intervening in the perpetuity of sex/gender.

In this section, I argue that traditional ideas of deliberation and consensus as intersubjective models intended to create conditions and outcomes of 'equality' and fairness in collective relations do not account for the ontological realities of inequality that sex/gender so clearly demonstrates. They over-presume the existence of a universalised rationality, and downplay the tacit and informal perpetuation of hierarchy and exclusion through intersubjective and social means. The modes of communication and relation that I propose instead to be more inherently enabling are, firstly, Foucault's 'curiosity' or 'problematization', which leads directly from the idea of the critical subject that I drew on in Chapter 7; and, secondly, Mouffe's agonism, alongside a particular anarchist formulation of consensus that prioritises 'productive dissensus'. These are models of relating or communicating that prequire, and concurrently co-constitute and foster (and therefore do not presume), the ideal capacities for self-determination considered in Chapter 7, and also have mechanisms to avoid collapse into hierarchy. These approaches, I argue, can take heed of the consideration that:

> ... if dialogue is 'essential' to the self, it is in turn important that this self create itself in shapes and forms that contribute to the

maintenance and development of social practices and institutions which enable dialogical modes of being and differences to flourish. (Coles 1992: 85)

I shall then outline how these enabling interactional ideals may be put into practice, discussing the means by which certain anarchist and radical communities attempt to implement and maintain reciprocal means of relating and making decisions. Various of the examples throughout Chapters 7 and 8 are drawn from anarchist communities or collectivities, which proceed from the contemporary perspective of anarchism as a relational ethic as opposed to a homogenous political ideology. As discussed previously, this is an ontologically *inter*subjective perspective, which conceptualises the self as potentiality, and it and ethics shaped in relation and situation. For Heckert, for example, anarchist practice 'means supporting each other to develop our capacities to listen, to cooperate, to connect, to share, to imagine. Nurturing autonomy, then, is empowerment – the realisation that power isn't something that other people *have*, its something we *do* together' (Heckert 2009: 3). What I wish to explore in this chapter is through what practices this positive, reciprocal, enabling power can be *done*. How can we foster reciprocal relations between subjects that allow for maximum purposive action, specifically in relation to identity and sexual identity?

The relational ideal: enabling, truly dialogical communication

I will outline here how Foucault's model of dialogism (1984) and Mouffe's ideal of 'productive dissensus' (Mouffe 1997) are emblematic of how the principles of the 'queer ethic' that I outlined in Chapter 5 could play out in practice in relations between people such that these relations are not led by the restrictions of sex/gender identity. These approaches are premised in the fundamentally interactional nature of being, but strive to consider how this could be as enabling as possible. Using them, I will outline how this mode of relating would need to centre on principle-based, procedural concerns rather than blueprints or end-points, and be guided by the 'universal particular' principle that 'people are different from one another' (Sedgwick 1990: 22). This represents a way of relating that does not need (and deconstructs) preconceptions of fixed identity, but could be ceaselessly open to the other 'in their otherness', allowing them maximum purposiveness in how they 'become', and thus is concurrently reconstructive. Mouffe articulates the non-foundational premises that models of democratic communication need to heed in per account:

> It is only by drawing all the implications of the critique of essentialism ... that it is possible to grasp the nature of the political and acknowledge the challenge to which the democratic project is today confronted. (Mouffe 1997: 24)

These models are developed in contradistinction from liberal models of supposedly free communication. Proponents of liberal ideals of consensus propose that consensus following deliberation is the best relation between people to guarantee as much self-determination as possible (Benhabib 1996; Gaus 2002; Michelman 2002). This model of communication they see as fundamental to the operation of democracy. However, they are forced to concede that the premise required for self-determined decision-making in these contemporary liberal models of democratic deliberation is unobtainable, and critics suggest that the ideal ends that they propose, that of a harmonious consensus, represent a homogeny and must necessarily privilege certain perspectives that will dominate dissenting perspectives. This is directly allegorical to the problem of closure identified as inherent to homogenous identity categories and the way that they shape what is possible in interaction, and thus for subjectivity. Solutions to the impasses of such homogenous consensus in communication between subjects, usually contrasted to value-free antagonism, are therefore usefully applied to my problem here of how. The problem is, then, how the other might be related to in a way that is proliferated enough to allow for self-determination without preconceptions of identity, but also underpinned by a universal ethic that means antagonism does not degenerate into negation. As my central argument proposes, conduct can be procedurally guided by thin universal principles that still allow for dissensus, proliferation and difference of internal perspectives, but with a mutual respect and without negation.

In the liberal model, 'a policy ... is justified only if it can, in some way, be embraced by all members of the public' (Gaus 2002: 206) – that is, there is the assumption that the ideal state is that of universal consensus. The universalism may be more or less gentle, for example, liberal feminist Benhabib proposes that this reaching of consensus should resemble 'wooing consent' (1992: 136). A key issue with this end-point of consensus, however, is that people cannot get along with or fully know *all* others – 'no single individual can anticipate and foresee all the variety of perspectives through which matters of ethics and politics would be perceived by different individuals' (Benhabib 1996: 71). Thus, substitutionalism must occur in this process of the 'social contract', and those with power universalise their own position and assume it applies to all others. Universal consensus is a utopian fantasy. The following definition from Della Porta of 'deliberative participatory democracy' as used in Social Movement Studies demonstrates what actually would be necessary for a *real* equality of this opportunity to exist in communication and such that true consensus could be reached:

> ... decisional processes in which, under conditions of equality, inclusiveness, and transparency, a communicative process based on reason (the strength of good argument) may transform individual preferences, leading to decisions oriented to the public good. (Della Porta 2009: 1)

However, these preconditions are much like those of the Rawlsian 'original position' that has been exhaustively critiqued, and such perfect conditions are not possible, and neither is an objective, universal reason or objectively 'good argument'. Further, if we take seriously the extent to which power dynamics can be tacit, and 'developmental' power can so easily congeal into dominating power in interaction, the intended outcome of transforming others could easily constitute a coercive process. Even 'wooing' indicates a process whereby one person attempts to convince another/others to their position, rather than equals coming to a joint decision.

I have argued that a key problem underpinning sex/gender is the extent that it negates the freedom of individuals by imposing a way of seeing on to them that is tacit and naturalised. I have proposed as an alternative an inexhaustible reciprocity that follows the lead from 'the other' in interaction with them. For the ideal of reciprocity to work, a form of intersubjective communication is required that is instead enabling to others and allows us to approach others 'in their otherness' (Beauvoir 1976a: 67), and does not hold the aim of homogenous consensus, or 'wooing the other' to our own way of seeing the world. Following the premises outlined in Chapter 5 that 'our capacity to imagine other people is very small' (Scarry 1996: 103), consensus as an ideal end-point is always going to result in homogenising others and imposing ideals upon them. So, what if we get rid of consensus, what kind of perspective or ethics can inform a more intersubjective, reciprocal code of conduct that can help us to 'get along' without closure or imposition of identity?

Here I build on the principle of the queer ethical axiom that 'People are different from one another' (Sedgwick 1990: 22) can be universally applied in an open-ended manner to each person in their particularity. Following this, I argue that the best outcome and guiding principle for a reciprocal mode of relating to the other 'in their [particular] otherness' (Beauvoir 1976a: 67) is approaching the other to achieve 'the maximum sense one can attain' of them (Coles 1992: 84). Consequently, this half of the chapter explores ways of communicating, deliberating and getting along socially with others that take 'productive dissensus' (Mouffe 1997) as an alternative guiding principle for truly enabling relations that might imbue people with the capacity to approach others without preconceptions of sex/gender, but still with enabling guiding principles. A key aspect of these alternative models is that they do not idealise a closed end-point where disagreement has been resolved: 'justice should always remain an open question' (Mouffe 1997: 27–28).

Drawing inspiration from relational anarchist ethics, Heckert (2009: 4) states that 'nurturing autonomy' requires getting beyond this unachievable consensus ideal and 'learning to get along with those I don't seek out'. In other words, this entails getting along with people who do not already share your perspective, and may never, without trying to force them to do so. That is, it entails dealing with dissensus in a productive manner. Exemplary here are Foucault's 'dialogical ethics', most practically outlined in an interview entitled 'Polemics, Politics, and Problematizations' (1984). This dialogical model for intersubjectivity is contrasted to Habermas's notion of consensus, which, Coles (1992) argues, inheres connotations of '*imposing* an agreement' (Coles 1992: 82). Foucault rejects the approach of polemicists whose 'final objective will be, not to come as close as possible to a difficult truth, but to bring about the triumph of the just cause he has been manifestly upholding since the beginning' (Foucault 1984: 382). In avoiding homogenisation and taking proliferation seriously, this practice, described as 'reciprocal elucidation', is exemplary of an approach 'that affirms both difference and solidarity' (Coles 1992: 73). In this way, Foucault describes this messy, perpetual process as a 'game [that] … is at once pleasant and difficult' (Foucault 1984: 381). Echoing the interminability that such an approach to relating necessitates, Le Guin proposes that 'intersubjectivity is mutual. It is a continuous interchange between two consciousnesses. Instead of an alternation of roles between box A and box B, between active subject and passive object, it is a continuous intersubjectivity that goes both ways all the time' (Le Guin 2004, in Heckert 2011: 163).

Instead of consensus, Mouffe (1997) and Foucault (1984) character-ise intersubjective conflict as not *a priori* negating and hierarchical, in the context of the 'ineradicable character' of 'power and antagonism' (Mouffe 1997: 24). Rather, it is the way that antagonism is carried out that determines this, that is, it is procedural, and these thinkers formu-late ways to foster *positive* antagonism. The question, for Mouffe,

> ... is not how to arrive at a rational consensus reached without exclu-sion. Indeed, this would mean establishing an 'us' that would not have a corresponding 'them' which, as I have argued, is impossible. What is at stake is how to establish the us/them discrimination in a way that is compatible with pluralistic democracy. (1997: 26)

Clarifying this approach that advocates universal principles, but proliferated practices, Mouffe calls for 'consensus on the principles and dissensus on their interpretation' (Mouffe 1997: 27–28). The question then becomes, how, in practice, can potential antagonism be positively rechannelled into this ideal agonism? Foucault's critical subject (outlined in the previous chapter) can be usefully extended as an ideal for intersubjectivity, as a critical mode of approaching the other. In this way, critique 'is something we must do to ourselves *and* to one another, for which we must constantly invent or re-invent the means, the techniques, the strategies and the spaces' (Rajchman 2007: 14 my emphasis). If Mouffe's 'productive dissensus' is the principle, then Foucault's anti-polemical idea of communication as 'dialogical' is the ideal elucidation of what the internal, procedural characteristics of Mouffe's broad principles might look like. Indeed, summarising this non-homogenising intersubjective ethic, Foucault elaborates: '*I insist on this difference as something essential*; a whole morality is at stake, the morality that concerns the search for the truth and the relation to the other' (Foucault 1984: 381, my emphasis).

Allegorically, Heckert (2010) theorises a central component of the practice of relational anarchism to be procedural, rather than prescrip-tive about particular behaviours or identities, centred on the process of *listening* to the other. Heckert draws inspiration for per vision of anarchist practice from Non Violent Communication: 'Through its emphasis on deep listening – to ourselves as well as others – NVC fosters respect, attentiveness and empathy' (NVC 2009). This is conceptualised by NVC as a *learned* practice that is dialogical, and thus I will consider below some practices through which different subcultures, collectives and groups have attempted to foster or enable this ethic.

Reciprocal relations in practice

Productive dissensus in communication

What, then, would a situation where there is 'consensus on the principles and dissensus on their interpretation' (Mouffe 1997: 27–28) look like? Many anarchist and radical political approaches to organising and communicating represent more radically and directly democratic means of organising and of understanding 'consensus' than would be possible in liberal models. While I do not deny that some anarchist and radical communities congeal into just the tyranny and lack of inclusivity that I have critiqued above (as noted in ethnographic studies of anarchist communities such as Graeber 2009), they are also the source of some imaginative progressive practices that, I argue, may represent enabling ways of interacting.

Anarchist approaches to consensus tend to contain a developmental aspect, wherein the capacities to participate are not assumed, but explicitly fostered. They often attempt to empower people to understand the 'rules', and in turn the 'rules' and their development are often intended to be transparent and open to criticism and alteration. Della Porta (2009) notes that understandings and uses of the idea of 'consensus' are as diverse among social movements as the movements themselves. It is one specific usage of consensus I draw on as particularly useful in forwarding the principles of a reciprocal ethic that evades negation and closure. I am keen not to create a strict typology of social movements, following much of the literature, particularly on social movement organisations (SMOs), that has shifted from overly agentic formulations of political actors to a more nuanced understanding of the ways that environmental and cultural influences combine with organisational agency (Della Porta 2009). However, in some anarchist and other activist communities there are examples of cultural practices that attempt to foster communication that evades closure and maintains intersubjectivity. These seem, as I will outline below, to hold a realistic conception of the intersubjective perpetuation of power.

For example, the following quotation concerns an approach to consensus by the British Climate Collective, which is *not* about a telos of homogenous closure, encourages a genuinely open disposition and is careful to avoid an ideal of convincing others to join a predetermined plan:

> The aim [of the consensus process] is not for one person to convince everyone else that they alone are right, but for the group to reach a collective decision that takes everyone's ideas, opinions

and concerns into consideration. It requires that people genuinely consider what will work best for the group, think about what others in the group would like and attempt to create a solution. (Climate Collective 2009: 3)

This valorises 'autonomy' alongside an understanding that autonomy is constituted in conjunction with others, which informs an ideal practice of *listening* to the perspective of others. For me, this evokes Piercy's utopian vision in *Woman on the Edge of Time*, of collective communication strategies that try to transcend the false dichotomy between homogenous community interest vs. atomised pluralistic interest. This is the ontology of 'being singular plural' (Nancy, in Muñoz 2009: 10). While conflict, disagreement and divergence of opinion, that is, dissensus, is an aspect of life in the fictional future utopian community of Mattapoisett, there is a practice of 'worming' to facilitate the airing and resolution of conflicts, based on attempting to understand the perspective of the other: 'we try to comprehend that hostility and see if we can defuse it' (Piercy 2001 [1979]: 207). Rather than departing from predetermined assumptions of commonality, these processes create temporal, strategic bonds. This is allegorical to the performative process that Noterman & Pusey (2012), drawing on Linebaugh, call 'a process of "commoning." Commoning is the "doing" of the common(s), a verb rather than a noun, a process rather than a static resource or product' (190).

Further, the Climate Collective emphasise the disposition that the individual must take on in order to participate in a reciprocal manner. It is an ethic of openness in which opinions are not pre-decided, and it is not about 'winning' the game of wooing:

Participants in the meeting should be ready to alter their positions as the meeting uncovers ideas and possibilities that they may not have considered before. It helps if people are respectful and trust each other: Think before you speak, listen before you object. (Climate Collective 2009: 3)

This reflects Foucault's rejection of polemics and valorisation of 'dialogical ethics' and a 'limit attitude', the process of which Coles describes as non-teleological, open-ended:

What is involved here is dwelling with a 'patient labour' at the limits of our being, where dialogically we consider that which and those who we are not, not in order to secure a universal rationality, but to explore the shapes of our lives and social practices at their limits with an eye to how it might be possible and desirable to fashion our lives and limits differently. (Coles 1992: 87)

Some of the practices engaged in by anarchist communities, while idealising 'equality' inhere an acknowledgment of the reality of different levels of agency with which individuals are imbued, and fostering these is sometimes part of their overall deliberative ideal. For example, 'progressive speaking lists' attempt to strategically acknowledge existing hierarchies resulting from existing dominant subject-positions and imbue confidence:

> ... the 'progressive speaking list', which allows the facilitators to be flexible in taking points, so that if someone who has not yet spoken raises their hand, the facilitator can take their point before that of someone else who has spoken more often. The purpose is to encourage as many people to participate and have their voices heard as possible, and attempts to overcome the domination of space by a small number of confident individuals. (Climate Collective 2009: 3)

In the various queer groups, meetings, workshops and anarchist and activist meetings and groups I have participated in, there are a number of variations on the progressive speaking list. These range from informal flexibility on the part of the facilitator of meetings/discussions, to more institutionalised, formal procedures, such as a list of priorities according to gender, ethnicity, (dis)ability and age. Additionally, many groups and collectives recognise the extent to which full agency is contingent on 'social techniques, skills and trainings' (Hurley 1990: 156). In this context, these can be fostered and made transparent through information and guidelines on the cultural norms of different decision-making styles that are distributed at actions/meetings and so on. These demonstrate the attempted explication of social norms that I have identified as key for preventing their hegemony, such that control does not become concentrated. This is something that I have witnessed, for example, at G8 counter summits, Climate Camps and Queer Symposiums. The Italian Social Justice Group *Rete Lilliput*, for example, understand that the capacity to participate is contingent on certain things, such as access to information, and states in its manifesto that it favours 'fast and complete circulation of information, in order to allow for the construction of processes based upon consensus' (Della Porta 2009: 84). Many groups are open to constant critique and have fully open, participatory working groups in which anyone can engage in developing organisational practices, and some groups implement rotation, such that people do not stay in working groups for too long and acquire (intentional or not) authority in that area.

I have discussed here some fairly institutional, political relationships that emblematise enabling intersubjectivity. The following section will consider some of the ways that intimate or dyadic relationships can be self-consciously reciprocal, and stay as such. This illustrates how relations can be structured without the predetermined roles and hierarchies of compulsory sexual difference and according to the principles of maximum pleasure, autonomy and reciprocity, which I argue are central to obviating sexual difference.

Anarchist and queer approaches to intimate relationships

Alternative approaches to relationships, for example, anarchist, queer, feminist, 'non-violent' approaches, are of interest here because they are explicitly concerned with *practical strategies* for how intersubjective, often dyadic, relationships may be engaged in such that they enable both participants. That is, without restricting the purposiveness of participants by becoming hierarchical around oppositional, antagonistic difference. Some of the strategies discussed in these accounts represent reciprocity, through the principles of non-coercive and nurturing relations, lack of presumptions and 'scrupulous visibility'.

A valuable aspect of much writing on alternative intimate relations that could be usefully extended to any intersubjective relationships is the idea that expectations of partners should not be assumed to correlate with dominant cultural expectations. In the case of sexual relationships, this is articulated in literature from largely monogamous societies in the minority world as not assuming that your partner also expects the relationship to be monogamous, ensuring that both parties talk to and listen to each other and reach agreement on the type of relationship both desire (Easton & Lizst 1997; Matik 2002). The principle of reciprocity could, of course, equally be applied to the inverse and still allows for monogamy so long as it is *consensual* monogamy. I have already mentioned that it is common in various alternative communities to encounter discussion and practice around 'different kinds of relationships'. I discussed in the previous chapter a workshop/discussion group of this name with the intention of fostering critical thinking in regard to dominant structures of relationships. Likewise, Free Skool Santa Cruz holds a discussion group entitled 'Love

Unabashedly: The undefining of relationships', and the ideas that they explore there are not identities, but rather *practices* and *principles* that are to do with maximum pleasure and maximum purposiveness: 'autonomy, consent, negotiation, respect, and pleasure' (Free Skool Santa Cruz). Reflecting this shift to the principle of purposiveness and away from evaluating identities seen in many radical communities, the authors of polyamory guide *The Ethical Slut* (Easton & Lizst 1997) propose that sexual relationships should be ethical relations, and call for less implicit assumption and prescription and greater agency for people in formulating their ideal ways of structuring relations. This is a strategy for avoiding the coercion and normatising of imposed, universalising dominant models of sexual relationships. The same principles of questioning presumptions and listening to the other outlined for collective intersubjective communication above are indispensable in maintaining reciprocity in an intimate relationship. This ethical ideal of a focus on responsibility to the other, of listening to the other in a relationship of reciprocity as opposed to a simplistic notion of two individuals in atomised autonomy is, I argue, what could prevent these models from assumptions of what Robinson calls 'unproblematic sexual agency' (Robinson 1997: 154). As such, this approach to non-monogamy or radical, chosen monogamy is premised on an intersubjectively constitutive understanding of power and capacities, and seems to evade the over- and under-emphases of agency, or negative associations that Robinson (1997) has identified in most discussions of the topic. In being an attempt to implement a positive relational ethic, these 'radical love' (Matik 2002) approaches are more like the more reflective 'conscious feminist politics which sees non-monogamy as a potentially radical act' (Robinson 1997: 154) that Robinson envisaged as more ideal. As ever, intersubjective ideals require the co-existence of subjective capacity, and enabling sociality: 'any potential that non-monogamous relationships have to enable more democratic, honest and less possessive ways of being, may also necessitate a degree of self-knowledge, if gendered relationships are to be more equal' (Robinson 1997: 155).

This correlation between subjects, interpersonal relationships and social context is also apparent in anarchist and queer community approaches to intersubjective consent, and specifically sexual consent. These approaches constitute prefigurative social practices and will be discussed in depth below, but I shall engage with some aspects of them here because they attempt to put into practice the anarchist ethic of intersubjective listening, described by Heckert (2010).

As I have discussed elsewhere (Nicholas 2009), anarchist, anarcho-queer and radical queer spaces often develop safer space policies to encourage their ethical ideals in interpersonal relations. While anarchism is sometimes understood as dogmatic and as a set of specific beliefs, such policies demonstrate an approach to anarchism that has more in common with Heckert's articulation of it as a relational ethic, discussed earlier. These policies demonstrate the self-conscious minimal normative ethic by calling for adherence to the principle of respect for others. The particular policies I have investigated are developed collectively and inclusively, and are open to critique by all members of the community/collective, akin to the working groups described above. Auckland Anarchist Conference 2007 developed an emblematic policy that demonstrates an ideal of collective freedom, akin to that of Beauvoir. This involves a valorisation of purposive or 'autonomous' action, and enabling intersubjectivity, and a disavowal of action that negates the purposive or 'autonomous' action of others. In the following statement/policy, the only behaviour that is regulated is that which imposes on others:

> People attending this conference are asked to be aware of their language and behaviour, and to think about whether it might be offensive to others. This is no space for violence, for touching people without their consent, for being intolerant of someone's religious beliefs or lack thereof, for being creepy, sleazy, racist, ageist, sexist, hetero-sexist, trans-phobic, able-bodiest, classist, sizist or any other behaviour or language that may perpetuate oppression. (aspaceinside 2008: n.p.)

Such 'safer spaces' policies are common in anarchist social centres or community events, for example the Cowley Club Libertarian Social Centre in Brighton, UK, at some DIY anarchist punk concerts, at queer club nights, queer sex parties, and at festivals, conferences and gatherings such as Queeruption and Queer Mutiny (which I will discuss in more detail in the next section). There are also cultural products such as zines (e.g. *Creating Safer Spaces*, *Support Zine* and *What Do We Do When?*), which engage the issue specifically of sexual consent and serve as enabling discourses.

The explicitly erotic spaces in queer communities such as play spaces, play parties or sex parties common at events such as Queeruption, or as one-off events organised by various collectives internationally, invariably entail such safer spaces policies. The policies themselves are usually collectively created, and participants are asked to consent to before entering the space (Nicholas 2012). Brown, in per ethnographic research in such communities, describes this as 'the process of collectively defining an ethics of care [which] was an important element of the gathering's experiment in queer social autonomy' (Brown 2007b: 2694). These policies 'impose' (ideally through collective deliberation and consensus) a principle-based (not identity-derived) queer sexual ethics, which I elaborated as reconstructive but minimally prescriptive in Chapter 5, their concern being ethical conduct, not what or who one does, but that *how* it is done is consensual.

This more prefigurative practice of fostering social contexts that are conducive to and nurturing of purposive, autonomous action and reciprocal relations is a useful segue into the discussion following. The next section is concerned more explicitly with how prefigurative social practices and cultural resources can allow for and foster – as much as possible – reciprocity and thus (as far as possible) autonomy. My principal argument is that they can do this by providing alternative cultural discourses that constitute subject-positions within which individuals can position themselves.

Enabling, post-gender cultural resources: 'transcending immanence in concert with others'

This section will consider how the more macro, societal and institutional level of intervention could be engaged by groups of individuals to foster enabling social contexts and try to preclude impulses to closure and domination. I will chart intersex activism that seeks to expand medical and legal categorisations of sex/gender. I will then draw on prefigurative practices that are intended to develop and maintain more androgynous modes of perception and reciprocal relational ethics. Given the extent to which individuals are enabled (or not) by norms and 'there is a desire for norms that might let one live' (Butler 2004: 3), the practices considered here will be discussed regarding the extent to which they are collectively effective and support the capacities necessary for partaking in them.

I have already charted how Gagne & Tewkesbury (1998) emphasise social and intersubjective 'conformity pressures' on transgender folk in some contexts, including sometimes within trans communities. I argued in Chapter 2 that it is the delimiting pre-existence of only two cultural and institutional categories of binary gender, *(re)produced* intersubjectively and subsequently internalised, that constitutes this pressure: 'Transgendered individuals' understandings of themselves and their ability to formulate alternative identities depended upon existing *cultural categories* as well as *institutional pressures* to be one gender or the other' (Gagne & Tewkesbury 1998: 95, emphasis added). Broader social and cultural norms are a co-constitutive site of social conservatism and therefore conversely of possible social change. Given that meanings are contingent on 'reading formations' (Hurley 1990) or a 'practice of reading' ... what we call "capacity"' (Butler 2005: 29), I will consider how collective discourses could be intervened within, without their recuperation by dominant discourses. I have discussed in Chapter 7 how subjects may be fostered who would have the capacities to engage in ways of being that do not rely on the cultural categories of agonistic difference, given conducive contexts. Here, I go on to consider what these equally necessary more proliferated, more enabling contexts themselves may look like.

Deregulating dimorphism: intersex rights

As Butler emphasises, the availability or not of both formal and informal 'modes of intelligibility' such as sex/gender categories makes life more or less liveable (2004). Returning us once again to the central motivation for this book, the lack of modes of intelligibility for intersex people who do not feel represented by male/female is for Butler a violence that renders those who transgress sex/gender duality as 'less-than-human' (Butler 2004: 2): 'I may feel that without some recognisability I cannot live. But I may also feel that the terms by which I am recognized make life unliveable' (Butler 2004: 4).

This makes the compulsarity of only two sex categories through which we come to be, and come to understand each other, perpetuated by legal and medical categories and medical practices, a key site for challenging the maintenance and dominance of 'bigenderism'. In terms of raising the visibility of bodies that challenge biological sexual difference, and of subjective identifications that exceed binary gender, Germany and Australia have recently made moves towards expansion of legal categories, and support for 'third sex' options is growing (Bibby 2013; Nandi 2013). India allows a third identification of 'E' for Eunuch on some official documents, and both India and Nepal have a third category on their census (Knight 2012). Australian Norrie May-Welby sees such acts as symbolically important for the subjective and social possibility of being recognised not as gendered, but simply as humyn (in Mitchell 2011), a strategy for raising awareness of such binary transgression more widely.

As identified in Chapter 1, it is still common medical practice in many places to 'assign' infants to definitive sex categories when they are physically ambiguous. For example, in my place of residence, 'The Royal Children's Hospital Melbourne currently performs one or two gonadectomies a year on infants with undescended testes [and] 10 to 15 genital reconstruction operations a year often on girls under the age of two' (Bock 2013). Chase argues that 'paediatric genital surgeries literalize ... the attempted production of normatively sexed bodies and gendered subjects through constitutive acts of violence' (Chase 1998: 189), and resistance to medically unnecessary surgery is visible and growing, with notable impact on the medical establishment (Greenberg 2012).

Considering political strategy, in per germinal statement of intersex politics, Chase also notes that as well as harming individuals and impacting on their autonomy in immediate contexts, this medical intervention results in the near-invisibility of intersexuality in public knowledge and thus the perpetuation of naturalised assumptions of dimorphism. Chase considers more awareness of intersexuality as an important strategy for undermining the false normalising assumptions that render intersex a problem, which may in turn minimise some of the psychological and social harm suffered by intersex people in the long term. Ze characterises awareness raising as 'an opportunity to deploy "nature" strategically to disrupt heteronormative systems of sex, gender and sexuality' (Chase 1998: 190).

However, Greenberg (2012) outlines how recent intersex rights strategies have become more varied and ze charts some tension in approaches. There are those who advocate an integrated approach with the medical institution. This approach tends to draw on the language of DSD (disorders of sex development), and they propose that working with the medical establishment will 'enhance the overall health and wellbeing of persons with DSD' (Consensus, in Greenberg 2012: 91). Greenberg characterises this as distinct from those who reject medicalisation and hold the aim of 'depathologizing gender nonconformity' (2012: 92). Activists following Chase's line of reasoning suggest that the adoption of DSD may be an attempt, or at least an occasion, to further invisibilise the existence of non-dimorphic sex and reinforce binary gender, for example, by parents who 'dislike the terms "intersex" because they believe it implies that their child is "in-between" sexes' (Greenberg 2012: 93). Greenberg suggests this may be illustrated by some intersex activists who seek to distance themselves from trans activism (2012: 95). However, ze also emphasises that it is important that the specific political struggles of intersex people are not 'co-opted' by other political agendas, of which mine is perhaps paradigmatic. Likewise, Dreger & Herndon (2009) remind academics to 'write about intersex people on their own terms rather than just appropriate intersex for talking about other issues like the social construction of gender' (2009: 218). However, there are intersex individuals and collectives who advocate expansion of understandings of sex and gender both on its own terms *and* as a more effective strategy for making life more liveable for those born with 'indeterminate' sex. Australian Organisation Intersex International (OII), for example, seeks to 'help people to understand that there are not just two pre-existing sexes' (Greenberg 2012: 94). It is Chase's more radical position, however, that 'intersex activists have deep stakes in allying with and participating in the sorts of post-structuralist cultural work that exposes ... foundational assumptions about personhood' (Chase 1998: 208).

Queer prefiguration: queeruption

I have made regular reference to contemporary radical queer communities such as Queer Mutiny and Queeruption, and I address here how it is that they attempt to function as prefigurative spaces. In the context of Butler's ontology, Allen suggests how social movements could form part of the picture of resistance and empowerment:

> Collective social movements, such as the feminist and the queer movements, generate conceptual and normative resources, create networks of psychological and emotional support, and foster counterpublic spaces, all of which aid individuals in their efforts to resist regulatory regimes by providing new modes of recognition, new possibilities for attachment and thus, new ways of becoming subjects. (Allen 2010: n.p.)

This is exactly the purpose of prefiguration, described as 'the demonstration or rehearsal or sample of how life could be in a better world [which] is usually but not always transgressive' (Greenway, in Bowen & Purkis 1997: 175). It is my position that, through the collective development of new norms, these subcultures maximise the critical relation that 'depends ... on a capacity, invariably collective, to articulate an alternative, minority version of sustaining norms or ideals that enable me to act' (Butler 2004: 3), which might allow greater autonomy of sexual and gender(/free) identity. The two movements named above act more as monikers than fixed entities. As with other contemporary anarchist or autonomist monikers that work in this way (Nicholas 2007), each can be taken up and engaged by groups anywhere for a variety of collective purposes such as the purpose of naming a collective that meets regularly and organises events in a town or a temporary collective for the purpose of a specific event or gathering. Queeruption is perhaps more continuous and less ephemeral as it has a more permanent central email list and has been held annually in different international locations for some years, but the organising committee is autonomous and changes yearly. To give some sense of their ethos, Queeruption describes itself as an a space for 'alternative/radical/disenfranchised queers' (in Nicholas 2009: 8) and the 'opportunity for Queers of all genders and sexualities to gather, celebrate queerness and diversity – to share experiences, fun stories, ideas, listen and learn from each other' (in Vanelslander 2007: 1; cf. Brown 2007b). Brown describes their 'affiliations' as 'broadly aligned with the anarchist and anticapitalist wings of the global justice movement' (Brown 2007b: 2685), and describes their 'usage of the term "queer" ... to refer to a variety of states of being that challenge both homonormativity and heteronormativity' (Brown 2007b: 2685). Also worth noting is the international nature of Queeruption, which is held in a different location annually, admittedly almost entirely in the minority world, but attempts have been noted to connect with 'radical queer groups in Argentina, Israel/Palestine, Serbia, and Turkey' (Brown 2007b: 2689).

These explicitly political spaces 'pose ... questions about what it means to be an activist' (Brown 2007b: 2686), and I characterise them as prefiguratively political, or ethico-political (Nicholas 2007), with a nuanced, multi-layered understanding of how norms and domination are perpetuated. Prefiguration has been considered in anarchist theory as practically nurturing and fostering the ontological *potentiality* for mutual aid and 'autonomy', in similar non-foundational and non-coercive terms to the pedagogical approaches discussed in Chapter 7 (Bowen & Purkis 1997; Franks 2006; Heckert 2009). Prefiguration has unsurprisingly been dismissed as individualistic 'lifestyle' anarchism by critics who restrict their understanding of 'power' to the state (Churchill 2004; Franks 2006: 268–269), but prefiguration can be characterised as politically effective if power is understood as relational or diffuse, as in many contemporary or poststructuralist approaches to anarchism (Heckert 2010; May 1994; Newman 2001). It is also inherently pedagogical insofar as it is a way that people can 'teach and learn' modes of being without explicit frameworks, according to more informal ethical principles and codes, and perhaps most importantly through voluntary association and without coercion. It provides alternative discourses and modes of thought to relate to, which ideally supplements and complements the development of autonomous subjects and reciprocal relations.

Ideally, prefiguration acknowledges ontological situatedness, emphasising the need to 'create a community of allies' (Bergoffen 2004: 85) and positive, enabling 'constitutive projects and attachments' (Sandel 1982: 181). I argue that the prefiguration noted as a historically continuous, but contemporaneously expanding aspect of anarchism can be understood as an ideal *re*constructive supplement to oppositional critique: 'breaking rules for the sake of breaking rules is merely transgressive. Breaking rules to produce new realities is prefigurative' (Heckert 2005: 42).

Queeruption and related spaces and communities demonstrate an attempt to practise this concurrent critical stance *and* reconstruction of new values by 'building alternatives and living our dreams' (Queeruption London, in Brown 2007b: 2693). They also represent a concurrently individual *and* collective prefigurative enabling function: 'queeruptors are interested in making modest, low-key attempts to re-engage their "power to-do", which is always part of a social process of doing with others' (Brown 2007a: 197). Like those resources outlined above intended to disseminate the knowledge required for participating in the consensus processes, Queeruption also entails a number of modes of communication, for example the Queeruption 'reader/guide/fanzine' (Vanelslander 2007: 1), which familiarises people with the general ethos and some of the language such that the playing field is more equal. Notably, the events also foster and reflect on their 'common perspective' through pre-event communications such as email lists, organising committees and during daily general meetings held at the event, which are collective and participatory (Vanelslander 2007). Vanelslander in particular notes the usefulness of 'structural preparation (such as mission statements, including definitions of "queer", decision making, violence etc.)' (2007: 3). The way that prefiguration interacts with the individual and enables new capacities in interaction with others is beautifully summarised in Vanelslander's (2007) autoethnographic reflections on 'putting the queer ideal into practice' at Queeruption 2004 in Amsterdam, which discusses the use in these spaces of gender-neutral language:

> a process of consciously dealing with gender in language could be observed, especially in the attempts of avoiding gender-specific expressions. Personally, I experienced Queeruption Amsterdam as an enormous challenge not to assume or even define people's identity (especially their gender), either in language or in thought.

If queers want the broader society to break down gender boundaries, I experienced Queeruption as an occasion to start with myself. (Vanelslander 2007: 2)

This quotation places Queeruption as a space that is attempting to be mindful of and enact a great many of the themes of this book. That is, the realities of the relationships between individuals and collectivities and the extent to which intersubjective reciprocity is a 'game ... [that is] is at once pleasant and difficult' (Foucault 1984: 381), as well as the importance of taking cues from the other about their selfhood in interaction to avoid imposition of preconceptions. Additionally, the extent to which this space attempted to foster gender neutrality *consciously* rather than tacitly, resonating with the argument that to be truly prefigurative and nurturing, rather than in some way coercive, strategies should be completely visible. There is also a clear ethic of self-critique in these spaces, as noted in the earlier example of a zine article about 'dogmas in the queer scene' (Les Panther Roses 2003). An example offered by Vanelslander (2007) is that of a reversal of a language hegemony that had come about, wherein a group of non-native English speakers noted that meetings had begun to sideline their ability to participate fully because of being consistently held in English with insufficient translation. They initiated a reflection on this, which led to a reversal of this dynamic, with Spanish as the primary language and English translation. In my own experience, a similar attempt was made by participants of Queeruption Vancouver who did not drink alcohol. There was a sense that alcohol consumption was beginning to take over the event and so, after a communal general meeting, the dynamic was reversed by making the designated drinking area the minority space. The effectiveness of such ideal strategies is, of course, not perfect and the constant struggle of attempting 'analysis interminable' (Fuss 1991: 6) should not be underestimated. As utopian speculative fiction to which I have already referred illustrates (Le Guin 1974; Piercy 2001 [1979]), the possibility of closure in idealistic communities is ever present, leading Vanelslander (2007) to argue that queer ideals seem to work better in temporal contexts. As one participant observed, 'queertopia was exhausting' (Lechat, in Brown 2007b: 2695).

Post-gender prefiguration and gender-neutral language

Gender-transcendent prefiguration is not restricted to queer or radical communities. There was controversy recently when a Swedish preschool opted to aim for an environment free of sex/gender distinctions.

They addressed this through selection of books, mixing of 'gendered' toys and use of gender-neutral language, such as the Swedish gender-neutral term 'hen', or by referring to each other 'as "friends" [or] by their first names' (Hebblethwaite 2011).

As well as being part of subcultural and grassroots politics, then, prefiguration can also be part of more institutional and mainstream political practice. Also in Sweden, an Advertising Standards Authority pressured a toy retailer to produce less gendered catalogues (Ditum 2012), and Sweden has also recently added gender-neutral pronoun 'hen' to their online National Encyclopaedia (NE 2013). As illustrated by Vanelslander's reflections above on the extent to which gender-neutral language challenged per perceptions, nowhere perhaps is the prefiguration of representation of sex/gender both 'in language or in thought' (Vanelslander 2007: 2) more explicit than in gendered language. Attempts to reconstructively foster more enabling language practices as an implicit deconstruction of the symbolic violence of negation through un-representation in language are exemplary of positive and creative – but undoubtedly challenging and difficult – prefigurative practices. I bear in mind Sedgwick's (2003: 6) broader textual claim that 'Many kinds of objects and events *mean*, in many heterogeneous ways and contexts, and I see some value in not reifying or mystifying the linguistic kinds of meaning unnecessarily.' However, putting aside the question of whether language is reflective or productive of modes of thought, language is an important element of meaning, culture, communication and socialisation:

> Regardless of whether sexism in language merely reflects or actually enhances sexism in societal practices, its continued existence is ensured by its availability as 'linguistic input' to the child acquiring language. (Blaubergs 1978: 245)

Thus I follow Mills' point that 'there is a complex dialectic process going on in language, whereby language items both affirm and contest the status quo, and changes in social structures necessitate the development of new vocabulary and forms of expression' (Mills 2003: n.p.). This is apparent in the queer communities outlined above, wherein new social norms and practices require *and* are catalysed by new vocabularies and forms of expression. In Chapter 2 I argued that gender-neutral language such as pronouns are useless out of context, as signifiers of something that cannot exist. However, evading linguistic determinism, what is of interest in this ontological picture is how the performative function of gender-transgressive language can be collectively wielded in a manner not reductive to individual agency, with an awareness of the requirement of reading capacities. This is something shared by third wave feminist linguists who are interested in linguistic habitus or 'communities of practice' that are 'more focused on the way that context and individual mutually shape the way that interaction takes place' (Mills 2003: n.p.). In acknowledging the necessity of speaking positions, Allen & Faigley are interested, like me, not only in the ways that language has been changed itself, that is, the content of such changes, but also in strategies concerned with 'perspectival change' (Allen & Faigley 1995: 145). As Mills emphasises, 'What something means in a particular context is the result of the actions of all of the individuals concerned, negotiating with the institutional constraints of status and institutionalised linguistic routines' (Mills 2003: n.p.).

My prefigurative use of gender-neutral pronouns is not without precedent in academic queer work (e.g. Feinberg 1998; Spade 2003; Wyss 2004), in speculative fiction (Piercy 2001 [1979]), or in contemporary trans and queer community contexts (Marinucci 2010; Risman, Lorber & Sherwood 2012: 15; Vanelslander 2007). Marinucci emphasises how gender-*inclusive* (as opposed to neutral) language replicates the necessarily exclusive prescriptions of identity politics because it 'specifies all categories intended for recognition' (2010: 74). I take this to be sufficient justification for gender-transcendent strategies, as these do not exclude but sidestep the issue of the 'add-on' strategy. However, given that 'institutionalised linguistic routines' (Mills 2003: n.p.) determine the effectiveness of alternatives, such strategies are most effective alongside explication and justification of the practice, and I hold that they make particular sense in works explicitly engaging in deconstructions of binary sex/gender such as this one.

Ethical sex: community responses to sexual assault

At the less symbolic end of the violence spectrum, the response of communities or collectives to negating behaviours or circumstances such as sexual assault or violence is a real test of the practicability of their ethical principles, as I discussed in Chapter 6. Responses to sexual assault illustrate some ways in which communities or collectives can implement a proliferated ethics of pleasure, but still draw value distinctions about conduct – that is, how post-gender ethics can be ethical. These practices one again illustrate that the fostering of different ways of being relies on an interplay between individuals, relationships and cultural contexts, and this discussion could have been placed just as easily in my discussions about ethically queer individuals in Chapter 7 or my discussion about reciprocal relationships above. Indeed, I have already commented on some of the safer spaces policies and community practices engaged in by anarchist and queer communities that attempt to foster maximum sexual consent and avoid sexual violence or domination. What is significant here is how these practices represent a collective ethos or 'minority version of sustaining norms' (Butler 2004: 3).

The approach that many anarchist and queer communities take to sexual consent and to violations of this through sexual assault demonstrate just this concomitant concern with positive construction of practices according to the principles held by the communities (as above), and the *de*construction of those at odds with this. Community responses to sexual assault attempt to equip individuals with cultural resources such that they do not *need* to negate others, and it becomes only a matter of culpable choice. There is a strong normative premise here, and should perpetrators of sexual assault reject this, they are sometimes ostracised from the community within which the assault took place. However, an important point is that this is perceived as valid and un-authoritarian because these are voluntary and informally maintained communities. That is, they are not premised on the liberal notion of 'complete freedom', but, as discussed in Chapter 4, on an ontologically situated, normative notion of freedom as the ability to 'transcend facticity' unhindered by the negation of as well as by others.

In this way, these practices directly illustrate the principle of reciprocity that I outlined in Chapter 6, by attempting to provoke reflection by perpetrators on their intersubjectivity and the responsibility that entails for others: Beauvoir's very definition of reciprocity. The examples I discuss here offer those who have perpetuated sexual assault the resources they would need to have the choice to take responsibility and be held accountable (in the language of the communities) for their behaviour. This is the fostering of culpability in the enabled sense that Beauvoir elaborates, which allows people the possible subject-position to 'freely recognize ... past faults, repent, and despair' (Beauvoir 2004: 249). It is after this is made possible that Beauvoir proposes that 'negation of negation' (Muñoz 2009: 12) may be justifiably and ethically undertaken in punishing this individual in some way, as in per account this restores the reciprocity that is lost through the domination or negation that they wilfully enacted.

An account of radical approaches to sexual assault comes from a collaboration between two community groups based in Philadelphia, USA: Philly's Pissed (PP) and Philly Stands-Up (PSU) (Coleman, Kelly & Squires 2008). These groups are attempting to collectively create new ways of relating for use in their own subcultures. Their communities are based around shared ethical aims of subjective 'autonomy' and positive relationships between subjects that allow for this autonomy of *all*:

> In a nutshell, PP provides direct support to survivors of sexual assault and PSU works with perpetrators of sexual assault to hold them accountable for their actions and to demand for changes in future behaviour ... as individuals and collectives, we are committed to survivor autonomy, perpetrator accountability, and to developing coordinated, radical and grassroots mechanisms to confront sexual assault in our communities. (Coleman, Kelly & Squires 2008: n.p.)

By addressing the survivor, the perpetrator and the community, this approach takes off from similar ontological assumptions to ways of relating that are co-constitutive with subjects, others and the social:

> *Restorative justice* deals with everybody's needs in a situation, because when a person hurts another person – whether it's *sexual assault*, theft, whatever – there are communities around that *survivor* who feel hurt and like they've been betrayed. *Restorative justice* tries to take the needs of anyone who has been hurt into account. It's a more holistic approach. (Coleman, Kelly & Squires 2008: n.p.)

An example of restorative justice in *What Do We Do When? #2* – a 'zine about community response to sexual assault' – states that the broadly anarchist community of which the survivor was a member recognises sexual assault as 'a violation of a person' (*What Do We Do When? #2*: 11) and does so in terms similar to the 'negation' of humanity theorised as 'absolute evil' by Beauvoir (2004: 257). Additionally, the writer of this article wanted per community to acknowledge and confront the rape so that ze could 'have my humanity restored' (*What Do We Do When? #2*: 12), which again resonates with Beauvoir's view that the restoration of balance should be the outcome of justice. The process that this community chose to engage with entailed the 'victim' confronting the 'perpetrator' in a public community gathering. This enabled the survivor 'Being able to tell the experience exactly as it happened for me, with my community and him to have to sit with ... Speaking my mind to him, looking him in the eye whilst expressing such rage, and having my peers also experience this' (*What Do We Do When? #2*: 15). This process is one of restoring reciprocity, of transforming what was a one-way relation of imposition of one person upon another into a dialogue. It has obvious parallels to the purpose of punishment as Beauvoir theorises it: justice is done when the 'perpetrator' will 'freely recognize its past faults, repent, and despair, but it must be an exterior necessity that compels this spontaneous movement' (Beauvoir 2004: 249). However, the outcome in this example was not so ideal, for 'He showed no remorse, expressed no sorrow' (*What Do We Do When? #2*: 15), and consequently the community excluded the 'perpetrator' from the community. This is the form of the 'last resort' also taken in response to the ultimate negations of sexual assault and murder in the fictional communities in feminist speculative fiction novels *The Dispossessed* and *Woman on the Edge of Time* (Le Guin 1974; Piercy 1979), which serve as thought-experiments through these ethical dilemmas.

Another example of these principles in practice concerns the San Francisco informal international Queeruption community, and the 'Latin@'[1] movement, who publicly informed organisers of a conference that a member of their own community who they had attempted to call to account for sexually predatory behaviour was planning to attend the conference. The problem was that 'multiple attempts at community accountability have failed' (Queeruption 2011: n.p.), and because he 'refuses to seek help, a group of survivors and community members have banned him from women-centered spaces and activist networks that prioritize women's safety' (Queeruption 2011: n.p.). What is of interest here is the considered, self-critical manner in which such action was taken and the awareness of the ethical nuances of 'banishment':

> ... we are seeking to challenge his entitlement to spaces that actively engage young women of color by effectively banishing him. This is a proactive attempt to make our community safer and make sure ******* does not retraumatize survivors of his abuse that belong to these communities.
>
> We understand the political and social ramifications of criminalization. We do not seek to criminalize *******; instead, we wish to nonviolently ban him from spaces that want to stop violence against women and transpeople. (Queeruption 2011: n.p.)

The processes of accountability, then, attempt to equip perpetrators with full awareness of the negating outcomes of their behaviour and that this behaviour is at odds with the ethics of the communities in which they are participating. This takes off from an awareness of the co-constitutive relationship between subjects, others and social practices, as well as being exemplary of an auto-critical practice that eschews congealment into authoritarianism. This is apparent in the reflexive relationship between the 'policies' and 'procedures' and members of the community in both directions, in that members of the community are held to account through these policies, and the policies are reflexively held to account by community members.

This chapter has considered how the ontological ethical theory developed and fine-tuned in the previous chapters can be made practicable, especially taking heed of the lessons of potential antinomies resolved in Chapter 6. As such, it has completed a thorough account of a reciprocal ethics to replace the negation of sexual difference by considering the practical 'how?' in light of my arguments in previous chapters that such an ethic is *theoretically* possible, by also demonstrating that it is *practically* possible too and can be suitably open and enabling, but still able to draw moral distinctions. In the Conclusion I will now recount how it is that we arrived here, and consider some of the possible sticking points, and some possible limitations to the account that I have argued for.

Conclusion: Utopian Realism

I have proposed in this book that radical deconstructions of biological sex and gender can be applied to reconstructive ethics to underpin a queer, post-gender ethics. This extends the project undertaken by queer theorists and gender-deconstructive theorists, and explicates the implications of these ideas for social change, towards a more inclusive and positive sociality than the heteronormative or gender-fundamentalist ones that provoked them. The strength of this utopian vision of an androgynous mode of being and relating that does not rely on the classifications of biological sex and gender is that it takes inspiration from queer theory by coalescing around an ethico-political *potentiality*, not an identity. The intention is that it serves as 'an ethos and mode of sociability that escapes ... dialectical determination or that emerges as a third term effectively exceeding the dialectical opposition which forms its condition' (Butler 2011a: n.p.). It is this key aspect that, I hope, can speak to some of the possible limits or problematic outcomes of a call for an end to sex/gender.

I hope that this work will not be judged as an account of biology. I am not a biologist, but I found great inspiration and saw great ethical and political potential in the exciting, well-argued and thorough work that has been done by feminist biologists around the potentiality of understanding bodies in less dimorphic and less fixed ways. It seemed to me necessary to consider its social and transformative implications, what it might mean for ethics, for how we conduct ourselves. These ideas offer a freeing potentiality for reconstructive thinking, and my intention has been to undertake a thorough consideration of how they may be extended metaphysically, normatively, politically and practically. Many theorists, such as the immensely popular Judith Butler (1990), have undertaken invaluable, exhaustive deconstructions of modes of perception, such as compulsory sex/gender, that are to be avoided in the quest for non-totalising modes of being but have been less forthcoming with non-totalising, non-essentialist alternatives. This often results from an understandable weariness of the ever-present risks of offering blueprints and teleological visions, given the deconstructive impulses that such studies depart from. Indeed, a great fear of mine is that a vision such as this might be construed as somehow authoritarian and imposing, and as denying the freedom of choice that it is intended to promote. Such reactions can be seen in media coverage of gender-neutral childrearing, sometimes framed as brainwashing or social engineering.

I think this can be a result of reductionist readings when academic or specialist ideas are taken up in more popular contexts, identified as a limit of the theoretically dense language of much queer studies (Duggan 1994). However, there are some theorists who are genuinely committed to sharing the exciting and democratising impulses of queer theory, new materialism – or whatever their conceptual bent – to a wider audience. Given the emphasis I have placed on 'reading capacities' as necessary individual and social skills to make new ethical modes workable, such careful communication is indispensable. Fausto-Sterling's accessible communication of per complex developmental ideas about biology and sex/gender across different fora, including the popular press and multiple academic disciplines, is inspirational in this regard (see Fausto-Sterling 1993a; 1993b). In journalism, Orenstein's (2011) newspaper article, which takes seriously the role of toys and environment in sex/gender development, is another great example.

This communication issue aside, I think that the danger of an imposed androgyny or a 'banning' of gender identity that may be a corollary of such ideas may be very real, and felt by many people who have a deep investment in their sex/gender identity. I cannot deign to know or presume the individual, subjective relationships of other people to their own sense of identity. And in reality, more thought needs to be put specifically to issues of what might happen to funding and support for surgeries and other services which, in the current social context, are contingent on dominant cultural notions of permanent and stable gender identity.

This I cannot solve here but, in being mindful of the dangers of imposition, my hope is that, by being a mode of recognition that is suitably non-specific, a principle-based 'universal particular' post-gender ethic, rather than identity, this ideal could allow a multiplicity of behaviours and expressions within it. The difference being, however, that these characteristics lose their sex/gendered significance. This is my attempt at filling out the ideal with which I opened the book, Weiner & Young's sketch of queer sociality (not identity) where 'identitarian positionings ... will remain forever incommensurate [and] ... differences ... may remain irreducible' (2011: 227). A key issue here is that the vision of androgynous ethics or queer sociality that I am proposing is not one of sameness to replace difference, but of limitless proliferated differenc*es*, united around broad values.

The reality of co-existing accounts of the world or of existence, united by ethos, is apparent in some of the real-world practices that I have charted in the book. These have been inspirational and are exemplary for my vision of how such ontological squabbles can be transcended and energy applied instead to finding a preferable, enabling mode of being and relating to that of compulsory sexual difference. This, I hope, also goes some way to addressing the utility of such an ethic and political practice in a global context where the urgency of deconstructing gender is somewhat sublimated to more immediate concerns. It can, as I charted in Chapters 5 and 6, be used to underpin a variety of political strategies and agendas with uniting principles. One of the key mechanisms that I have drawn on for maintaining such a non-homogenising 'dissensus' (Mouffe 1997) is that of 'reciprocity' as an inexhaustible mode of approaching the other 'in their otherness' (Beauvoir 1976a: 67) so as not to impose one's one preconceptions. However, 'if we do want to promote an alternative vision of human life, to what extent are we accountable for the practicality of this vision?' (Suissa 2010: 2).

In a utopian context, and in temporary communities or isolated contexts, this inexhaustibly open, universal post-gender principle makes sense, but a second critique of such utopian ideas tends to go along the lines of 'it's a laudable goal ... *but* the notion of gender is deeply ingrained' (the words of a child psychologist cited in Birkeland 2012, my emphasis). Such reasoning can also be seen in academic accounts that share the ontological premises that nature does not even *lend* itself to oppositional sex/gender, but that the social strength is such that attempts to challenge it are not worth the energy (Gatens 1994; Van Lenning 2004). This seems to me a defeatist realism that leaves all of the work to those who benefit least from gender and, in the words of Duggan, 'let[s] everyone else off the hook' (1994: 6).

Hence, practices that appear imposing, such as that of the universal application of gender-neutral pronouns that I have applied to all people discussed in the book, are intended to provoke non-normative readings in those whose sex/gender may usually be unquestioned, to queer, as a site of attempted 'dissonant and denaturalized performance that reveals the performative status of the natural itself' (Butler 2007: 200). That is, they are attempts at least to *try*.

But, of course, such a vision *is* utopian. A real concern of mine is that of the energy required for such an inexhaustible mode of being in the world, for this critical capacity, a danger attested to by the phenomenon of 'activist burnout'. While my ideal for reciprocity is inexhaustible, humyns are not inexhaustible. Recall the queer activist who noted after an exhilarating social experiment that nonetheless 'Queertopia was exhausting' (Lechat, in Brown 2007b: 2695). The ideal of a proliferated reciprocity that I characterise as the crux of androgyny, as opposed to the tyrannical closure feared by some (above), necessitates a labour-intensive and engaged mode of being in the world. The critical subject that I outlined in Chapter 7 as the ideal disposition for post-gender ethics has the potential to be exhausting, with its

> dwelling with a 'patient labour' at the limits of our being, where dialogically we consider that which and those who we are not, not in order to secure a universal rationality, but to explore the shapes of our lives and social practices at their limits with an eye to how it might be possible and desirable to fashion our lives and limits differently. (Coles 1992: 87)

But my response can only be, why don't we try? We haven't tried it, so we don't know how we might feel, and be able to behave, without the determinations of oppositional sex and gender. Shifts in thinking about the body and 'sex' indicate that it might at least be a possibility. I am heartened that there are people who do try, who keep experimenting and trying to better carry out their values, and consider 'what maximizes the possibility for a liveable life' (Butler 2004: 8), not just for them, but for all.

Notes

Introduction

1. The book is written using gender-neutral pronouns and language, replacing human with 'humyn', s/he with 'ze' and her/him with 'per'. This practice has precedents (e.g. Feinberg 1998; Spade 2003; Wyss 2004), and I discuss gender-neutral pronouns as part of post-gender practice in Chapter 8.
2. A zine is an amateur handmade publication, commonly made and distributed in DIY punk and anarchist communities, as well as a common feature of the riot grrrl movement.

1 The Resilience of Bigenderism

1. In this case Hill-Meyer replaced 'he/she' with 'ze' and 'him/her' with 'hir' (pronounced 'here').
2. '"majority world" (a term used as an alternative to "developing countries") ... "minority world" (primarily Western, industrialized nations)' (Raffaelli et al. 2013).
3. 'Cis is the Latin prefix for "on the same side." It compliments trans, the prefix for "across" or "over." "Cisgender" replaces the terms "nontransgender" or "bio man/bio woman" to refer to individuals who have a match between the gender they were assigned at birth, their bodies, and their personal identity' (Schilt & Westbrook 2009: 461).

2 Diagnosing and Transcending Sexual Difference

1. NB: I will discuss 'strategic essentialism' and return to the issue of identity politics in Chapter 5 when discussing examining strategies for change and overcoming such dualisms as means/ends, idealism/realism.

4 Philosophical Arguments for Post-Gender Ontological Ethics

1. I use the gendered pronoun here as the gender of this character has been argued to be a significant choice by Beauvoir (Holveck 1999) for illustrating feminine ethics.

7 The Fully Armed Self: Cultivating Post-Gender Subjects

1. See http://www.cowleyclub.org.uk/

8 Ethical Post-Gender Sexual Relationships and Communities

1. An alliance of anarchist members of the Latin@ community. It is spelled as such to undermine the gendering of language and to incorporate anarchism into the word.

Bibliography

Abraham, Kera 2004, 'Minority Students Share Their Life Stories', *Oregon Daily Emerald*, http://media.www.dailyemerald.com/media/storage/paper859/news/2004/05/24/News/Minority.Students.Share.Their.Life.Stories-1969992.shtml, accessed 6/11/09.

Alaimo, Stacy 2008, 'Trans-Corporeal Feminisms and the Ethical Space of Nature' in Alaimo, Stacy & Hekman, Susan (eds) *Material Feminisms*, Indiana University Press, Bloomington, pp. 237–264.

Allen, Amy 1998, 'Power Trouble: Performativity as Critical Theory', *Constellations*, 5 (4), pp. 456–471.

Allen, Amy 1999, *The Power of Feminist Theory: Domination, Resistance, Solidarity*, Westview Press, Boulder.

Allen, Amy 2005, 'Dependency, Subordination, and Recognition: On Judith Butler's Theory of Subjection', *Continental Philosophy Review*, 38, pp. 199–222.

Allen, Amy 2010, 'Rethinking resistance: Feminism and the politics of our selves', Eurozine, http://www.eurozine.com/articles/2010-05-05-allen-en.html accessed 31/7/14

Allen, Julia M. & Faigley, Leicester 1995, 'Discursive Strategies for Social Change: An Alternative Rhetoric of Argument', *Rhetoric Review*, 14 (1), pp. 142–172.

Anarchist Free University Toronto. (n.d.). *Anarchist Free University Toronto*, http://anarchistu.org/cgi-bin/twiki/view/Anarchistu accessed 24/11/10

Anderson, S. & McIntyre, V. (eds) 1976, *Aurora: Beyond Equality*. Connecticut: Fawcett.

Andrews, Naomi J. 2003, 'Utopian Androgyny: Romantic Socialists Confront Individualism in July Monarchy France', *French Historical Studies*, 26 (3), pp. 437–457.

Antrobus, Peggy, Harcourt, Wendy & Sen, Gita 2010, 'Power, Respect and Solidarity: In Conversation with Peggy Antrobus and Gita Sen', *Development*, 53 (2), pp. 150–155.

Archer, Margaret Scotford 1996, *Culture and Agency: The Place of Culture in Social Theory*, Cambridge University Press, Cambridge.

Arp, Kristina 2004, 'Introduction to An Eye for An Eye' in Beauvoir, Simone de (ed.) *Simone de Beauvoir: Philosophical Writings*, (Margaret A. Simons ed.), University of Illinois, Illinois, pp. 239–244.

Aspaceinside 2008, 'Creating a Safer Space', http://aspaceinside.googlepages.com/saferspacepolicy

Bahadur, Nina 2013, 'Swedish Gender-Neutral Pronoun, "Hen," Added to Country's National Encyclopaedia', *Huffington Post*, 4/11/13, http://www.huffingtonpost.com/2013/04/11/swedish-gender-neutral-pronoun-hen-national-encyclopedia_n_3063293.html

Bakunin, Michael 1970, *God and the State*, Dover Publications, London.

Barad, Karen 2003, 'Posthumanist Performativity: Toward an Understanding of how Matter Comes to Matter', *Signs. Journal of Women in Culture and Society*, 28 (3), pp. 801–831.

Barker, Chris 2008, *Cultural Studies: Theory and Practice*, Sage, London.

Baumrind, Diana 1982, 'Are Androgynous Individuals More Effective Persons and Parents?' *Child Development*, 53 (1), pp. 44–75.

Baynes, Kenneth 1987, *After Philosophy: End or Transformation?* MIT Press, London.

Beauvoir, Simone de 1968, *Force of Circumstance*, (Trans. Richard Howard), Penguin, Middlesex.

Beauvoir, Simone de 1976a, *The Ethics of Ambiguity*, (Trans. B. Frechtman), Citadel Press, New York.

Beauvoir, Simone de 1976b, *The Prime of Life*, (Trans. Peter Green), Penguin, Middlesex.

Beauvoir, Simone de 1978, *The Blood of Others*, (Trans. Yvonne Myse and Roger Senhouse), Penguin, Middlesex.

Beauvoir, Simone de 1987, 'Selections from Towards a Morals of Ambiguity, according to Pyrrhus and Cineas', (Trans. Jay Miskowiec), *Social Text*, 17, pp. 135–142.

Beauvoir, Simone de 1997, *The Second Sex*, (Trans. H.M. Parshley), Vintage, London.

Beauvoir, Simone de 2004, *Simone de Beauvouir: Philosophical Writings*, (Margaret A. Simons ed.), University of Illinois Press, Illinois.

Beauvoir, Simone de 2005, *The Mandarins*, (Trans. Leonard M. Friedman), Harper Perennial, London.

Beauvoir, Simone de 2006, *She Came to Stay*, (Trans. Yvonne Moyose & Roger Senhouse), Harper Perennial, London.

Beauvoir, Simone de 2011, *'The Useless Mouths' and Other Literary Writings*, (Margaret A. Simons and Marybeth Timmermann eds), University of Illinois Press, Illinois.

Belkin, Lisa 2011, 'Gender Neutral Parenting', *NY Times*, http://parenting.blogs.nytimes.com/2011/05/09/gender-neutral-parenting/?_r=0

Bem, Sandra 1975, 'Sex Role Adaptability: One Consequence of Psychological Androgyny', *Journal of Personality and Social Psychology*, 31 (4), pp. 634–643.

Bem, Sandra 1995, 'Dismantling Gender Polarization and Compulsory Heterosexuality: Should We Turn the Volume Down or Up?' *Journal of Sex Research*, 32 (4), pp. 329–334.

Benhabib, Seyla 1985, 'The Generalized and the Concrete Other: The Kohlberg-Gilligan Controversy and Feminist Theory', *PRAXIS International*, (4), pp. 402–424.

Benhabib, Seyla 1992, *Situating the Self: Gender, Community and Postmodernism in Contemporary Ethics*, Polity Press, Cambridge.

Benhabib, Seyla (ed.) 1996, *Democracy and Difference: Contesting the Boundaries of the Political*, Princeton University Press, Princeton, N.J.

Berger, Charles R. & Calabrese, Richard J. 1975, 'Some Explorations in Initial Interaction and Beyond: Toward a Developmental Theory of Interpersonal Communication', *Human Communication Research*, 1 (2), pp. 99–112.

Bergoffen, Debra 2004, 'Introduction to Pyrrhus and Cineas' in Beauvoir, Simone de (ed.) *Simone de Beauvoir: Philosophical Writings*, (Margaret A. Simons ed.), University of Illinois, Illinois, pp. 79–87.

Berlin, Isaiah 1969, *Four Essays on Liberty*, Oxford University Press, London.

Bey n.d. 'The Dinner Party', *The Temporary Autonomous Zone*, http://delza.alliances.org/taz/taz13.html, accessed 19/11/09.

Bhabha, Homi K. 1999, 'Liberalism's Sacred Cow' in Okin, Susan Moller (ed.) *Is Multiculturalism Bad for Women?*, Princeton University Press, Princeton, N.J. pp. 79–84.

Bhave, Vinoba 2008, 'Intimate and Ultimate' in Hern, Matt (ed.) *Everywhere All The Time: A New Deschooling Reader*, AK Press, Edinburgh, pp. 7–12.

Bibby, Paul 2013, 'Please, Just Call me Norrie, This is a Whole New Agenda', *The Age* 1/6/13, accessed at, http://www.theage.com.au/national/please-just-call-me-norrie-this-is-a-whole-new-agenda-20130531-2nhmo.html on 18/7/13.

Bijker, Wiebe E. & Law, John (eds) 1992, *Shaping Technology/Building Society: Studies in Sociotechnical Change*, MIT Press, London.

Birkeland, Charlene Prince 2012, 'Can Kids Be Raised in a Gender-neutral Society? Sweden Thinks So', *Team Mom*, http://shine.yahoo.com/team-mom/kids-raised-gender-neutral-society-sweden-thinks-033400030.html#!oZSxW

Blaubergs, Maija S. 1978, 'Changing the Sexist Language: The Theory Behind the Practice', *Psychology of Women Quarterly*, 2 (3), pp. 244–261.

Bock, Andrew 2013, 'Being Man and Woman', *The Age* 20/6/2013, accessed at http://www.theage.com.au/national/being-man-and-woman-20130625-2ou9g.html on 18/7/13.

Bordo, Susan 1993, *Unbearable Weight: Feminism, Western Culture, and the Body*, University of California Press, Berkeley.

Bornstein, Kate 1994, *Gender Outlaw*, Routledge, London.

Bornstein, Kate 1998, *My Gender Workbook*, Routledge, London.

Bourdieu, Pierre 2004, 'Gender and Symbolic Violence' in Scheper-Hughes, Nancy & Bourgois, Philippe (eds) *Violence in War and Peace: An Anthology*, Blackwell, Oxford, pp. 339–342.

Bowen, James & Purkis, Jonathan (eds) 1997, *Twenty-First Century Anarchism: Unorthodox Ideas For the New Millennium*, Cassell, New York.

Braidotti, Rosi 1994, *Nomadic Subjects: Embodiment and Difference in Contemporary Feminist Theory*, Columbia University Press, New York.

Braidotti, Rosi 1996, *Cyberfeminism with a Difference*, http://www.let.uu.nl/womens_studies/rosi/cyberfem.html, accessed 9/3/07.

Britzman, Deborah P. 1998, *Lost Subjects, Contested Objects: Toward a Psychoanalytic Inquiry of Learning*, State University of New York Press, Albany.

Brown, Gavin 2007a, 'Autonomy, Affiliation and Play in the Spaces of Radical Queer Activism' in Browne, Kath, Lim, Jason & Brown, Gavin (eds) *Geographies of Sexualities: Theory, Practice and Politics*, Ashgate, Hampshire, pp. 195–206

Brown, Gavin 2007b, 'Mutinous Eruptions: Autonomous Spaces of Radical Queer Activism', *Environment & Planning A*, 39, pp. 2685–2698.

Browne, Kath 2004, 'Genderism and the Bathroom Problem: (Re)Materialising Sexed Sites, (Re)Creating Sexed Bodies, *Gender, Place and Culture*, 11 (3), pp.331–346.

Browne, Kath & Nash, Catherine, J. (eds) 2010, *Queer Methods and Methodologies: Intersecting Queer Theories and Social Science Research*, Ashgate, Surrey.

Butler, Judith 1990, *Gender Trouble: Feminism and the Subversion of Identity*, Routledge, New York.

Butler, Judith 1993a, *Bodies That Matter: On the Discursive Limits of Sex*, Routledge, New York.

Butler, Judith 1993b, 'Extracts from Gender as Performance: An Interview with Judith Butler', Theory.org, http://www.theory.org.uk/but-int1.htm, accessed 14/09/2011.

Butler, Judith 1997, *The Psychic Life of Power: Theories in Subjection*, Stanford University Press, California.

Butler, Judith 2004, *Undoing Gender*, Routledge, New York.

Butler, Judith 2005, *Giving an Account of Oneself*, Fordham, New York.

Butler, Judith 2007 [1990], *Gender Trouble: Feminism and the Subversion of Identity*, 4th edn., Routledge, London.

Butler, Judith 2011(a), 'Queer Anarchism & Anarchists Against the Wall', *Anarchist Developments in Cultural Studies*, http://www.anarchist-developments. org/index.php/adcs/article/view/24/18, accessed 11/07/2011.

Butler, Judith 2011(b), 'On Anarchism: An Interview with Judith Butler' in Heckert, Jamie & Cleminson, Richard (eds) *Anarchism and Sexuality: Ethics, Relationships and Power*, Routledge, Oxon.

Butler, Judith 2011(c), 'Remarks on "Queer Bonds" ', *GLQ*, 17(2–3), pp. 381–387.

Cain, Joey 2003, 'Who are the Radical Faeries?', Mooncircle.org, http://www. mooncircle.org/Index/WhatRFaes.html

Campisi, Caitlin 2013, *Homonationalism on TV?: A Critical Discourse Analysis of Queer and Trans* Youth Representations on Mainstream Teen Television Shows*, Master thesis, University of Ottawa, accessed at https://ruor.uottawa.ca/en/ bitstream/handle/10393/24263/Campisi_Caitlin_2013_thesis.pdf?sequence=1

Camus, Albert 1983, *The Myth of Sisyphus, and Other Essays*, Vintage Books, London.

Carlson, Åsa 2010, '"Gender and Sex: What Are They?" Sally Haslanger's Debunking Social Constructivism', *Distinktion: Scandinavian Journal of Social Theory*, 11(1), pp. 61–72.

Chase, Cheryl 1993, 'Intersexual Rights', *The Sciences*, July/August 1993, p. 3.

Chase, Cheryl 1998, 'Hermaphrodites with Attitude: Mapping the Emergence of Intersex Political Activism', *GLQ*, 4 (2), pp. 189–211.

Chomsky, Noam 2003, *Chomsky on Democracy and Education*, Routledge, New York.

Chomsky, Noam & Foucault, Michel 1971, *Justice Vs. Power*, http://www.youtube. com/watch?v=WveI_vgmPz8, accessed 28/1/11.

Churchill, Ward 2004, *Pacifism as Pathology*, Beating Hearts Press, Wollongong.

Claes, Tom & Reynolds, Paul 2014, 'Why Sexual Ethics and Politics? Why Now? An Introduction to the Journal', *Journal of the International Network of Sexual Ethics and Politics*, 1 (1), pp. 5–18.

Climate Collective 2009, *Action Guide to COP15*, www.climate-justice-action. org/wp-content/.../ActionGuideEn_web.pdf accessed 16/06/2011.

Colebrook, Claire 2000, 'From Radical Representations to Corporeal Becomings: The Feminist Philosophy of Lloyd, Grosz, and Gatens', *Hypatia*, 15 (2), pp. 76093.

Coleman, Timothy, Kelly, Esteban & Squires, Em 2008, 'Philly's Pissed & Philly Stands Up- Collected Materials', *In the Middle of a Whirlwind*, http://inthe middleofthewhirlwind.wordpress.com/philly%E2%80%99s-pissed-philly-stands-up-collected-materials/

Coles, Romand 1992, 'Communicative Action and Dialogical Ethics: Habermas and Foucault', *Polity*, 25 (1), pp. 71–94.

Connell, R. W. 1995, *Masculinities*, Polity Press, Cambridge.

Connell, R. W. 1996, 'Politics of Changing Men', *Australian Humanities Review* December 1996–February 1997, http://www.australianhumanitiesreview.org/ archive/Issue-Dec-1996/connell

Connell, R. W. 2003, *Gender*, Polity Press, Cambridge.

Cooper, Martha & Blair, Carole 2002, 'Foucault's Ethics', *Qualitative Inquiry*, 8, pp. 511–531.

Cooper, Robbie 2007, *Alter Ego: Avatars and their Creators*, Chris Boot Ltd, London.

Cowan, Sharon 2004, ' "That Woman Is a Woman!" the Case of Bellinger v. Bellinger and the Mysterious (Dis)appearance of Sex', *Feminist Legal Studies*, 12 (1), pp. 79–92.

Cowan, Sharon 2005, ' "Gender Is No Substitute for Sex": A Comparative Human Rights Analysis of the Legal Regulation of Sexual Identity', *Feminist Legal Studies*, 13/1, pp. 67–96.

CrimethInc n.d. [a], *Harbinger (of a new dawn)*, CWC, Olympia, http://www.crimethinc.com/tools/downloads/zines.html, accessed 2/8/13.

CrimethInc n.d [b], *Gender Subversion Kit*, CWC, Olympia, http://www.crimethinc.com/tools/posters/gender_subversion_front.pdf, accessed 2/8/13.

Critchley, Simon 1999, *The Ethics of Deconstruction: Derrida and Levinas*, Edinburgh University Press, Edinburgh.

Dahl, Ulrika 2010, 'Femme on Femme: Reflections on Collaborative Methods and Queer Femme-inist Ethnography' in Browne, K. & Nash, C.J. (eds) *Queer Methods and Methodologies: Intersecting Queer Theories and Social Science Research*, Ashgate, Surrey, pp. 143–166.

Daly, Mary 1979, *Gyn/Ecology: The Metaethics of Radical Feminism*, The Women's Press, London.

Davidson, Helen 2014, 'Third Gender Must be Recognised by NSW After Norrie Wins Legal Battle', *The Guardian*, 2/4/14, http://www.theguardian.com/world/2014/apr/02/third-gender-must-be-recognised-by-nsw-after-norrie-wins-legal-battle

de Lauretis, Teresa 1987, *Technologies of Gender: Essays on Theory, Film, and Fiction*, Macmillan Press, Basingstoke.

de Lauretis, Teresa 1991, 'Queer Theory: Lesbian and Gay Sexualities', *Differences: A Journal of Feminist Cultural Studies*, 3 (2), pp. iii–xviii.

de Lauretis, Teresa 1994, 'The Essence of the Triangle or, Taking the Risk of Essentialism Seriously' in Schor, Naomi & Weed Elizabeth (eds) *The Essential Difference*, Indiana University Press, Bloomington, pp. 1–39.

de Lauretis, Teresa 2011, 'Queer Texts, Bad Habits, and the Issue of a Future', *GLQ*, 17 (2–3), pp. 243–263.

De Miguel, V. 2012, 'Sasha and Storm: Is Gender-Neutral Parenting Right?', *Voxxi*, http://www.voxxi.com/sasha-and-storm-is-gender-neutral-parenting-right-mujer/

della Porta, Donatella (ed.) 2009, *Democracy in Social Movements*, Palgrave Macmillan, Basingstoke.

Delphy, Christine 1993, 'Rethinking Sex and Gender', *Women's Studies International Forum*, 16 (1), pp. 1–9.

Derrida, Jacques 1976, *Of Grammatology*, (trans. Spivak, Gayatri Chakravorty), The John Hopkins University Press, Baltimore & London .

Diagnosing Difference 2011, *Diagnosing Difference*, http://www.diagnosing difference.com, accessed 18/06/2011.

Ditum, Sarah, 'Sweden Makes my Gender-Free Toy Christmas with Wish Come True', *The Guardian* 27/11/12, http://www.theguardian.com/commentisfree/2012/nov/27/sweden-christmas-gift-girl-nerf-gun

Dreger, Alice 1998, *Hermaphrodites and the Medical Invention of Sex*, Harvard University Press.

Dreger, Alice & Herndon, April 2009, 'Progress and Politics in the Intersex Rights Movement: Feminist Theory in Action', *GLQ*, 15 (2), pp. 199–224.

Driver, Susan (ed.) 2008, *Queer Youth Cultures*, SUNY, New York.

Duggan, Lisa 1994, 'Queering the State', *Social Text*, 39, pp. 1–14.

Dynes, Wayne R. 1995, 'Queer Studies: In Search of a Discipline', *Academic Questions*, 8 (4), pp. 34–52.

Easton, Dossie & Lizst, Catherine A. 1997, *The Ethical Slut: A Guide to Infinite Sexual Possibilities*, Greenery Press, Eugene.

Edelman, Lee 2004, *No Future: Queer Theory and the Death Drive*, Duke University Press, Durham.

Enslin, Penny & Tijattas, Mary 2006, 'Educating For a Just World Without Gender', *Theory and Research in Education*, 4, pp. 41–68.

Ettling, Alex 2005, *Homohistories – PAN speech*, http://groups.yahoo.com/group/appetitefordeconstruction/files/, accessed 22/10/2007.

Fanon, Frantz 1974, *The Wretched of the Earth*, Penguin, Harmondsworth.

Fausto-Sterling, Anne 1993a, 'The Five Sexes: Why Male and Female Are Not Enough', *The Sciences*, March/April 1993. pp. 20–25.

Fausto-Sterling, Anne 1993b, 'How Many Sexes Are There?' *New York Times*, 12/3/93, http://www.nytimes.com/1993/03/12/opinion/how-many-sexes-are-there.html

Fausto-Sterling, Anne 2000, 'The Five Sexes, Revisited', *The Sciences*, 40, July/Aug 2000, pp. 18–23.

Fausto-Sterling, Anne 2003, 'The Problem with Sex/Gender and Nature/Nurture' in Williams, Simon J., Birke, Lynda, & Bendelow, Gillian A. (eds) *Debating Biology: Sociological Reflections on Health, Medicine and Society*, Routledge, London, pp. 123–132.

Fausto-Sterling, Anne 2007, 'Dueling Dualisms' in Cook, Nancy (ed.) *Gender Relations in Global Perspective*, Canadian Scholars' Press, Toronto, pp. 25–36.

Fausto-Sterling, Anne 2012, *Sex/Gender: Biology in a Social World*, Routledge, New York.

Feinberg, Leslie 1993, *Stone Butch Blues*, Firebrand Books, Ithaca, N.Y.

Feinberg, Leslie 1998, *Trans Liberation: Beyond Pink or Blue*, Beacon Press, Boston.

Fenstermaker, Sarah & West, Candace (eds) 2002, *Doing Gender, Doing Difference: Inequality, Power and Institutional Change*, Routledge, London.

Fidler, Geoffrey 1989, 'Anarchism and Education: Education Intégrale and the Imperative Towards Fraternité', *History of Education: Journal of the History of Education Society*, 18 (1), pp. 23–36.

Firestone, Shulamith 1972, *The Dialectic of Sex*, Bantam, NY.

Foucault, Michel 1980, *Herculine Barbin: Being the Recently Discovered Memoirs of a Nineteenth-century French Hermaphrodite*, (trans. Richard McDougall), Harvester Press, Brighton.

Foucault, Michel 1983, *Michel Foucault on 'Pleasure vs. Desire'*, YouTube, http://www.youtube.com/watch?v=uNcQA3MSdIE

Foucault, Michel 1984, *The Foucault Reader*, (Paul Rabinow ed.), Pantheon, New York.

Foucault, Michel 1991, *The Foucault Reader: An Introduction to Foucault's Thought*, (Paul Rabinow ed.), Penguin, London.

Foucault, Michel 1997, *Ethics: Subjectivity and Truth* (ed. Paul Rabinow, Trans. Robert J. Hurley), New Press, New York.

Foucault, Michel 2007, *The Politics of Truth*, Semiotext(e), Los Angeles.

Franks, Benjamin 2006, *Rebel Alliances: The Means and Ends of Contemporary British Anarchisms*, AK Press, Edinburgh.

Fraser, Lin, Karasic, Dan H., Meyer, Walter J. & Wylie, Kevan 2010, 'Recommendations for Revision of the DSM Diagnosis of Gender Identity Disorder in Adults', *International Journal of Transgenderism*, 12 (2), pp. 80–85.

Fraser, Nancy 1995, 'False Antitheses: A Response to Seyla Benhabib and Judith Butler' in Butler, Judith, Benhabib, Seyla, Cornell, Drucilla & Fraser, Nancy (eds) *Feminist Contentions: A Philosophical Exchange*, Routeledge, London, pp. 59–74.

Fraser, Nancy 2000, 'Rethinking Recognition', *New Left Review*, 3 May–June 2000, http://newleftreview.org/II/3/nancy-fraser-rethinking-recognition, accessed 14/8/13.

Freeman, Jo 1996 [1970], 'The Tyranny of Structurelessness', http://flag.blackened. net/revolt/anarchism/pdf/booklets/structurelessness.html, accessed 8/2/10.

Friedan, Betty 1965, *The Feminine Mystique*, Penguin, Harmondsworth.

Friedman, Marilyn 1993, *What Are Friends For? Feminist Perspectives on Personal Relationships and Moral Theory*, Cornell, London.

Frosh, Stephen, Phoenix, Ann & Pattman, Rob (eds) 2002, *Young Masculinities: Understanding Boys in Contemporary Society*, Palgrave, Basingstoke.

Fukuyama, Francis 1992, *The End of History and the Last Man*, Hamish Hamilton, London.

Fullbrook, Edward 2004, 'Introduction to Two Unpublished Chapters From "She Came To Stay" ' in Beauvoir, Simone de (ed.) *Simone de Beauvouir: Philosophical Writings*, (Margaret A. Simons ed.), University of Illinois Press, Illinois, pp. 33–40.

Fullbrook, Kate & Fullbrook, Edward 1994, *Simone de Beauvoir and Jean-Paul Sartre: The Remaking of a Twentieth Century Legend*, Basic Books, New York.

Fuss, Diana 1989, *Essentially Speaking: Feminism, Nature and Difference*, Routledge, London.

Fuss, Diana 1991, *Inside/Out: Lesbian Theories, Gay Theories*, Routledge, London.

Gagne, P. & Tewkesbury, R. 1998, 'Conformity Pressure and Gender Resistance among Transgendered Individuals', *Social Problems*, 45 (1), pp. 81–101.

Gagnon, John & Simons, William 1974, *Sexual Conduct: The Social Sources of Human Sexuality*, Aldine, Chicago.

Gamson, Joshua 1995, 'Must Identity Movements Self-Destruct? A Queer Dilemma', *Social Problems*, 42 (3), pp. 390–407.

Garfinkel, Harold 1967, *Studies in Ethnomethodology*, Prentice-Hall, New Jersey.

Garnets, Linda & Pleck, Joseph H. 1979, 'Sex Role Identity, Androgyny, and Sex Role Transcendence: A Sex Role Strain Analysis', *Psychology of Women Quarterly*, 3 (3), Spring 1979, pp. 270–283.

Gatens, Moira 1994, 'A Critique of the Sex/Gender Distinction' in Gunew, Sneja (ed.) *A Reader in Feminist Knowledge*, Routledge, London, pp. 139–157.

Gaus, Gerald F. 2002, 'Reason, Justification and Consensus: Why Democracy Can't Have It All' in Bohman, James & Rehg, William (eds) *Deliberative Democracy: Essays on Reason and Politics*, MIT Press, Massachusetts, pp. 205–242.

Giddens, Anthony 2009, *Sociology*, Polity, Cambridge.

Giffney, Noreen 2004, 'Denormatizing Queer Theory: More Than (Simply) Lesbian and Gay Studies', *Feminist Theory*, 5 (1), pp. 73–78.

Gilbert, Miqqi Alicia 2009, 'Defeating Bigenderism: Changing Gender Assumptions in the Twenty-first Century', *Hypatia*, 24 (3), pp. 93–112.

Gilligan, Carol 1982, *In a Different Voice: Psychological Theory and Women's Development*, Harvard University Press, London.

Gilligan, Carol 2003, 'Hearing the Difference: Theorizing Connection', *Anuario de Piscologia*, 34 (2), pp. 155–161.

Goffman, Erving 1956, *The Presentation of Self in Everyday Life*, University of Edinburgh Press, Edinburgh.

Goldman, Emma 1969, *Anarchism*, Kennikat Press, New York.

Goldman, Russell 2014, 'Here's a List of 58 Gender Options for Facebook Users', *ABC News* 13/2/14, http://abcnews.go.com/blogs/headlines/2014/02/heres-a-list-of-58-gender-options-for-facebook-users/

Gordon, Uri 2009, 'Utopia in Contemporary Anarchism' in Davis, Laurence & Kinna, Ruth (eds) *Anarchism and Utopianism*, Manchester University Press, Manchester, pp. 260–275.

Gosine, Andil 2005, *Sex for Pleasure, Rights to Participation, and Alternatives to AIDS: Placing Sexual Minorities and/or Dissidents in Development. IDS Working Paper 228*, Institute of Development Studies, http://www.ids.ac.uk/files/Wp228.pdf accessed on 27/8/13.

Graeber, David 2009, *Direct Action: An Ethnography*, AK Press, Edinburgh.

Greed, Clara 2003, *Inclusive Urban Design: Public Toilets*, Architectural Press, Oxford.

Greenberg, Julie A 2012, Intersexuality and the Law, New York University Press, New York.

Green, Fiona Joy & Friedman, May 2013, *Chasing Rainbows: Exploring Gender Fluid Parenting Practices*, Demeter Press, Bradford.

Gunnarson, L. 2011, 'A Defence of the Category "Women" ', *Feminist Theory*, 12 (1), pp. 23–37.

Gutmann, Amy 1985, 'Communitarian Critics of Liberalism', *Philosophy and Public Affairs*, 14 (3), pp. 308–322.Halberstam, Judith 2011, *The Queer Art of Failure*. Duke University Press, Durham.

Gutterman, David S. 2001, 'Postmodernism and the Interrogation of Masculinity' in Whitehead, Stephen & Barret, Frank (eds) *The Masculinities Reader*, Polity, Cambridge, pp. 56–72.

Halberstam, Judith 1998, *Female Masculinity*, Duke University Press, Durham & London.

Halperin, David 1995, *Saint Foucault: Towards a Gay Hagiography*, Oxford University Press, Oxford.

Hanssesn, Beatrice 2000, *Critique of Violence: Between Poststructuralism and Critical Theory*, Routledge, London.

Hausman, Bernice L. 1999, 'Virtual Sex, Real Gender: Body and Identity in Transgender Discourse' in O'Farrell, May Ann & Vallone, Lynne (eds) *Virtual Gender: Fantasies of Subjectivity and Embodiment*, University of Michigan Press, Ann Arbor, pp. 190–204.

Hebblethwaite, Cordelia 2011, 'Sweden's "Gender-Neutral" Pre-School', BBC News, 7/11/11, http://www.bbc.co.uk/news/world-europe-14038419

Heckert, J. 2002, 'Maintaining the Borders: Identity and Politics, http://www.academia.edu/234259/Maintaining_the_Borders_identity_and_politics, accessed 19/8/13.

Heckert, Jamie 2009 'Nurturing Autonomy', *The Anarchist Library*, http://theanarchistlibrary.org/HTML/Jamie_Heckert__Nurturing_Autonomy.html, accessed 10/06/2011.

Heckert, J. 2010, 'Listening, Caring, Becoming: Anarchism as an Ethics of Direct Relationships' in Franks, B. & Wilson, M. (eds) *Anarchism and Moral Philosophy*, Palgrave: Basingstoke, pp. 186–207.

Heckert, Jamie, 2011, 'Fantasies of an Anarchist Sex Educator' in Heckert, Jamie & Cleminson, Richard (eds) *Anarchism and Sexuality: Ethics, Relationships and Power*, Routledge, London, pp. 154–180.

Heinamaa, Sara 1999, 'Simone de Beauvoir's Phenomenology of Sexual Difference', *Hypatia*, 14 (4), pp. 114–132.

Hennen, Peter 2004, 'Fae Spirits and Gender Trouble: Resistance and Compliance among the Radical Faeries', *Journal of Contemporary Ethnography*, 33, pp. 499–533.

Hern, Matt (ed.) 2008, *Everywhere All The Time: A New Deschooling Reader*, AK Press, Edinburgh.

Higginbotham, Emma 2012, 'Why I Decided to Raise my Son "Gender-Neutral"', *Cambridge News*, http://www.cambridge-news.co.uk/Health/Family/Hes-pretty-in-pink-to-make-you-think-20012012.htm

Hindess, Barry 1986, 'Actors and Social Relations' in Wardell, M. L. & Turner, S. P. (eds) *Sociological Theory in Transition*, Allen and Unwin, Boston, pp. 113–126.

Hine, Christine 2003, *Virtual Ethnography*, Sage, London.

Hird, Myra J. 2000, 'Gender's Nature: Intersexuality, Transsexualism and the "Sex"/"Gender" Binary', *Feminist Theory*, 1 (3), pp. 347–364.

Hird, Myra J. 2004a, *Sex, Gender and Science*, Palgrave, Hampshire.

Hird, Myra J. 2004b, 'Feminist Matters: New Materialist Considerations of Sexual Difference', *Feminist Theory*, 5 (2), pp. 223–232.

Hirvonen, Onni 2012, 'Taylor and the Problem of Recognizing Cultural Groups', *Distinktion: Scandinavian Journal of Social Theory*, 13 (1), pp. 109–124.

Hoagland, Sarah 1990, 'Some Concerns About Nel Noddings' Caring', *Hypatia*, 5 (1), pp. 109–114.

Hobbes, Thomas 1994 [1668], *Leviathan: With Selected Variants from the Latin Edition of 1668*, (Edwin Curley ed.), Hackett Publishing, Indianapolis, Indiana.

Holloway, John 2002, *Change the World Without Taking Power: The Meaning of Revolution Today*, Pluto Press, London.

Holveck, Eleanore 1999, 'The Blood of Others: A Novel Approach to The Ethics of Ambiguity', *Hypatia*, 14 (4), http://www.iupjournals.org/hypatia/hyp14-4.html, accessed 12/08/08.

Hood-Williams, John 1996, 'Goodbye to Sex and Gender', *Sociological Review*, 44 (1), pp. 1–16.

Hsueh-Hao Chiang, Howard 2007, 'Epistemic Gender, Sex Beyond the Flesh: Science, Medicine, and the Two-Sex Model in Modern America', *E-Sharp*, 9 (Spring 2007), http://www.gla.ac.uk/departments/esharp/issues/9/, accessed 15/3/10.

Hubbard, Ruth 1996, 'Gender and Genitals: Constructs of Sex and Gender', *Social Text*, 46/47, pp. 157–165.

Hunter, Ian 1988, *Culture and Government: The Emergence of Literary Education*, Macmillan, London.

Hurley, Michael 1990, 'Homosexualities: Fiction, Reading and Moral Training' in Threadgold, Terry & Cranny-Francis, Anne (eds) *Feminine/Masculine and Representation*, Allen and Unwin, Sydney, pp. 154–170.

Hutcheon, Linda 1994, *Irony's Edge: the Theory and Politics of Irony*, Routledge, London.

Hutchings, Kimberly 2007, 'Simone de Beauvoir and the Ambiguous Ethics of Political Violence', *Hypatia*, 22 (3), pp. 111–133.

Irigaray, Luce 1985, *This Sex Which Is Not One*, (trans. Catherine Porter) Cornell University Press, New York.

ISNA 2013, 'Intersex Society of North America', http://www.isna.org/

Jackman, Mary 2002, 'Violence in Social Life,' *Annual Review of Sociology*, 28, p. 387–415.

Jagose, Annamarie 1998, *Queer Theory*, Melbourne University Press, Victoria.

James, Susan Donaldson 2011, 'Baby Storm Raised Genderless is Bad Experiment, Say Experts', *ABC News*, http://abcnews.go.com/Health/baby-storm-raised-genderless-gender-dangerous-experiment-child/story?id=13693760

Johnson, Greg 2002, 'The Situated Self and Utopian Thinking', *Hypatia*, 17 (3), pp. 20–44.

Jolly, Susie 2007, 'Why the Development Industry Should Get Over its Obsession With Bad Sex and Start to Think About Pleasure', *IDS Working Paper 283*, http://citeseerx.ist.psu.edu/viewdoc/download?doi=10.1.1.109.7494&rep=rep1&type=pdf

Jones, Gerard 2003, *Killing Monsters: Why Children Need Fantasy, Super Heroes and Make-Believe Violence*, Basic Books, New York.

Jun, Nathan 2012, 'Paideia for Praxis: Philosophy and Pedagogy as Practices of Liberation' in Haworth, Robert (ed.) *Anarchist Pedagogies: Collective Actions, Theories, and Critical Reflections on Education*, PM Press, Oakland, pp. 283–302.

Kabeer, Naila 2005, 'Gender Equality and Women's Empowerment: A Critical Analysis of the Third Millennium Development Goal', *Gender and Development*, 13 (1), pp. 13–24.

Kaufman, Michael 1999, 'Men, Feminism, and Men's Contradictory Experiences of Power' in Kuypers, Joseph A. (ed.) *Men and Power*, Fernwood Books, Halifax, pp. 59–83.

Kenney, Rick & Akita, Kimiko 2013, ' "Is She a Man? Is She a Transvestite?" Critiquing the Coverage of Intersex Athletes' in Campbell, Jane & Carilli, Theresa (eds) *Queer Media Images: LGBT Perspectives*, Lexington, Plymouth, pp. 137–146.

Kessler, Suzanne J. 1993, 'Letters from Readers: Intersexual Rights', *The Sciences*, July/August 1993, p. 3.

Kessler, Suzanne & McKenna, Wendy 1978, *Gender: An Ethnomethodological Approach*, John Wiley & Sons, New York.

Kessler, Suzanne & McKenna, Wendy 2000, 'Who Put the "Trans" in Transgender? Gender Theory and Everyday Life', *The International Journal of Transgenderism*, 4 (3), July–September 2000, http://www.iiav.nl/ezines/web/ijt/97-03/numbers/symposion/kessler.htm, accessed 31/01/07.

Kimmel, Michael S. 2007, 'Masculinity as Homophobia: Fear, Shame, and Silence in the Construction of Gender Identity' in Cook, Nancy (ed.) *Gender Relations in Global Perspective*, Canadian Scholars' Press, Toronto, e-book pp. 73–82.

Kisby, Ben 2007, 'New Labour and Citizenship Education', *Parliamentary Affairs*, 60 (1), pp. 84–101.

Knight, Kyle 2012, 'Dividing by Three: Nepal Recognizes a Third Gender', *World Policy Blog*, http://www.worldpolicy.org/blog/2012/02/01/dividing-three-nepal-recognizes-third-gender

Kollman, Kelly & Waites, Matthew 2009, 'The Global Politics of Lesbian, Gay, Bisexual and Transgender Human Rights: An Introduction', *Contemporary Politics*, 15 (1), pp. 1–17.

Kopelson, Karen 2002, 'Dis/Integrating the Gay/Queer Binary: "Reconstructed Identity Politics" for a Performative Pedagogy', *College English*, 65 (1), Special Issue: Lesbian and Gay Studies/Queer Pedagogies, pp. 17–35.

Korsgaard, Christine M. 1995, 'A Note on the Value of Gender-Identification' in Nussbaum, Martha C. & Glover, Jonathan (eds) *Women, Culture and Development: A Study of Human Capabilities*, Oxford University Press, Oxford, pp. 401–405.

Kropotkin, Petr 2007, *Mutual Aid*, BiblioBazaar, www.bibliobazaar.com.

Kruks, Sonia 1987, 'Simone de Beauvoir and the Limits to Freedom', *Social Text*, 17, pp. 111–122.

Kruks, Sonia 2005, 'Living on Rails: Freedom, Constraint, and Political Judgement in Beauvoir's "Moral" Essays and The Mandarins' in Scholz, Sally J. & Mussett, Shannon M. (eds) *Philosophical Essays on Simone de Beauvoir's The Mandarins*, State University of New York Press, Albany, pp. 67–86.

Laqueur, Thomas 2003, *Making Sex: Body and Gender from the Greeks to Freud*, Harvard University Press, Massachusetts.

Le Doeuff, Michèle 1995, 'Simone de Beauvoir: Falling into (Ambiguous) Line' in Simons, Margaret A. (ed), *Feminist Interpretations of Simone de Beauvoir*, Pennsylvania State University Press, Pennsylvania, pp. 59–66.

Le Guin, Ursula K. 1974, *The Dispossessed*, Gollancz, London.

Le Guin, Ursula 1976 'Is Gender Necessary?' In Vonda N. McIntyre and Susan Janice Anderson (eds.), *Aurora: Beyond Equality*, Fawcett,?, pp.130–139.

Le Guin, Ursula K. 1978, *The Lathe of Heaven*, Granada Publishing, London.

Leonard, T. 2011, 'The Baby Who Is Neither Boy Nor Girl: As Gender Experiment Provokes Outrage, What About the Poor Child's Future?' *The Daily Mail*, accessed at http://www.dailymail.co.uk/news/article-1391772/Storm-Stocker-As-gender-experiment-provokes-outrage-poor-childs-future.html on 9/7/13.

Les Panther Roses, 2003, 'Queer is Hip, Queer is Cool – Dogmas in the Queer Scene', *Queeruption*, http://www.queeruption.org/queeriship.htm, accessed 30/08/11.

Linden, Merrit 2003, 'Neutral Bathrooms', *The Campanil*, http://www.thecampanil.com/2003/02/27/neutralbathrooms/ accessed 10/11/09.

Lombardi, Emilia L, Riki Anne Wilchins, Dana Priesing & Malouf, Diana 2001, 'Gender Violence: Transgender Experiences with Violence and Discrimination' *Journal of Homosexuality*, 42 (1), pp. 89–101.

Lorber, Judith 1986, 'Dismantling Noah's Ark', *Sex Roles*, 14 (11/12), pp. 567–580.

Lorber, Judith 1993, 'Believing is Seeing: Biology as Ideology', *Gender & Society*, 7 (4), pp. 568–581.

Lorber, Judith 2000, 'Using Gender to Undo Gender: A Feminist Degendering Movement', *Feminist Theory*, 1 (1), pp. 79–85.

Luhmann, Susanne 1998, 'Queering/Querying Pedagogy? Or, Pedagogy is a Pretty Queer Thing' in Pinar, William (ed.) *Queer Theory in Education*, Lawrence Earlbaum Associates, NJ, pp. 141–156.

Lykke, Nina 2010a, 'The Timeliness of Post-Constructionism', *NORA: Nordic Journal of Feminist and Gender Research*, 18 (2), pp. 131–136.

Lykke, Nina 2010b, *Feminist Studies: A Guide to Intersectional Theory, Methodology and Writing*, Taylor & Francis, Hoboken.

MacIntyre, Alasdair C. 1985, *After Virtue: A Study in Moral Theory*, Duckworth, London.

Marinucci, Mimi 2010, *Feminism is Queer: The Intimate Connection Between Queer and Feminist Theory*, Zed Books, London.

Martin, Emily 2006, 'The Egg and The Sperm: A Scientific Fairy Tale' in Grewal, Inderpal & Kaplan, Caren (eds) *An Introduction to Women's Studies: Gender in a Transnational World*, McGraw Hill, New York.

Martin, Karin 2005, 'William Wants a Doll. Can He Have One? Feminists, Child Care Advisors, and Gender-Neutral Child Rearing', *Gender & Society*, 29, pp. 456–479.

Matik, Wendy-O. 2002, *Redefining Our Relationships: Guidelines for Responsible Open Relationships*, Regent Press, Oakland.

May, Todd 1994, *The Political Philosophy of Postsructuralist Anarchism*, Pennsylvania State University Press, Pennsylvania.

McDermott, Daragh 2011, 'It's a Boy! Coupe Reveal Sex of their "Gender Neutral" Kid After Five Years', *The Sun*, http://www.thesun.co.uk/sol/home page/news/4075523/Its-a-boy-Couple-reveal-sex-of-their-gender-neutral-kid-after-five-years.html

McLaren, Margaret A. 2001, 'Feminist Ethics: Care as a Virtue', in DesAutels, Peggy & Waugh, Joanne (eds) *Feminists Doing Ethics*, Rowan and Littlefield, Oxford, pp. 101–118.

McLaughlin, Ken 2005, 'Door No. 1 or door No. 2?: Bathroom Ambiguity a Hot Topic with gay, Lesbian Community', *Spokane7*, http://www.spokane7.com/culture/stories/?ID=87010, accessed 26/8/05.

McNay, Lois 2008, *Against Recognition*, Polity Press, Cambridge.

Mead, George Herbert 1934, *Mind, Self and Society: From the Standpoint of a Social Behaviorist*, University of Chicago Press, Chicago.

Michelman, Frank I. 2002, 'How Can the People Ever Make the Laws?: A Critique of Deliberative Democracy' in Bohman, James & Rehg, William (eds) *Deliberative Democracy: Essays on Reason and Politics*, MIT Press, Massachusetts, pp. 145–171.

Mills, Sara 2003, 'Third Wave Feminist Linguistics and the Analysis of Sexism', *Discourse Analysis Online*, http://extra.shu.ac.uk/daol/articles/open/2003/02/mills2003001-01.html

Mitchell, Natsha 2011, 'End of Gender', *Life Matters*, ABC Radio, Broadcast on 12/7/11, http://www.abc.net.au/radionational/programs/lifematters/end-of-gender/2923338

Morris, Alex 2011, 'The Prettiest Boy in the World', *New York Magazine*, Fall 2011, http://nymag.com/fashion/11/fall/andrej-pejic/

Mouffe, Chantal 1997, 'Decision, Deliberation and Democratic Ethos', *Philosophy Today*, 41 (1), pp. 24–28.

Muñoz, José Estaban 2009, *Cruising Utopia: The then and There of Queer Futurity*, New York University Press, New York.

Naji, Catherine & Stanley, Liz (2011), 'Translation of The Useless Mouths by Simone de Beauvoir' in Simons, Margaret A. (ed.) *Simone de Beauvoir: Literary Writings*, University of Illinois Press, Urbana, pp. 1–27.

Nakata, Martin 2012, 'CDSI Plenary: Widening Participation, Social Inclusion, Closing the Gap', *Journal of Academic Language & Learning*, 6 (12), pp. 1–8.

Nandi, Jacinta 2013, 'Germany got it Right by Offering a Third Gender Option on Birth Certificates', *The Guardian* 10/11/13, http://www.theguardian.com/commentisfree/2013/nov/10/germany-third-gender-birth-certificate

NE 2013, 'Hen', http://www.ne.se/hen/1826342

Newman, Saul 2001, *From Bakunin to Lacan: Anti-Authoritarianism and the Dislocation of Power*, Lexington Books, Oxford.

Nicholas, Lucy 2007, 'Approaches to Gender, Power and Authority in Contemporary Anarcho-punk: Poststructuralist Anarchism?', *E-Sharp Journal*, (9) (Spring 2007), http://www.gla.ac.uk/departments/esharp/issues/9/

Nicholas, Lucy 2009, 'A Radical Queer Utopian Future: A Reciprocal Relation beyond Sexual Difference', *Thirdspace: A Journal of Feminist Theory and Culture*, 8 (2), http://www.thirdspace.ca/journal/article/viewArticle/lnicholas/248.

Nicholas, Lucy 2012 'Anarchism, Pedagogy, Queer Theory and Poststructuralism: Towards a Positive Ethical Theory of Knowledge and the Self' in Haworth, Robert (ed.) *Anarchist Pedagogies: Collective Actions, Theories, and Critical Reflections on Education*, PM Press, Oakland, pp. 242–259.

Nietzsche, Friedrich 1998, 'On Truth and Lying' in Rivkin, Julie & Ryan, Michael (eds) *Literary Theory: An Anthology*, Blackwell, Oxford, pp. 358–361.

Noddings, Nel 2003, *Caring: A Feminine Approach to Ethics and Moral Education*, University of California Press, London.

Noddings, Nel 2006, 'Principles, Feelings and Reality', *Theory and Research in Education*, 4 (1), pp. 9–21.

Noterman, Elsa & Pusey, Andre 2012, 'Inside, Outside, and on the Edge of the Academy: Experiments in Radical Pedagogies' in Haworth, Robert (ed.) *Anarchist Pedagogies: Collective Actions, Theories, and Critical Reflections on Education*, PM Press, Oakland, pp. 175–199.

Nowak, K. L. & Rauh, C. 2005, 'The Influence of the Avatar on Online Perceptions of Anthropomorphism, Androgyny, Credibility, Homophily, and Attraction', *Journal of Computer-Mediated Communication*, 11 (1), article 8, http://jcmc.indiana.edu/vol11/issue1/nowak.html, accessed 6/11/08.

Nozick, Robert 1974, *Anarchy, State and Utopia*, Blackwell, Oxford.

Nussbaum, Martha C. (ed) 1996, *For Love of Country: Debating the Limits of Patriotism*, Beacon Press, Boston.

Nussbaum, Martha C. 1999a, 'The Professor of Parody', *The New Republic*, 22/2/1999, pp. 37–45.

Nussbaum, Martha C. 1999b, *Sex and Social Justice*, Oxford University Press, Oxford.

Nussbaum, Martha C. & Glover, Jonathan (eds) 1995, *Women, Culture and Development: A Study of Human Capabilities*, Oxford University Press, Oxford.

NVC 2007, 'NVC Concepts', *The Center for Non-Violent Communication*, http://www.cnvc.org/Training/NVC-Concepts, accessed 1/07/2011.

NVC 2009, 'Foundations of NVC', *The Center for Non-Violent Communication*, http://www.cnvc.org/learn/nvc-foundations, accessed 28/06/2011.

Oakley, Ann 1972, *Sex, Gender and Society*, Maurice Temple Smith Ltd., London.

O'Brien, Jodi 1999, 'Writing in the Body: Gender (re)Production in Online Interaction' in Smith, Marc A. & Kollock, Peter (eds) *Communities in Cyberspace*, Routledge, London, pp. 75–106.

OII 2013, 'Intersex Australia', http://oii.org.au/

Okin, Susan Moller 1987, 'Justice and Gender', *Philosophy and Public Affairs*, 16 (1), pp. 42–72.

Okin, Susan Moller 1989, *Justice, Gender and the Family*, Basic Books, New York.

Okin, Susan Moller 1999, *Is Multiculturalism Bad for Women?*, Princeton University Press, Princeton, N.J.

Olly 2004, 'Reply to: More About Hir', *The Oregon Commentator: A Conservative Journal of Opinion*, http://oregoncommentator.com/2004/10/14/more-about-hir/, accessed 15/3/10.

Orenstein, Peggy 2011 'Should the World of Toys Be Gender-Free?' *The New York Times*, http://www.nytimes.com/2011/12/30/opinion/does-stripping-gender-from-toys-really-make-sense.html?_r=0

Ortner, Sherry 1972, 'Is Female to Male as Nature to Culture?', *Feminist Studies*, 1 (2), pp. 5–31.

Pacteau, Francette 1986, 'The Impossible Referent: Representations of the Androgyne' in Burgin, Victor, Donald, James & Kaplan Cora, *Formations of Fantasy*, Methuen, London, pp. 62–84.

Parafianowicz, L. 2009 'Swedish Parents Keep 2-year-old's Gender Secret', *The Local*, http://www.theloacl.se/article.php?ID=20232&print=true, accessed 8/5/2012.

Parafianowicz, Lydia 2009, 'Swedish Parents Keep 2-year-old's Gender Secret', *The Local*, http://www.thelocal.se/20090623/20232, accessed 8/5/2012.

Parpart, J. 1993, 'Who is the "Other"? A Postmodern Feminist Critique of Women and Development Theory and Practice', *Development and Change*, 24, pp. 439–464, http://onlinelibrary.wiley.com/doi/10.1111/j.1467-7660.1993.tb00492.x/pdf

Pascoe, C. J. 2007, *Dude, You're a Fag: Masculinity and Sexuality in High School: Masculinity and Sexuality in High School*, University of California Press, California.

Patton, Paul 1994, 'Foucault's Subject of Power', *Political Theory Newsletter*, 6, pp. 60–71.

Pauline, Park 2006, 'S/he's Not Heavy, Zie's my Non-Gendered Sibling: Why Gender-Neutral Pronouns Don't Work for Me', *Transgender Tapestry*, (111), pp. 44–45.

Pearson, Carol 1977, 'Women's Fantasies and Feminist Utopias', *Frontiers: A Journal of Women Studies*, 2 (3), pp. 50–61.

Peppers, Margot 2013, 'It's Easier to Model as a Man Than a Woman': Casey Legler, the First Female to be Signed as Male Model, on her Knack for Gender-Bending', *The Daily Mail*, 15/413, http://www.dailymail.co.uk/femail/article-2309598/Its-easier-model-man-woman-Casey-Legler-female-signed-male-model-knack-gender-bending.html

Phelan, Shane 2004, 'Alliances & Coalitions: Nonidentity Politics' in Carlin, Deborah & DiGrazia, Jennifer (eds) *Queer Cultures*, Prentice Hall, New Jersey, pp. 700–720.

Piercy, Marge 2001[1979], *Woman on the Edge of Time*, Women's Press, London.

Pike, Mark 2007, 'The State and Citizenship Education in England: A Curriculum for Subjects or Citizens?' *Journal of Curriculum Studies*, 39 (4), pp. 471–489.

Poisson, Jayme 2011, 'Parents Keep Child's Gender Secret', *Parentcentral.ca*, May 21st 2011, http://www.parentcentral.ca/parent/babiespregnancy/babies/article/995112--parents-keep-child-s-gender-secret

Proudhon, Pierre-Joseph 1994,*What is Property*, Cambridge University Press, Cambridge.

Queeruption 2011, 'Boycott Sexist Violators in Hardcore!' *Queeruption Mailing List*, Wednesday, 15 June 2011, http://lists.queeruption.org/cgi-bin/mj_

wwwusr?user=s0675026%40sms.ed.ac.uk&passw=38A8-333F-0C04&list= queeruption&brief=on&func=archive-get-part&extra=201106/25

Raffaelli, Marcela, Lazarevic, Vanja, Koller, Silvia H., Nsamenang, A. Bame & Sharma, Deepali 2013, 'Introduction: Special Issue on Adolescents in the Majority World', *Journal of Research on Adolescence*, 23 (1), pp. 1–8.

Rajchman, John 2007, 'Enlightenment Today' in Foucault, Michel (ed.) *The Politics of Truth*, Semiotext(e), Los Angeles, pp. 9–25.

Rak, Julie 2005, 'The Digital Queer: Weblogs and Internet Identity', *Biography*, 28 (1) (Winter 2005), pp. 166–182.

Rawls, John 1973, *A Theory of Justice*, Oxford University Press, Oxford.

Reid, Elizabeth 1995 'Virtual Worlds: Culture and Imagination' in Jones, Steven G. (ed.) *Cybersociety: Computer Mediated Communication and Community*, Sage, London, pp. 164–183.

Reynolds, Andrew 2005, *The New Utopian Politics of Ursula K. Le Guin's The Dispossessed*, Lexington Books, Oxford.

Risman, Barbara J. 2004, 'Gender as a Social Structure: Theory Wrestling with Activism', *Gender & Society*, 18 (4), pp. 429–450.

Risman, Barbara J., Lorber, Judith & Sherwood, Jessica Holden 2012, *Toward a World Beyond Gender: A Utopian Vision*, Paper prepared for the 2012 American Sociological Society Meetings, http://www.ssc.wisc.edu/~wright/ASA/Risman-Lorber-Sherwood%20Real%20Utopia%20Proposal%20--%20Beyond%20Gender.pdf, accessed 23/5/12.

Robinson, Kerry H. 2005, '"Queerying" Gender: Heteronormativity in Early Childhood Education', *Australian Journal of Early Childhood*, 30 (2), pp. 19–28.

Robinson, Victoria 1997, 'My Baby Just Cares for Me: Feminism, heterosexuality and non-monogamy', *Journal of Gender Studies*, 6 (2), pp. 143–157.

Rosinsky, Natalie Myra 1984, *Feminist Futures–Contemporary Women's Speculative Fiction*, UMI Research Press, Ann Arbor.

Roth, Zachary 2011, 'Parents Keep Child's Gender Under Wraps', *Yahoo News*, May 24th 2011, http://news.yahoo.com/s/yblog_thelookout/20110524/ts_yblog_thelookout/parents-keep-childs-gender-under-wraps

Rothblatt, Martine 1995, *The Apartheid of Sex: Manifesto on the Freedom of Gender*, Rivers Oram Press, London.

Rubin, Gayle 1993 [1984], 'Thinking Sex: Notes for a Radical Theory of the Politics of Sexuality' in Abelove, Henry, Barale, Michele Aina & Halperin, David M. (eds) *The Lesbian and Gay Studies Reader*, Routledge, New York, pp. 3–44.

Ruddick, Sara 1980, 'Maternal Thinking', *Feminist Studies*, 6 (2), pp. 342–367.

Sandel, Michael J. 1982, *Liberalism and the Limits of Justice*, Cambridge University Press, Cambridge.

Sandland, Ralph 2005, 'Feminism and the Gender Recognition Act 2004', *Feminist Legal Studies*, 13 (1), pp. 43–66.

Santa Cruz, Free Skool 2008, 'About', *Free Skool Santa Kruz*. Retrieved from, http://santacruz.freeskool.org/e107_plugins/content/content.php?content.1 accessed 4/6/08

Sargisson, Lucy 1996, *Contemporary Feminist Utopianism*, Routledge, London.

Sartre, Jean-Paul 1974, 'Preface' in Fanon, Frantz (ed.) *The Wretched of the Earth*, Penguin, Middlesex, pp. 7–26.

Scarry, Elaine 1996 'The Difficulty of Imagining Other People' in Nussbaum, Martha C. (ed.) *For Love of Country: Debating the Limits of Patriotism*, Beacon Press, Boston, pp. 98–110.

Scheper-Hughes, Nancy & Bourgois, Philippe (eds) 2004, *Violence in War and Peace: An Anthology*, Blackwell, Oxford.

Schilt, Kristen and Westbrook, Laurel 2009, 'Doing Gender, Doing Heteronormativity: "Gender Normals," Transgender People, and the Social Maintenance of Heterosexuality', *Gender & Society*, 23 (4), pp. 440–464.

Scullyadams n.d., *No Labels: A Post-Queer Manifesto*, self published.

Sedgwick, Eve Kosofsky 1990, *Epistemology of the Closet*, University of California Press, Berkeley.

Sedgwick, Eve Kosofsy 2003, *Touching Feeling: Affect, Pedagogy, Performativity*, Duke University Press, London.

Seidman, Steven 1995, 'Deconstructing Queer Theory or the Under-Theorisation of the Social and the Ethical' in Linda Nicholson & Steven Seidman (eds) *Social Postmodernism: Beyond Identity Politics*, Cambridge University Press, Cambridge, pp. 116–141.

Seidman, Steven 1997, *Difference Troubles: Queering Social Theory and Sexual Politics*, Cambridge University Press, Cambridge.

Sennett, Richard 2012, *Together: The Rituals, Pleasures and Politics of Cooperation*, Yale University Press, New Haven.

Simons, Margaret A. 1999, 'The Origins of Beauvoir's Existential Philosophy', in Giles, James (ed.) *French Existentialism: Consciousness, Ethics and Relations with Others*, Rodopi, Amsterdam.

Simons, Margaret A. 2001, *Beauvoir and the Second Sex: Feminism, Race and the Origins of Existentialism*, Rowan and Littlefield, Oxford.

Soffel, Jenny 2011, ' "Gender-Neutral" Pre-school Accused of Mind Control', *The Independent*, http://www.independent.co.uk/news/world/europe/genderneutral-preschool-accused-of-mind-control-2305983.html

Spade, Dean 2003, 'Resisting Medicine, Re/Modeling Gender', *Berkeley Women's Law Journal*, 18, pp. 15–40.

Spivak, Gayatri Chakravorty 1976, 'Translators Preface' in Derrida, Jacques (ed.) *Of Grammatology*, (trans. Spivak, Gayatri Chakravorty), The John Hopkins University Press, Baltimore & London, pp. ix–lxxxiii.

Spivak, Gayatri Chakravorty 1994, 'In a Word: Interview. Gayatri Chakravorty Spivak with Ellen Rooney' in Schor, Naomi & Weed Elizabeth (eds) 1994, *The Essential Difference*, Indiana University Press, Bloomington, pp. 151–184.

Spivak, Gayatri Chakravorty 1996, 'More on Power/Knowledge' in Landry, Donna & MacLean, Gerald (eds) *The Spivak Reader*, Routledge, New York, pp. 141–174.

Spurlin, William J. 2002, 'Theorizing Queer Pedagogy in English Studies after the 1990s', *College English*, 65 (1), Special Issue: Lesbian and Gay Studies/Queer Pedagogies, pp. 9–16.

Stanley, Liz 1984, 'Should "Sex" Really Be "Gender" – or "Gender" Really Be "Sex"?' in Anderson, R. J. & Sharrock, W.W. (eds) *Applied Sociological Perspectives*, Allen & Unwin, London, pp. 1–19.

Stanley, Liz 1996, 'Rejecting the Legend, Rereading de Beauvoir, Reworking Existentialism: The Case for Ontological Ethics', *European Journal of Women's Studies*, 3, pp. 423–449.

Stanley, Liz 2001, 'A Philosopher Manqué? Simone de Beauvoir, Moral Value and "The Useless Mouths"', *European Journal of Women's Studies*, 8 (2), pp. 201–220.

Stanley, Liz (ed.) 2013, *Feminist Praxis: Research, Theory and Epistemology in Feminist Sociology*, Routledge, London.

Stein, A. & Plummer, K. 1994, ' "I Can't Even Think Straight" "Queer" Theory and the Missing Sexual Revolution in Sociology', *Sociological Theory*, 12 (2), pp. 178–187.

Stoetzler, Marcel 2005, 'Subject Trouble: Judith Butler and Dialectics,' *Philosophy & Social Criticism*, 31 (3), pp. 343–368.

Stone, Bob 1987, 'Simone de Beauvoir and the Existential Basis of Socialism,' *Social Text*, 17, pp. 123–133.

Suissa, Judith 2010, *Anarchism and Education: A Philosophical Perspective*, PM Press, Oakland, CA.

Sumara, Dennis & Davis, Brent 1999, 'Interrupting Heteronormativity: Toward a Queer Curriculum Theory', *Curriculum Inquiry*, 29 (2), pp. 191–208.

Taylor, C 1992, *Multiculturalism and 'The politics of recognition': An Essay*, Princeton University Press, Princeton, N.J.

Testa, Rylan J., Sciacca, Laura M., Wang, Florence, Hendricks, Michael L. 2012, 'Effects of Violence on Transgender People', *Professional Psychology: Research and Practice*, 43 (5), pp. 452–459.

Tolstoy, Leo 2008, 'On Education' in Hern, Matt (ed.) *Everywhere All The Time: A New Deschooling Reader*, AK Press, Edinburgh, pp. 1–6.

Travers Scott, D. 1997, 'Le Freak, C'est Chic! Le Fag, Quelle Drag!: Celebrating The Collapse of Homosexual Identity' in Queen, Carol & Schimel, Lawrence (eds) *Pomosexuals: Challenging Assumptions About Gender and Sexuality*, Cleis Press, Berkeley, pp. 62–69.

Turner, Stephanie S. 1999, 'Intersex Identities: Locating New Intersections of Sex and Gender', *Gender and Society*, 13 (4), pp. 457–459.

Vade, Dylan n.d, 'Beyond the Women's Room', *Curve Magazine*, 13, p. 3, http://www.curvemag.com/Detailed/346.html, accessed 6/11/08.

Vaneslander, B. 2007, 'Long Live Temporariness: Two Queer Examples of Autonomous Spaces', *Affinities: Theory, Culture, Action*, 1 (1), pp. 1–4, http://affinitiesjournal.org/index.php/affinities/article/view/3/41

Van Lenning, Alkeline 2004, 'The Body as Crowbar: Transcending or Stretching Sex?' *Feminist Theory* 5 (1), pp. 25–47.

Vintges, Karen 2001, ' "Must We Burn Foucault?" Ethics as Art of Living: Simone de Beauvoir and Michel Foucault', *Continental Philosophy Review*, 34, pp. 165–181.

Wain, Kenneth 1996, 'Foucault, Education, the Self and Modernity,' *Journal of Philosophy of Education*, 30 (3), pp. 345–360.

Waites, Matthew 2009, 'Critique of 'sexual orientation' and 'gender identity' in Human Rights Discourse: Global Queer Politics Beyond the Yogyakarta Principles', *Contemporary Politics*, 15 (1), pp. 137–156.

Wajcman, Judy 2004, *Technofeminism*, Polity, Cambridge.

Walzer, Michael 1985, *Spheres of Justice: A Defence of Pluralism and Equality*, Blackwell, Oxford.

Warhol, Robyn R. 2002, 'The Inevitable Virtuality of Gender: Performing Femininity on an Electronic Bulletin Board for Soap Opera Fans', in O'Farrell, Ann & Vallone, Lynne (eds) *Virtual Gender: Fantasies of Subjectivity and Embodiment*, University of Michigan Press, Ann Arbor, pp. 91–109.

Warner, Michael 1991, 'Fear of a Queer Planet', *Social Text*, 29, pp. 3–17.

Webster, Frank 2006, *Theories of the Information Society*, Routeledge, Abingdon.

Weeks, Jeffery 2003, 'Necessary Fictions: Sexual Identities and the Politics of Diversity', in Weeks, Jeffery, Holland, Janet & Waites, Matthew (eds) *Sexualities and Society: A Reader*, Blackwell, Cambridge, pp. 122–131.

Weiner, Joshua J. & Young, Damon 2011, 'Queer Bonds', *GLQ*, 17 (2–3), pp. 223–241.

West, C & Zimmerman, D 1987, 'Doing Gender', *Gender and Society*, 1 (2), pp. 125–151.

What Do We Do When? , *What Do We Do When?* http://www.phillyspissed.net/node/27

Whitbeck, Caroline 1989 'A Different Reality: Feminist Ontology' in Garry, Ann & Pearsall, Marilyn (eds) *Women, Knowledge and Reality: Explorations in Feminist Philosophy*, Routledge, London, pp. 51–76.

Widerberg, Karin 1998, 'Translating Gender', *NORA: Nordic Journal of Feminist and Gender Research*, 6 (2), pp. 133–138.

Witterick, Kathy 2011, 'Baby Storm's Mom on Gender, Parenting and the Media', *Ottawa Citizen*, May 28 2011, http://www.ottawacitizen.com/Baby+Storm+gender+parenting+media/4856804/story.html

Wittig, Monique 1993, 'One is not Born a Woman' in Abelove, Henry & Barale, Michèle Aina & Halperin, David M. (eds) *The Lesbian and Gay Studies Reader*, New York, Routledge, pp. 103–109.

Wolf, John & Schweisberger, Valerie 2013, 'Should We Stop Believin'? Glee and the Cultivation of Essentialist Identity Discourse' in Campbell, Jane & Carilli, Theresa (eds) *Queer Media Images: LGBT Perspectives*, Lexington, Plymouth, pp. 157–170.

Wolf, Naomi 1998, *The Beauty Myth: How Images of Beauty are Used Against Women*, Vintage, London.

Woodcock, George (ed.) 1980, *The Anarchist Reader*, Fontana, Glasgow.

Woodcock, George 2004, *Anarchism: A History of Libertarian Ideas and Movements*, Broadview Press, Plymouth.

Woodhill, Brenda Mae & Samuels, Curtis A. 2004, 'Desirable and Undesirable Androgyny: A Prescription for the Twenty-First Century', *Journal of Gender Studies*, 13 (1), pp. 15–28.

Woodward, Kathryn 1997, *Identity and Difference*, Sage, London.

Wyss, Shannon E. 2004, 'This Was My Hell: The Violence Experienced by Gender Non-Conforming Youth in US High Schools', *International Journal of Qualitative Studies in Education*, 17 (5), pp. 709–730.

Young, Iris Marion 1995, 'The Ideal of Community and the Politics of Difference' in Friedman, Marilyn & Weiss, Penny A. (eds) *Feminism and Community*, Temple University Press, Philadelphia, pp. 300–323.

Index

Printed and bound by CPI Group (UK) Ltd, Croydon, CR0 4YY